What the Bible Says about the

What the Bible Says about the

HOLY Spirit

Stanley M. Horton

REVISED EDITION

GPH™
Gospel Publishing House
Springfield, Missouri
02-0650

All Scripture quotations, unless otherwise indicated are taken from the HOLY BIBLE, NEW INTERNATIONAL VERSION®. NIV®. Copyright © 1973, 1978, 1984 by International Bible Society. Used by permission of Zondervan. All rights reserved.

Scriptures marked KJV are from the King James Version.

©2005, 1976 by Gospel Publishing House, Springfield, Missouri 65802-1894. All rights reserved. No part of this book may be reproduced, stored in a retrieval system, or transmitted in any form or by any means—electronic, mechanical, photocopy, recording, or otherwise—without prior written permission of the copyright owner, except brief quotations used in connection with reviews in magazines or newspapers.

First edition 1976
Revised edition 2005. 3rd printing 2007.

The text revision of *What the Bible Says about the Holy Spirit* was undertaken to include the New International Version of the Holy Bible. Corresponding adjustments were made to the author's text.

ISBN: 0-88243-359-8
Library of Congress Catalog Card Number: 75-43154

Printed in the United States of America

Contents

In-Depth, Spiritually Satisfying Bible Study without Hours of Research

The Pentecostal Library
from the works of Stanley M. Horton

28FQ5000

From highly respected Pentecostal author and theologian Stanley M. Horton comes this digital treasury of outstanding systematic theology and biblical commentary. Combining extensive research with practical experience, each book in this collection offers solid teaching that will bring a deeper understanding of the Holy Spirit and His ministry to every believer.

Powerful and easy-to-use for study, research, and sermon preparation, **The Pentecostal Library** interfaces with the PC Study Bible®. These Pentecostal reference materials are searchable and can be easily cut and pasted into text documents or slide presentations. The content is also hyperlinked to other search tools within the PC Study Bible® library, such as dictionaries, lexicons, and encyclopedias for in-depth searches and results in seconds.

The following Pentecostal works are included in this library:

- *Acts*
- *1 & 2 Corinthians*
- *Systematic Theology*
- *Bible Doctrines: A Pentecostal Perspective*
- *What the Bible Says about the Holy Spirit*

REQUIREMENTS: This add-on module is only compatible with PC Study Bible® Version 4 or higher. It will not operate as a stand-alone unit or as an add-on for any previous version of PC Study Bible®.

Available at
www.GospelPublishing.com/PCStudyBible

Foreword

With the events of what is happening in our world politically, economically and on the religious scene, it is certainly evident that we are living in the days that Peter spoke about on the Day of Pentecost when he quoted the prophet Joel, "In the last days, saith God, I will pour out of my Spirit upon all flesh" (Acts 2:17, KJV).

This promise was fulfilled when Jesus said it was expedient for Him to go away for if He did He would send the Holy Spirit. Jesus went and the Holy Spirit was sent. It is a joy to stand on the threshold of the soon return of our Lord Jesus Christ and see the role the Holy Spirit is playing in this great end-time harvest.

One will capture the deep appreciation the author, Dr. Stanley Horton, has for the Third Person of the Godhead, the Holy Spirit and His work. This book is written as a result of a life lived in the presence of the Holy Spirit. As one reads and studies the contents of Dr. Horton's writings, one will come to a deeper and fuller revelation of the Holy Spirit's ministry in one's own life. It is a book that can be given to others so that they might more fully understand and enjoy the work, teachings, and giftings of the Holy Spirit.

Dr. Horton is viewed by many in and out of this church as one of the great Bible scholars of our day and has been used by God to unfold eternal truths contained in the Word of God. His writings have brought instruction and inspiration to Bible readers. We would encourage everyone reading *What the Bible Says about the Holy Spirit* to open one's heart, mind, and spirit to what the Holy Spirit would have us to know.

The Scriptures state in the Book of Revelation: "He that hath an ear, let him hear what the Spirit saith unto the churches" (Revelation 2:7, KJV). This is a most timely book for the Church of Jesus Christ at large.

Thomas E. Trask
General Superintendent of the Assemblies of God

The Spirit
in the World Today

"It seemed good to the Holy Spirit and to us" (Acts 15:28). How clearly this indicates the reality of the Holy Spirit and the personal relation the first-century believers enjoyed with Him!

The scene was the Jerusalem Council, the first council of the Early Church. The question had arisen: How could the Jewish believers maintain fellowship with Gentile Christians who were not circumcised, who ate nonkosher food, and who came out of the highly immoral Greek culture of the day? Apostles, elders, and a whole multitude of believers had gathered together to resolve the question. Some converted Pharisees insisted that the Gentile converts must be circumcised and keep the Law of Moses. Peter reminded them how God gave the Holy Spirit to the Gentiles at the house of Cornelius before they had any opportunity to do good works, to say nothing of keeping the Law! Paul and Barnabas told of the miracles God had performed through them among the Gentiles.

James, the brother of Jesus, finally gave a message of wisdom that pleased the whole church. Then they wrote letters telling of their decision. But they did not say, "It seemed good to James, as the chief elder of the Jerusalem church," nor did they say, "It seemed good to Peter and the apostles," nor even, "It was the consensus of the brethren as indicated by a majority vote." In all their "discussion" (investigation, debate; Acts 15:7), they were conscious of the presence of a divine Person among them, leading them, guiding them into truth. Thus, it was not mere pious

9

language when they said, "It seemed good to the Holy Spirit and to us."

This consciousness of the reality of the Holy Spirit pervades the entire Bible from Genesis to Revelation. Many Old Testament writers refer to the Spirit, and only three of the New Testament books do not allude to Him (and these are all very short—Philemon and 2 and 3 John).

It is true that Jesus Christ is the key figure in all God's plan. The Holy Spirit himself focuses attention on Christ and seeks to glorify Him (John 15:26; 16:14). But this does not mean that the Holy Spirit is ever ignored in the Bible or that He is ever treated as some vague influence or imperceptible energy. He is recognized as a real person with intelligence, feeling, and will.

Both explicitly and implicitly the Bible treats the Holy Spirit as a distinct Person. "He who searches our hearts knows the mind of the Spirit, because the Spirit intercedes for the saints in accordance with God's will" (Romans 8:27). "The Spirit searches all things" (1 Corinthians 2:10). He thus acts with intelligence and wisdom. (See Ephesians 1:17; Isaiah 11:2.) He has emotions and can be grieved or vexed (pained, hurt; Ephesians 4:30; Isaiah 63:10). He distributes gifts "to each one, just as he determines" (1 Corinthians 12:11). He guided the Early Church and directed the key missionary movements in definite, specific, personal ways. (See Acts 13:2; 16:6.) John even uses masculine personal pronouns to draw attention to the Spirit's personality. (The word *spirit* in Greek is neuter and grammatically calls for a neuter pronoun.)

More importantly, it is evident from the Bible that men and women who were moved by the Spirit knew Him in a definite, personal way. If you were to ask the judges or prophets of the Old Testament if the Holy Spirit had come upon them, they would never say, "I think so," or, "I hope so." We read that "the Spirit of the LORD came upon [clothed himself with] Gideon, and he blew a trumpet" (Judges 6:34). This was no mild, secret touch. When a young lion roared against Samson, "the Spirit of the LORD came [rushed] upon him in power so that he tore the lion apart with his bare hands as he might have torn a young goat" (Judges 14:6).

When the Spirit of the Lord came upon Saul, he prophesied and was "changed into a different person" (1 Samuel 10:6,10). Amos, after a series of cause-and-effect illustrations, said, "The lion has roared—who will not fear? The Sovereign LORD hath spoken—who can but prophesy?" (Amos 3:8). There was an inner compulsion moving him that was as strong as the fear a lion puts in a man when it chases him. Micah knew he was "filled with power, [even] with the Spirit of the LORD" to deal with Israel's sins (Micah 3:8).

There is no guesswork concerning the reality and definiteness of action of the Holy Spirit in the New Testament either. For the sake of John the Baptist, the Spirit came upon Jesus in visible form as a dove. The sound of a wind and tongues of fire heralded His presence on the Day of Pentecost.

Though His other manifestations to the Church were invisible, they were just as definite. On three occasions it is specifically recorded that the believers spoke with other tongues (Acts 2:4; 10:46; 19:6). Once the place was shaken (Acts 4:31) and they all spoke the word of God with boldness. The comfort (encouragement) of the Holy Spirit was a very important factor in the growth of the Early Church (Acts 9:31). They did not have to guess whether He was there or not. They knew.

The Holy Spirit provided the warmth, the dynamic, and the joy that characterized the whole movement of the gospel in the first century. Every part of the daily life of the believers, including their work and worship, was dedicated to Christ Jesus as Lord and was under the direction of the Holy Spirit. This does not mean, of course, that their own minds or intelligence had no place, or that they were moved by emotion only. Emotion did have "a vital place, which the exaggerated intellectual emphasis of many Protestants today does not adequately value."[1] But they were expected to search the Scriptures, accept reasonable proofs, and in understanding (thinking) be men (become mature). (See 1 Corinthians 14:20; Acts 17:11; 28:23.)

Nevertheless, the whole of their Christian life and worship transcended the merely natural and human. The supernatural was a part of all experience. In their daily lives they did not try to carry out some things on the human level and some on the level of the Spirit. The qualities they needed in order to work together and bear testimony by their lives were not ordinary graces, but the fruit of the Spirit (Galatians 5:22,23). They never supposed that if a person tried hard enough he could live a good life and please God. They knew they needed the constant help of the Spirit. In their worship they knew they were quite insufficient in themselves to praise and glorify the Lord. They expected singing in the Spirit, praying in the Spirit, and gifts and ministries of the Spirit (1 Corinthians 14:15,26). They did not claim external miracles every day, but every day was a miracle as they lived and walked in the Spirit.

This personal experience with the Holy Spirit is still one of the distinguishing marks of Christianity. In a course which introduced me to the study of comparative religions, the professor pointed out that non-Christian religions do say good things. Some have high moral standards. A few emphasize one true God. Others even have some sort of trinity (really a triad). Many present a way of salvation of some kind. Some even speak of a resurrection. But none of them offers anything like the Holy Spirit. They all leave people to do in their own strength the good things they ask. You might say they ask people to try to lift themselves out of the mire by their own shoelaces.

Jesus said, "I will not leave you as orphans" (John 14:18). He went on to promise a Counselor, Helper, Advocate, Teacher, and Guide. The Holy Spirit is all of these. He is a personal Friend who is adequate for all our needs.

More and more writers and scholars are recognizing this. John V. Taylor, in his book *Go-Between God*, draws attention to Trevor Ling's argument that what distinguishes Old and New

Testament religion from the great religions of Asia is "the nature of the prophetic experience . . . the prophet, in the experience of revelation, is made aware of the personal nature of the transcendent reality which has taken hold of him."[2]

Dependence on the Holy Spirit and on wisdom from above may not have been very popular with the teachers and philosophers of New Testament times, however. Paul warned Timothy against "the opposing ideas [objections, contradictions, antitheses] of what is falsely called knowledge" (1 Timothy 6:20). Some of the objections may have been along this very line of rejecting the person and personal relationship of the Holy Spirit. At least, it was not long before false teachers were claiming that the Spirit was only "the exerted energy of God."[3] But all the objections and antitheses of these teachers only lead to confusion. Dependence on Christ and the Holy Spirit is the only way to peace.

More and more the world today has taken God off the throne and put self and human reason in His place. The tendency is to exalt the ego with success, money, status, fame. Even projects to help others or relieve the world's suffering are often motivated by a desire for satisfaction over what one has accomplished in himself. Like Pharaoh of old, the world says, "Who is the LORD, that I should obey him?" (Exodus 5:2). It is terribly humbling for the secular man of today to bow before Christ and accept the fact that he is a sinner who can do nothing to save himself. Yet the fact is that "the high and lofty One . . . who lives forever, whose name is holy" and who dwells "in the high and holy place [heaven]," still delights to come and dwell "with him who is contrite and lowly in spirit" (Isaiah 57:15).

The recognition that we are not self-sufficient, but totally dependent on Christ and the Holy Spirit to do anything that pleases God, and the willingness to give Him all the praise, is the secret of the success of the Pentecostal Movement today. More than that, the Pentecostals stand firm at the point that marks off Bible-believers from so-called liberals. The line of demarcation is not the acceptance simply of the Virgin Birth, the Cross, or the Resurrection. It is rather the supernatural itself. Those who oppose the simple gospel of Christ, who try to strip the Bible of its miracles, and who cut up the New Testament and make Jesus an empty figure—a pale, mistaken teacher—all build their theories on an antisupernaturalistic bias.

Most of these antisupernaturalists argue that they must remove the supernatural from the Bible in order to make the gospel acceptable and applicable to modern man. Actually, the reverse is true. I am constantly meeting people whose lives have been changed and revitalized by the Holy Spirit. One example is an Episcopal priest from Florida. When he was called on to read the funeral service, he would mumble as rapidly as possible such passages as "the dead in Christ will rise first. After that, we who are still alive and are left will be caught up together with them in the clouds to meet the Lord in the air" (1 Thessalonians 4:16, 17). He hoped no one would understand what he was saying, for he could not believe it and he did not believe anyone else could either.

He was reading Bishop Robinson's book *Honest to God* along with the works of other "God-is-dead" theologians and existential philosophers trying, as he said, "to find some excuse for an egghead like myself to stay in the ministry."

Finally, he determined one day he had performed his last service in the church. He decided he was through with the ministry. That night he was invited to a home where he found a group of happy, Spirit-filled Christians. In the presence of the genuine moving of the Holy Spirit all his arguments and presuppositions fell apart. He found Christ, received the baptism in the Holy Spirit, and entered into a new and wonderful Pentecostal ministry. After that, he loved the Bible and looked forward to the coming of Jesus with joyful anticipation. Such incidents could be multiplied hundreds of times over.

It is worth noting also that all the major denominations in the United States in their early days put up barriers of creeds against liberalism and against the destructive criticism of the Bible. Few have succeeded in keeping this sort of unbelief out. Today the Pentecostals are in the frontline of the battle against the enemy of the truth who is also the enemy of our souls. Modern man needs the full illumination that comes through the person of the Spirit when He dwells within in power.

Thank God, there is increasing interest today both in the gospel of our Lord Jesus Christ and in the person and work of the Holy Spirit. A number of years ago when I was in seminary, one of my professors asked a New Testament class of one hundred people from about twenty-five different denominations, "How many have heard a sermon on the Holy Spirit in the last five years?" Only three or four of us put up our hands. He added, "In the last ten years?" Two or three more put up their hands. Few books on the Holy Spirit were available at that time. Owing in part to the faithful witness of the Pentecostals, this is no longer true. In increasingly large segments of the Church, literature on the Holy Spirit is proliferating.

The purpose of this book is simply to go through the Bible book by book and take a fresh look at what it teaches about the Holy Spirit and His work. Then a final chapter will summarize and apply further what we discover.

The book-by-book approach was chosen because it fits in well with the way the Bible was written. In the Bible we find a progressive, step-by-step revelation of God and His plan.

In the Old Testament the chief emphasis needed was on the one true God. Israel was an island in the midst of a whole world of polytheism. It was necessary to deal with this first. As long as idols were worshipped "under every green tree," as was the case in the days of Jeremiah and Ezekiel, Israel was not ready for the full revelation of the deity of the Messiah and the personality of the Holy Spirit. So these are only hinted at in the Old Testament.

By New Testament times the Jews had learned their lesson. They were known the world over as worshipers of one God. It was time for the next step in God's revelation and plan.

The Spirit in the Pentateuch

The Bible introduces us almost at once to the Spirit of God. "In the beginning God created the heavens and the earth. Now the earth was formless and empty [uninhabited], darkness was over the surface of the deep [the primeval ocean], and the Spirit of God was hovering over the waters" (Genesis 1:1,2). Thus, the Spirit of God is associated with God's creative activity.

Actually, the Bible ascribes all the works of God in an absolute sense to each member of the Trinity both individually and collectively. Each of the divine Persons has His specific function. Yet they all work in perfect harmony and cooperation at all times.

Creation is a prime example. The Bible speaks of God the Father as the Maker of the heaven, earth, sea, and all that is in them (Acts 4:24). It also speaks of the Son (the same life-giving Word who became flesh and dwelt among us) as the secondary Agent in creation. "Through him all things were made; without him [apart from Him] nothing was made that has been made" (John 1:3). Here the phraseology is of God speaking through the Son just as He spoke through the prophets. He was the living Word through whom God spoke the worlds into existence. From the beginning He was the mediator between God and man (1 Timothy 2:5).

The Spirit also is recognized in other places. The Psalmist said, "When you send your Spirit, they are created, and you renew the face of the earth" (Psalm 104:30). The Spirit is thus connected with both creation and God's continuing providence. (See also Isaiah 40:12,13.) Other passages that refer to the Spirit also use terminology indicating the breath of God (Job 26:13; 33:4; Psalm 33:6).

The Bible also emphasizes that the heavens and earth were created by His power and wisdom (Psalm 136:5; Proverbs 3:19; 8:23–30; Jeremiah 10:12; 51:15). His power is pictured by mentioning in a concrete way His hands and His fingers (Psalms 8:3; 95:5; 102:25; Isaiah 45:12; 48:13). This is balanced by an emphasis that they were all made by His word (Psalms 33:6,9; 148:5).

Spirit, Wind, Breath

Most scholars take "spirit" in Isaiah 34:16 to mean breath, since it is parallel to "mouth." Many today also find difficulty in rendering Genesis 1:2 as "Spirit." *The New English Bible,* following some Jewish and most liberal scholars, reads, "The earth was without form and void, with darkness over the face of the abyss, and a mighty wind that swept over the surface of the waters," possibly to keep the waters in check.

Actually, the Hebrew word for spirit *(ruach)* like the Greek word *(pneuma)* can mean wind, breath, or spirit. It is used to represent a wide range of expressions in relation to nature, the life of animals and man, and God. Someone has figured up that there are at least thirty-three different shades of meaning that the word may have in different contexts.[1]

In Exodus 14:21, the word *ruach* is used of the strong east wind that kept blowing until the Israelites could cross on dry land. "The cool of the day" (Genesis 3:8) is the "wind" of the day, referring to the cool breezes of the afternoon. In the wilderness "a wind went out from the LORD" and brought quail from the sea (Numbers 11:31). Poetically, the Psalmist speaks of "the wings of the wind" (Psalms 18:10; 104:3). The Lord also sent "a great wind" when Jonah fled toward Tarshish (Jonah 1:4).

Genesis 2:7 uses a different word for "the breath of life" (Hebrew, "lives"). But 6:17 uses *ruach* for breath, and 7:22 combines the two words for "the breath of life" (Hebrew, "the spirit of the breath of life"), showing the close relationship of the ideas of spirit and breath. Job also uses this word when he speaks of taking his breath (Job 9:18; see also 19:17).

Most writers take the original sense of the word for spirit *(ruach)* to be wind, breeze, moving air.[2] Some insist that, in both Greek and Hebrew, it always keeps this basic meaning in the sense of either wind or breath, that is, air moving either inside or outside man.[3] Others take it that whether translated spirit or breath, when related to living things, it is always God's gift coming from Him and returning to Him (Genesis 6:3,17; 7:15,22; Job 33:4; 27:3; Psalm 104:29,30; Ecclesiastes 12:7). In this sense "spirit" can be taken as a life energy or life-giving energy that God alone possesses permanently by His very nature (Isaiah 31:3; John 5:26).[4] It is generally accepted, therefore, that in the Old Testament the separate personality of the Holy Spirit is not fully revealed. He is equated with God's power or personal presence in action.[5]

In the light of this, the reading "a mighty wind" does not seem to be suitable in Genesis 1:2. Liberal commentators who think "the Spirit of God" is a wrong translation possibly are influenced too much by naturalistic and evolutionary presuppositions. Some try to compare it to Genesis 8:1 where God did cause a wind to pass over the earth so that the waters of the Flood began to subside.

Some liberals do admit that *The New English Bible* translation "mighty" is insufficient. They agree that if the word "God" is used adjectively "a god of a wind," it must mean at least "divine, supernatural, awesome."[6]

The Hovering Spirit

Bible words must be studied in their own context. The phraseology of Genesis 1:2 is not at all like that of Genesis 8:1. The verb is entirely different. Genesis 1:2 states: "the Spirit of God was hovering (continually) over the waters." The word "moved" is used in this form in only one other place (Deuteronomy 32:11). There it describes a mother bird hovering or fluttering over her young in a vibrant, protective way. (The meaning is not "brooding." There is no thought here of mythology or of hatching eggs.) "A mighty wind" does not hover. It is contradictory, almost absurd, to picture a violet wind, which some even compare to a tornado, as gently hovering over the waters.[7]

Closer examination of the entire first chapter of Genesis shows that God is the subject of most of the sentences in the chapter. We read that God created, God saw, God called, God made, God blessed. The whole picture is one of God in action—not just any god, but the one true God. From this we see also that the Hebrew looks at the word "God" here as a definite noun. A common rule for Hebrew grammar makes the word *Spirit* definite also.[8] Thus, the only translation that fits the whole context is "the Spirit of God." As we have seen, this fits the clear teaching of the rest of the Bible that the Father, Son, and Holy Spirit worked in perfect cooperation in the totality of the work of creation.

Genesis, of course, does not emphasize this. The world was not ready for the revelation of the Trinity. Because of the polytheism that surrounded Israel, it was more important to show that creation had its source in the one true God and not in the many gods of the nations of that day. For the same reason, Genesis 1:2 does not explain exactly what the work of the Spirit of God was. It was evidently preparatory for the order and purpose that was brought out by God in the six creation days that followed. It lets us know that though all was darkness, God was active. Though the earth did not yet have its final form and was uninhabited, it was not chaos. God was there.

God, however, remains separate from His creation. He acts upon it, but does not become part of it. The emphasis as creation proceeds is on the fact that it is all from God. Life does not rise from the earth of itself, but is the result of the creative Word. At every step God speaks, God creates, God makes. Though He calls on the sea and the dry land to bring forth living creatures ("souls of life"; living souls, living beings each with its own life as an individual), He steps in to create or make them.[9] (See Genesis 1:20,21,24,25.)

The Creation of Man

The climax comes when God says, "Let us make man in our image, in our likeness" (Genesis 1:26). Though nothing is said about the Holy Spirit here, the Bible shows that the image and likeness have to do with the spiritual and moral nature of man. Paul prays that God would "strengthen [believers] with power through his Spirit in [their] inner being" and goes on to urge them to "put on the new self, created to be like God [in the image and likeness of God] in righteousness and holiness" (Ephesians 3:16; 4:24). It is reasonable, therefore, to believe that the Holy Spirit was just as active in Genesis 1:26–28 as He was in Genesis 1:2, if not more so.

Genesis 2:7 gives more details. "The LORD God formed [molded, shaped as a potter would] the man from the [moist] dust of the ground [red earth], and breathed into his nostrils the breath of life [Hebrew, "lives"], and the man became a living being [person, individual]." Again, though the Holy Spirit is not mentioned, it is reasonable to believe He was active along with the Father and the Son.

Older commentaries tend to find significance in the Hebrew plural, "breath of lives," taking it to refer to animal and intellectual life, or physical life and spiritual life.[10] The Bible does show that a person's own spirit comes from God and will return to Him (Ecclesiastes 12:7; Luke 23:46; see also John 19:30 where Jesus gave up His Spirit). Other passages also emphasize that God is the source of life and that His Spirit produces it (Job 27:3; 33:4). If He were to withdraw it, all life would come to an end (Job 34:15).[11]

However, possession of the "breath of lives" is used to describe all those who died in the Flood (Genesis 6:17; 7:22), as well as the animals who entered the ark (Genesis 7:15). Thus, a more logical view recognizes that the Hebrew plural is not speaking of different kinds of life here. In Hebrew, the plural is often used of fullness or of something that flows. (Water is always plural in Hebrew.) It is also used of something that shows many aspects or expressions. (The words *face* and *heaven* are also always in the plural in Hebrew.) The attention in Genesis 2:7 is, therefore, not so much on the kind of life as on the source of life. The "breath of life" may simply mean God's breath or Spirit which produces life, which gives man his "life-breath" or "faculty of life."[12] In any case, the New Testament contrasts what Adam received to what Christ is. He, the last Adam, is more than a living soul. He is a life-giving Spirit (1 Corinthians 15:45).

The Spirit Striving, Judging

When he sinned, man was cut off from the fellowship with God he enjoyed in the Garden of Eden. But that God's Spirit continued to deal with man after the Fall is brought out in Genesis 6:3 where an end is proclaimed. "My Spirit will not contend with man forever, for he [mankind] is mortal; his [mankind's] days will be a hundred and twenty years."

This passage is a difficult one in many respects. The one hundred-twenty years probably refers to a period of grace God was giving mankind before the Flood would come and destroy them all (except for Noah and his family). The word "contend" is variously interpreted as rule, judge, shield, abide in, or act in. The translation "abide in" chosen by some modern versions (including the Revised Standard Version) as well as by a number of ancient versions is a pure guess. There seems to be nothing in the Hebrew to give any grounds for it. Yet many scholars still accept it, taking the verse to mean that God's Spirit (as a vital principle or as the breath of Genesis 2:7) would not continue to abide (or be established) in man because of his sin and weakness. But most who take this view are quite hesitant and uncertain about it.[13]

The translation rule is an application of the meaning "to judge." (The fact that the judges judged came to mean that they ruled.) Shield is another aspect of "judge" in the sense that a judge should be a protector of the weak. This meaning has some support from related Semitic languages.[14] Most modern interpreters take "my Spirit" to mean the spirit God breathed into man. This may be possible, but it is a usage not found elsewhere in the Bible. Everywhere else, "my Spirit" means the Holy Spirit, the Spirit of God.[15]

Actually, the simplest meaning of the verb translated "contend with" is "judge among." The name Dan ("judge") is derived from the same root (Genesis 49:16). Though not the most common word for judge, it is used of the Lord judging and vindicating Israel (Deuteronomy 32:36; Psalms 50:4; 72:2; 135:14) as well as judging the world (1 Samuel 2:10; Psalm 110:6). This seems to fit better than any of the other proposed meanings.

In a sense, "to judge" also corresponds with the traditional interpretation of "to contend with." As Leupold points out, mankind before the Flood was not without the Word of God given through godly men such as Enoch and Noah. The Holy Spirit would act as judge, using the Word given up to that time to instruct, exhort, reprove, and convict men. In this sense, the judging of the Spirit would truly be a striving with men "to restrain them from their evil ways."[16]

Another question arises when some writers attempt to tie this passage with Jude 6 and make angels that sinned have a part in the cause of the Flood. This raises more problems because of the great emphasis on mankind and on flesh (weak, frail, unregenerate human flesh) here. At least, it has little bearing on the Spirit's ceasing to judge here.

Abraham and the Patriarchs

After man again failed at the tower of Babel and the new variety of languages brought confusion and scattering, the Book of

Genesis ceases to deal with mankind as a whole. The remainder of the book is concerned with Abraham and the chosen line that comes from him. Most mentions of the Holy Spirit in the rest of the Old Testament have to do with Israel.

Someone has said, "The story of the Bible is the story of Spirit-filled men."[17] This may not seem very apparent in the history of the patriarchs, but it would be very strange if Abraham, whom Paul upholds as one of the greatest examples of faith (Romans 4:1–22; Galatians 3:6–18), were not a man of the Spirit.

Actually, there is one clear indication that he was, though the circumstances are somewhat strange. Abraham had called his wife his sister (actually, she was his half-sister) and allowed her to be taken into King Abimelech's harem. When a treaty was made allowing a powerful man with a large following to stay in a neighbor's country, custom demanded that the treaty be sealed by depositing a daughter or sister in the harem as a hostage to guarantee the good behavior of the guest. God took them where they were and undertook to protect Sarah by warning Abimelech to return her to Abraham. Since Abraham was a prophet he would then pray for Abimelech (Genesis 20:7).

Prophet means a spokesman for God. (See Exodus 7:1; 4:16; Deuteronomy 18:18–22.) More importantly, prophets were men of the Spirit: "men spoke from God as they were carried along [borne along, led along] by the Holy Spirit" (2 Peter 1:21).

Abraham deserved the designation of prophet, for God spoke to him often and gave him directions not only for himself but for others as well. Abraham also spoke to others and called on others to worship God. His altars were invitations to public worship where he witnessed to the truth of the one God. His intercession for Sodom also was the sort of thing that characterized the prophets. Most prophets were intercessors, especially Moses (Numbers 14:13–20; Deuteronomy 9:20); Samuel (1 Samuel 7:5; 12:19,23); Jeremiah (7:16); and Amos (7:2,5).

God answered Abraham's prayer for Abimelech (Genesis 20:17). Later, the Psalmist applied the principle taught in this passage to the rest of the patriarchs: Isaac, Jacob, and Joseph (Psalm 105:9–22). Concerning them this psalm says (105:15), "Do not touch my anointed ones; do my prophets no harm." Joseph especially was recognized for the anointing of which the psalm speaks. After he interpreted Pharaoh's dream, Pharaoh said, "Can we find anyone like this man, one in whom is the spirit of God?" (Genesis 41:38). Pharaoh saw there was no other explanation of the wisdom and insight this Hebrew slave and recent convict demonstrated. Joseph truly was a Spirit-filled man, equipped by the Spirit of God for the work he was called to do.

Building the Tabernacle

The Israelites who followed Joseph to Egypt were made slaves, and the man God chose to deliver them was also a Spirit-filled man. God himself recognized Moses as the greatest prophet of his time. Other prophets of the day would experience God speaking to them in dreams and visions only, but to Moses God spoke directly, "face to face," just as a man would carry on a conversation with a friend (Numbers 12:6–8).

It is true that at the burning bush Moses complained that he could not speak well and God designated Aaron as Moses' prophet or spokesman. But God still spoke to Moses, and Moses would then speak to Aaron. Thus, Moses was still the real prophet (Exodus 3:4; 4:10–16).

At every point in Moses' dealings with Pharaoh and Israel, God continued to speak to Moses. At Mt. Sinai God did speak directly to the people in the initial giving of the Ten Commandments (Exodus 20:1–17). But the people were so filled with terror and awe caused by the voice of God and all the accompanying sights and sounds that they backed off to the far side of the valley. Then they begged Moses to speak with them instead of having God speak (Exodus 20:18,19). Thus, Moses alone was permitted to ascend to the top of Mount Sinai where he received the Law written on tables of stone, as well as directions for the tabernacle.

The tabernacle was a project intended to help the Israelites learn to work together, as well as a place where God would continually manifest His presence. All could participate. Those whose hearts made them willing could bring gold or silver. If they had none, they could bring brass (copper). Blue, purple, scarlet, and fine linen were needed, but so was goat's hair. They could also bring their skills (Exodus 25:1–9; 35:5–9,20–26). But in every situation there are always people who do not have anything and cannot do anything. These were to come and be taught. God promised to fill two men, Bezalel and Oholiab, with the Spirit to sharpen their own skills and to enable them to teach others also (Exodus 31:2,3; 35:30,31).

This filling with the Spirit would be the source of "skill, ability and knowledge in all kinds of crafts" (Exodus 31:3) In other words, the Spirit would supply them with supernatural help in connection with the practical tasks of preparing materials for the tabernacle that would be both useful and beautiful.

"Skill" in the Old Testament usually includes practical wisdom that makes it possible to reach one's goals. "Ability," also translated "understanding," usually includes insight and intelligent decisions. "Knowledge" includes "know-how" that sees what needs to be done and how best to do it. All this came from the Spirit. Bezalel and Oholiab were not to depend on their natural abilities and skills alone. They would still work hard, but at the same time they would depend on the Spirit and receive help from Him. Note, however, that not all the workers were filled— only those two who were specially named and chosen by the Lord.

Moses and the Elders of Israel

Not until Numbers 11:10–30 does the Bible specifically mention the Spirit in connection with Moses himself. The Israelites had moved out from Sinai into the wilderness and were murmuring (complaining) about the manna. They were tired of manna for breakfast, manna for lunch, manna for dinner. All they could think of was the fish, melons, leeks, and garlic they formerly ate so freely in Egypt. Actually, the manna was not that bad. It could be prepared in a number of ways. But unbelief and self-pity made them forget the bondage that went with all that spicy food in Egypt. Unbelief also filled them with a rebellious spirit that did not want to accept God's provision or direction. They were unwilling to commit themselves into God's hands. Soon the whole multitude was weeping for "flesh" (meat or fish).

This upset Moses. The pressure was too great. He told God he was not capable of taking care of this crowd of spiritual babies. In fact, if God was going to make him carry the whole load alone, He might as well kill him now. The job was going to kill him sooner or later anyway.

God's answer was, in a sense, a gentle rebuke. He told Moses to select seventy elders of Israel, mature men, with proven ability and make them officers over the people. (See Exodus 18:18–26.) He was to bring them to the tabernacle where they would stand in a semicircle with Moses. Then the Lord would come down and take of the Spirit which was on Moses and put the same Spirit on them. They would help Moses bear the burden of the people (Numbers 11:17).

In other words, God was saying to Moses, "What makes you think this is your burden or that you have to bear it in your own strength? The Spirit of God is big enough and fully sufficient to carry the load and meet the need." Nor would Moses lose by doing this. The infinite Spirit is not made less when He is shared with others. Ancient writers (as Origen) compared the Spirit on Moses to a lamp used to light seventy others without losing any of its brightness.

The prophesying of the seventy is not described. Some today insist they fell into some sort of frenzy (as King Saul did when he was resisting the Holy Spirit; 1 Samuel 19:23,24).[18] But this again supposes wrongly that it was too early in Israel's history for prophecy in the sense of exhortation of men or supplication to God. Frenzy was never a characteristic of Hebrew prophecy as such. All that is indicated here is a gentle yielding to the Spirit by the seventy and a willing response to His illumination.

The phrase "but they did not do so again" (Numbers 11:25) accurately portrays what the Hebrew says: "and they did not add, increase, do again." Deuteronomy 5:22 uses the same verb and it is translated "and he added nothing more." The most common use of the verb is to do something again that one has done before. Thus, it is generally agreed that the experience of these elders was temporary. The Spirit came upon them as an anointing for service and to teach Moses he could and must depend on the Spirit. The ministry of the elders was to help him carry the burden and responsibility of teaching and exhorting the people. But Moses remained the chief prophet or speaker for God in Israel.

Living below Their Privileges

That Moses learned his lesson is shown by his response to Joshua in an incident shortly after this (Numbers 11:29). Two of the elders, Eldad and Medad, called by Moses did not go to the tabernacle, but the Spirit came upon them just the same (v. 26). More than this, the Spirit continued to rest upon them as they prophesied out in the camp of Israel. Then Joshua ran to Moses and reported that, unlike the others, these had not ceased. They were still prophesying in the camp. (The Hebrew uses a participle here indicating continuous action.) Joshua very earnestly asked Moses to "stop them."

Moses' answer was a gentle rebuke to Joshua. "Are you jealous for my sake?" (v. 29). In other words, "Are you jealous over my authority or my ministry as a prophet?" Moses recognized that the move of the Spirit was not under his control nor was it limited to particular places or times. Joshua ought not to think Moses' authority was being undermined because these two did not come to the right place. Nor was he to think Moses' ministry was in any way threatened or diminished because the Spirit rested on them and they kept prophesying.

Moses also recognized something even more important when he added, "I wish that all the LORD's people were prophets and that the LORD would put [give] his Spirit upon them." He saw that the complaining, rebellious, unbelieving people were living far below their privileges. The normal level for all God's people ought to be one where they would all be like Eldad and Medad. They should all be prophets with the Spirit of God continually resting upon them. Later on, Jeremiah (31:31–34) and Ezekiel (36:25–27) caught a glimpse of a time when this would indeed be true of Israel. Joel (2:28,29) also prophesied it for all flesh. But for Moses it was only a wish he never saw fulfilled. Not until the Day of Pentecost did the Spirit come and begin the fulfillment of the prophecy of Joel by filling every believer present with the Spirit (Acts 2:4,16).

Israel Protected by the Spirit

The Holy Spirit was not only able to deal with Moses and the people of Israel; He was able to deal with their enemies as well. To reach the plains of Moab across the Jordan from Jericho, the Israelites went around the country of Moab. Then they moved north and won great victories over the people of Gilead and Bashan on the east side of the Jordan River. King Balak was afraid he would be next (Numbers 22:2,3). He was wrong, of course; the next step would be for Israel to cross the Jordan into the Promised Land; but Balak did not know that. He did realize, however, that Israel did not win their victories because of superior numbers or equipment. It had to be what Israel was saying it was: their God was with them.

Balak determined, therefore, that the only way to stop Israel was to turn their God against them. So he sent messengers in all directions looking for someone who had power with Jehovah. Finally, near the Euphrates River not far from where Abraham's relatives lived, they discovered an evil prophet named Balaam (2 Peter 2:15;

Jude 11; Revelation 2:14) also practiced divination (Joshua 13:22). He was really a heathen fortune-teller and adviser who used various means to conjure up spirits or find omens or make incantations for a price. Somehow, he had heard of the power of Jehovah and apparently had added His name to his list.

It may seem strange that God would use such a man. But God was protecting His people from an enemy they did not know about, and He purposed to use His Holy Spirit to do it.

Balak's purpose was to hire Balaam to get God to curse Israel instead of blessing them. The Bible shows God dealt with Balaam in strange ways. First, He showed that a dumb animal had more spiritual sense than Balaam did (Numbers 22:21–35). Second, God gave Balaam such a scare that he would not dare tell King Balak anything but what the Lord told him to say. Balaam was so greedy for money that he would have told Balak anything he wanted to hear, if the price was right, but now God could count on him.

Balaam still thought he could persuade God to curse Israel. His heathen attitude is shown by the way he approached the problem. He called for seven sacrifices to be offered on the top of a mountain overlooking the camp of Israel. Then he tried his sorcery (enchantments, incantations, omens). But God's word was one of blessing for Israel, not a curse.

Balaam then went to another mountain and offered seven more sacrifices. The heathen had the idea that the gods needed the sacrifices. They thought, therefore, that if they offered the right sacrifice in the right place, they could force a god to do anything they wished. In Balaam's thinking there could be nothing wrong with the sacrifice. Seven was a perfect number and bullocks and rams were the most expensive sacrifices they could offer. So he concluded the place must be wrong. He would try another mountain.

Again, God gave a word of blessing. So they tried a third mountain and another seven sacrifices. But this time Balaam gave up his sorcery, looked out over the camp of Israel, and the

Spirit of God came upon him. The Spirit did more than put a word in his mouth (as in Numbers 23:5,16). This time his whole being was affected. By the Spirit the Lord was revealed to him, and the vision of the Almighty caused him to fall before Him in awe (Numbers 24:1–9). (Note: In the King James Version, the words "into a trance" in verses 4 and 16 are in italics indicating they are not in the Hebrew. Actually, there is no thought of trance or frenzy here. Balaam's eyes remained open. He was aware of what was going on around him.)

As he lay prostrate before the Lord Balaam's eyes were open in a new way. He saw Israel's fair tents stretching out like prosperous orchards and gardens with victory and strength as their portion. In conclusion, he repeated for Israel the promise that was first given to Abraham (Genesis 12:3), "I will bless those who bless you, and whoever curses you I will curse" (Numbers 24:9).

At this, Balak was greatly angered and told Balaam to go home without the promised reward. But Balaam, still prostrate before the Lord, gave one more prophecy. No longer was he trying to manipulate God or control His purposes. He was simply yielded—and he saw the distant future. "A star will come out of Jacob; a scepter will rise out of Israel" (Numbers 24:17). Most older writers see this as a prophecy of the Messiah. In view of the context, however, some today take "star" and "scepter" as collective nouns referring to Israel and to the time the kingdom would rise and conquer Moab.[19] Yet it is still possible to take Balaam's emphasis on the distant future and see Moab as a type of God's enemies who will be conquered by Christ. In any case, it is clear that Balaam for once truly yielded to the Spirit. Unfortunately, the yielding was only temporary. His greed for money overpowered him. Later, he sold his services to the Midianites and died fighting against Israel (Numbers 31:8).

Joshua, a Man in Whom Is the Spirit

In strong contrast to Balaam, whose experience was so fleeting, Joshua was a man in whom the Spirit was continually resident

(Numbers 27:18). Balaam caught only a glimpse of God's blessing on Israel and never learned to treasure it for himself. Joshua was a faithful servant of the Lord and was chosen to lead Israel into Canaan to claim the blessing.

Joshua was probably not one of the seventy upon whom God put the Spirit around the tabernacle. They are called elders. He is specially designated as one of the young men who were servants of Moses (Numbers 11:28). But somewhere during the forty years of wilderness journeyings, he was filled with the Spirit of God and wisdom (Deuteronomy 34:9). More importantly, he remained full and learned to depend on the Spirit for wisdom (insight, ability to carry out God's purposes and bring them to completion).

We see then that though Moses was about to die, God had a leader ready to take his place. Moses had been the prophet, the man of the Spirit for forty years. The entrance into the Promised Land would be a critical time and it would not be easy for anyone to take Moses' place. Joshua was well-trained. He had already won victories (Exodus 17:9–14). Yet the key was the Spirit. The same Spirit who moved Moses would now move Joshua.

Some take the phrase "because Moses had laid his hands on him" (Deuteronomy 34:9) to mean that the Spirit filled Joshua because or as a result of the fact that Moses laid his hands on him.[20] But this was surely not the case. From Numbers 27:18 it is clear that Joshua was already filled with the Spirit. The word "because" (Deuteronomy 34:9) can also mean "so that." Thus, the laying on of hands, like New Testament ordination, was simply a public recognition of the ministry God had already given. As the result of the laying on of hands, the people listened to Joshua and accepted him as Moses' successor. Thus, with God-given leadership they were able to go forward.

The Spirit in the History of Israel

As we come into the Historical Books there is no specific mention of the Holy Spirit until we get to the Book of Judges. Though Joshua was Spirit-filled, there was a quiet presence in his life rather than noticeable outward manifestations. At times, however, it seems he fell back into trusting in his own judgment instead of seeking the guidance the Spirit of God could give (Joshua 7:2–4; 9:14). But these were the exceptions. On the whole Joshua obeyed the Lord, saw God fulfill many promises, and left Israel with a challenge to serve the Lord and Him alone (Joshua 24:14,15).

All went well as long as Joshua lived and as long as the elders lived who had crossed the Jordan and had seen the glory and power of God. In three great campaigns, Joshua subdued the land so that "the land had rest from war" (Joshua 11:23). Then, he proceeded to divide the land among the tribes. All the Canaanite cities had not been conquered, however, nor did the Israelites follow God's command to drive them out (Numbers 33:55; Joshua 23:12,13). Actually, each tribe was given the task of completing the conquest of its own territory. As the Lord reminded Joshua, there was still much land to be possessed (Joshua 13:1).

The individual tribes also failed to obey the Lord in this. Again and again the Book of Judges repeats that the various tribes did not drive out the Canaanites (Judges 1:21,27–31,33).

Some cities they were not able to conquer. But the Canaanites they conquered were put to work chopping wood or bringing in water from the wells (Joshua 9:23). As Israel became stronger they could have driven them out, but they preferred to take money from them as tribute (Joshua 16:10; 17:13; Judges 1:28). Only on a very few occasions did they step out in faith and see God's power manifested again. Most of the time they were quite content to settle back and enjoy the fruit of their new prosperity. Unfortunately, the Israelites had never learned how to handle prosperity.

With this increased prosperity came spiritual decline. The older generation was so taken up with their own pleasures that worship became formal. The training of the young was either neglected or the bad example of the parents made their words meaningless. As a result, a new generation arose "who knew neither the LORD nor what he had done for Israel" (Judges 2:10).

This does not mean these young people had never heard about the Lord or the miracles. They knew about the deliverance from Egypt. Undoubtedly, they had heard the story of the fall of Jericho again and again. But the word "knew" (Judges 2:10) means more than "knew about." The tragic fact is that though they had heard of these things they did not know the Lord for themselves. They had never seen any of His miracle-working power in their own experience.

As a result, the young generation were attracted to the feasting, drunkenness, and lax morals of the Canaanite culture as well as to the prestige of their ancient temples and high places. When this happened, God withdrew His blessing and sent armies to bring His judgment on the various tribes. These enemies were the very Canaanites whose religion and immorality they had followed. Again and again this happened throughout the period of the Judges.

Though the tribes of Israel had an established leadership in the elders and priests, these were of little help. In fact, they too were influenced by Canaanite ways all too often. A comparison of Judges 10:6,7; 13:1; 16:31; and 1 Samuel 4:18; 7:1 shows that the forty years of Eli's priesthood in Shiloh overlapped the judgeship of Jephthah in Gilead and Samson in Dan. Thus it seems evident that the permissiveness and heathen influence that characterized Eli and his sons were all too common during the whole period. It was a time when "everyone did as he saw fit," as Judges twice declares (17:6; 21:25).

God-Chosen Judges

Even the ones God chose to help and deliver the people during this time were not entirely free from its failings. But the Spirit of God worked, sometimes in spite of them. In fact, it seems God chose people who were unimportant and not well known so that it could be seen that the power was of God and not of man. It seems God often chooses to use the lowly and the despised as His agents to bring deliverance and spiritual restoration, "the foolish things of the world to shame the wise . . . so that no one may boast before him" (1 Corinthians 1:27,29). When these men and women were aroused, moved, and filled by the Spirit of the Lord they turned the hearts of the people to God, led them to victory, and inspired them to serve the Lord.

The judges, then, were not simply national heroes. Nor did they make attempts to retain their power or found a dynasty. When the people wanted to make Gideon their king he refused. "I will not rule over you, nor will my son rule over you. The LORD will rule over you" (Judges 8:23). God was their King. He was also their Savior, and the Spirit of God was active in men and women to bring His redeeming, saving power to the people and to rule for Him.[1] The political life and the spiritual life of the people were closely related. In fact, every part of their lives was shown to be related to the Lord, the one true God. They were not allowed to compartmentalize their lives, putting religion in one compartment and business and politics in another. In everything they needed the help that could come only by the outpouring of the Spirit.[2]

As we have already seen, the times of some of the judges overlapped. Other judges (Tolah, Jair, Ibzan, Elon, and Abdon) are barely mentioned. Obviously, it is not the intent of the book to give a complete history.[3] Rather it seems to concentrate on the judges who are specifically stated to be moved by the Holy Spirit.

Some suppose the action of the Spirit on these judges was only in the physical sphere. The Jewish Targums even spoke of the Spirit on the judges as "the Spirit of heroism." But it is evident in many cases, as we shall see, that the judges did more than win victories and do exploits. They judged or ruled the people and restrained idolatry. For this, they needed wisdom, understanding, and knowledge by the Spirit of the Lord. Salvation and redemption, not mere victory over enemies, was the real purpose of what the Spirit was doing through the judges.[4]

The Spirit of the Lord is first mentioned in connection with Othniel. By the Spirit he judged and ruled Israel. By the Spirit also he was used to deliver them from a northern Mesopotamian or Aramaean conqueror (Judges 3:10).[5]

Some commentators point out that where we read that the Spirit came upon him, the Hebrew may be translated "was upon him." By this they imply that the Spirit of the Lord was already on Othniel before the Lord called him. But the Hebrew actually indicates historical sequence. The Spirit proceeded to come upon him and remained on him while he did his judging, ruling, and delivering work. It is worth noting, however, that Othniel was already a hero in Israel before God called him to be a judge. Much earlier Othniel had responded to Caleb's challenge to capture Kirjath Sepher (Book Town) and received the additional prize of Caleb's daughter to be his wife (Joshua 15:15–17; Judges 1:11–13). It is quite possible for acts of faith and obedience to precede the coming of the gift of the Spirit. (See Acts 5:32.)[6]

The greater amount of space in the Book of Judges is given to Deborah, Gideon, Jephthah, and Samson. Of these Deborah is unusual in many ways. Not only was she a judge, she was a prophet (Judges 4:4,6). Miriam before her was a prophet.

Moved by the Spirit, Miriam had led the women of Israel with music and praise as they beat their timbrels and danced for joy before the Lord (Exodus 15:20). Miriam's ministry was temporary, however. Jealousy of her younger brother, Moses, caused her to criticize him unfairly. God struck her with leprosy, and though she was healed after seven days, her ministry was apparently at an end. She is not mentioned again until her death (Numbers 12:1–15; 20:1).

Deborah's Wisdom

As a prophet, Deborah was a speaker for God, speaking as she was "carried along" (borne along, led along) by the Spirit of God (2 Peter 1:21). Her prophetic gift qualified her to lead, judge, and rule the nation. (See Deuteronomy 17:18,19.)

Deborah was, in fact, the only judge who was recognized and accepted as a judge before winning any military victories or delivering God's people from their enemies. So many commentaries suppose the only work of the Spirit in the time of the judges was the production of a kind of divine ecstasy or enthusiasm. But we do not find that to be so in Deborah's case. She sat under a palm tree between Ramah and Bethel (probably about fifteen miles north of Jerusalem) and the people came to her with their problems, disputes, and questions. They came because they recognized she was in touch with the Lord. She was married, and there is no indication that she neglected her farmer husband. But she found time for this ministry. The Spirit of God continually gave her wisdom to exhort the people and to comfort them, challenge them, and settle their differences. She needed no prompting to do this, no fleeces to encourage her faith. Many consider her the most spiritual of all the judges.

When the Spirit indicated it was God's time to deliver Israel from the Cannanites who then oppressed them, she called a man, Barak, to lead the army. Barak's faith was not up to hers, however, and he insisted that she come along. He was not a coward, but he saw the strength of the enemy and he wanted to be sure he had someone with him who was in touch with God. Others also feared the well-equipped armies of the Canaanites and refused to join Deborah and Barak. On the inhabitants of Meroz (in the tribe of Naphtali) she had to call down a curse "because they did not come to help the LORD" (Judges 5:23).

Clothes for the Spirit

Gideon, in contrast to Deborah, had to be encouraged again and again. He was from an unimportant family in the tribe of Manasseh. (Ephraim, though descended from the younger son of Joseph, took the leadership and made the people of Manasseh feel left out and forgotten.) God had to encourage Gideon with an angel, fire from a rock, fleeces, and a Midianite's dream before he finally dared take the leadership and believe God for victory. Yet he did respond to the angel and destroyed the idolatry in his father's household.

This act of faith and obedience was soon followed by a most unusual experience with the Spirit of the Lord. We read, "the Spirit of the LORD came upon Gideon" (Judges 6:34). But the Hebrew word for "came upon" is quite different from that in Judges 3:10. Here it means "put on, was clothed with, clothed himself with."

Many Bible scholars do not see the full significance of this. The most common interpretation of Judges 6:34 is that the Holy Spirit clothed Gideon. Keil falls short when he says that the Spirit "descended upon him, and laid itself around him as it were like a coat of mail, or a strong equipment, so that he became invulnerable and invincible in its might."[7] Similarly, A. B. Davidson says it implies "the complete enveloping of all the human faculties in the divine."[8] Knight, though giving the correct translation of the Hebrew, interprets it to mean that Gideon "wore upon himself the spirit of the living God! The mighty action which he then performed in saving Israel was not just his own action; it was God's saving action as well."[9]

The Jewish Targum explains it simply as the Spirit of strength from the Lord coming upon Gideon. Some modern writers treat it as just another sudden or violent seizure by the Spirit,[10] while others (as Bertheau, Fuerst, and Ewald) give an interpretation similar to Keil's.

A few do recognize, however, that the Hebrew can only mean that the Spirit filled Gideon. Gideon did not put on the Spirit, the Spirit put on Gideon.[11] For Gideon to be clothed with the Spirit, another form of the Hebrew verb would most probably be used. Gideon was just the clothes, "the covering of the Spirit, which rules, speaks, and testifies in him."[12]

Used in Spite of Mistakes

The increasing moral and spiritual decline that came with Israel's repeated backslidings is more and more obvious as we come to the time of Jephthah and Samson. Jephthah was indeed one of the despised of this world. His father was a leader in Gilead, but his mother was a prostitute (possibly one of the Canaanite priestesses who were so-called "sacred" prostitutes as part of their religion). His brothers drove him out when he was grown, and he was forced to become a warrior or independent raider in order to maintain himself. He built up quite a reputation for his leadership, however, and when the Ammonites to the east threatened Gilead, his brothers begged him to come back and be their head and leader.

Jephthah tried to settle the matter by a letter to the Ammonites, but when they refused to respond it became necessary to act. Then the Spirit of the Lord came upon Jephthah and he moved quickly into battle. The same Hebrew phrase is used of the Spirit coming on Jephthah as was used of His coming on Othniel (Judges 3:10; 11:29). But he failed to depend on the Holy Spirit and thought he had to bargain with the Lord with a foolish vow. Even so, the Holy Spirit did not desert him and the victory was won.

Samson the Nazirite

Samson had all the advantages Jephthah did not have. His parents were godly. The angel of the Lord appeared to them commanding his mother to drink no wine or beer and to eat nothing unclean, for their son was to be a Nazirite from his birth (Judges 13:7,14). As Samson grew, the Lord blessed him. Yet his actions after he reached maturity are not easy to understand. As Keil says:

> The nature of the acts which he performed appears still less to be such as we should expect from a hero impelled by the Spirit of God. His actions not only bear the stamp of adventure, foolhardiness, and willfulness, when looked at outwardly, but they are almost all associated with love affairs; so that it looks as if Samson had dishonored and fooled away the gift entrusted to him, by making it subservient to his sensual lusts, and thus had prepared the way for his own ruin, without bringing any essential help to his people.[13]

Liberal theologians, also looking at the acts of Samson outwardly, sometimes call his visitations of the Spirit "fits of demonic rage," "excesses," or "abnormal."[14]

Those who look at the moves of the Spirit as abnormal miss the point, however. We need not look at this outwardly. From a point of view that is sensitive to God's patient dealings with His people, we can see in Samson an object lesson of the grace and power of the Holy Spirit that shines all the more brightly because of its dark background. Again, Keil puts it very well:

> In Samson the Nazarite, however, not only did the Lord design to set before His people a man towering above the fallen generation in heroic strength, through his firm faith in and confident reliance upon the gift of God committed to him, opening up before it the prospect of a renewal of its own strength, that by this type he might arouse such strength and ability as were still slumbering in the nation; but Samson was to exhibit to his age generally a picture on the one hand of the strength which the people of God might acquire to overcome their strongest foes through the faithful submission to the Lord their God, and on the other hand of the weakness into which they had sunk through unfaithfulness to the covenant and intercourse with the heathen.[15]

Moved into Powerful Action

Too much attention is often given to Samson's hair. But nothing is said about this in the beginning of the story. Instead, the whole attention is on the way the Lord blessed him and began to move him or excite him to action. The verb "stir" (Judges 13:25) has the idea of thrust or impel. It also implies that he was aroused out of the sphere of the natural into the supernatural. This does not mean, as some suppose, that the Spirit overpowered him and forced him to do things that were totally outside his control.[16] It means rather that when the Spirit came upon him, he could not be satisfied to accept things as they were. He was impelled to take action in the power of the Spirit.

Three more times the Bible mentions the Spirit's coming on Samson (Judges 14:6,19; 15:14). In each of these cases a verb is used that is still different from those used previously. This one means "to rush upon or break in upon." Just when Samson needed it, the Spirit brought Samson a great burst of mighty power and strength. Also implied is the fact that the Spirit moved at exactly the right time. Again, this does not mean that Samson was forced to do anything against his will. He was in control of his faculties and simply yielded to the mighty power of the Spirit, which he had learned to expect. Even after his lack of inner consecration finally caught up with him, we read that he said, "I'll go out as before and shake myself free" (Judges 16:20). Each time he took a step of faith and expected the Spirit of God to move with him, and up to that final time he was not disappointed.

In every case, therefore, Samson's cooperation with the Spirit was the secret of his strength. There is, in fact, no indication that Samson was a giant of a man or that he had unusual or impressive muscles. The Philistines were entirely at a loss to explain the secret of his strength, which would not have been the case if he were a model of physical culture.

Nor does the Bible actually say that Samson's strength was in his hair as such. Samson told Delilah he was a Nazirite unto God. The hair was the outward symbol of the Nazirite vow and consecration. We read that after the seven locks of his hair were shaved off his strength went from him. However, when Samson awoke, the Bible does not say he failed because his hair had been cut, but because "the LORD had left him" (Judges 16:20).

When his hair grew again, his strength did not return automatically. He made it a symbol of a renewed consecration to God and to the work of deliverance to which God had called him. Then he prayed and asked God to strengthen him or give him strength once more. "With all his might" (Judges 16:30) is actually a Hebrew phrase more often used of the power of God, especially in deliverance and judgment. We could translate it, "with all His [God's] might." Samson's final victory was not due in any measure to his own might. Rather, it came by another mighty move of the Spirit of God bringing the same power Samson had known on every previous occasion.

In the Book of Judges the Spirit of God is never presented as a mere influence coming from a God who is far away. God himself is always present personally and in power in His Spirit. To those who were open to Him, He also came as Isaiah prophesied He would come to the Messiah: as "the Spirit of wisdom and of understanding, the Spirit of counsel and of power, the Spirit of knowledge and of the fear of the LORD" (Isaiah 11:2). Thus, there was a fullness available which all did not appropriate.

Samuel, Saul, and David: Anointed by the Spirit

Though Samuel was a judge and a prophet, it is not specifically stated that the Spirit moved him. The attention in the Books of Samuel is more upon the way the Spirit anointed the kings.

Symbolic of this anointing was the anointing with oil. Prophets were sometimes anointed with oil (1 Kings 19:16) in order to set them apart and consecrate them for their ministry. Priests were always anointed with oil (Exodus 30:30; 40:13–15; Leviticus 8:12,30; 16:32). Kings often were (1 Samuel 10:1; 16:3,13; 2 Samuel 5:3; 1 Kings 1:34; 19:15; 2 Kings 9:3). The oil used was a special oil, a holy oil not to be imitated, made of olive oil compounded with four spices (Exodus 30:23,24). It was used to anoint sacred vessels and furniture in the tabernacle and temple symbolizing their dedication to the service of God. But in those passages dealing with people, the oil clearly represents the anointing of the Spirit. Throughout the Bible, oil continues to be an important symbol of the Holy Spirit. It speaks of the real "anointing from the Holy One" (1 John 2:20) which in the New Testament is extended to every believer.[17]

Samuel the prophet and anointer of kings was surely a man of the Spirit. God spoke to him frequently, putting him in a class with Moses (Numbers 12:6–8). When Samuel was a young man, God was with him and repeatedly revealed himself to him, giving him prophecies that were soon fulfilled. Thus, Israel accepted him as a prophet, and he was established as a voice for God in a very dark period of the nation's history. The ark had been stolen. Shiloh and its temple had been destroyed (Jeremiah 7:12; 26:6,9). Philistines dominated the land.

Revival Unites the Tribes

After twenty years of Samuel's ministry we find that Israel "mourned and sought after the LORD" instead of merely after the ark. (Compare 1 Samuel 4:21,22 and 7:2.) That is, Samuel's ministry turned the people from the forms of religion to the Lord himself. This finally led to a spiritual revival that brought all twelve tribes together in unity for the first time since Joshua.

Many of the judges ruled only a few tribes, Samson only one. Samuel persuaded all the tribes to give up the idolatry that had crept in and serve the Lord only. Then he gathered them all to Mizpah where they fasted and confessed their sins (1 Samuel 7:6). The Philistines took this for a political gathering. Their policy had been to keep the people apart and prevent them from uniting. When the Philistine army appeared, the people did not scatter. They asked Samuel to pray. Samuel offered a lamb as a burnt offering, and God thundered against the Philistines, throwing them into confusion. All Israel had to do was mop up the remains. From then on Samuel judged the people, traveling in a regular circuit (1 Samuel 7:15–17). Again, the work of the Spirit is evident though He is not mentioned.

Toward the end of Samuel's life, Israel wanted a king. Samuel was not happy about it. He felt rejected and he knew the people wanted a king for the wrong motive. But God gave him a ministry as an anointer of kings and intercessor for Israel.

Saul Anointed

A comparison of the anointings of Saul and David brings out some significant likenesses and differences. In both cases, God prepared Samuel in advance to do the anointing. In both cases also, God followed the symbolic action of pouring out the oil with a real outpouring of the Spirit.

Saul, however, seems more surprised by the anointing than David was. Saul, though a mature man, had not learned to seek the Lord. His servant was the one who suggested they seek out Samuel as a seer (one who sees with supernatural insight) or prophet (1 Samuel 9:6,9). After anointing him, Samuel told Saul he would meet several people, then a company of prophets with lyres (small triangular harps), tambourines, flutes, and harps (guitar-like lyre). They would be prophesying (speaking for God in song). The Spirit of the Lord would come upon Saul and he would prophesy with them and "be changed into a different person" (1 Samuel 10:6).

Actually, an inner change came before Saul met the prophets. As soon as he left Samuel, God gave him another heart (1 Samuel 10:9). For a time then he prophesied among these prophets.

Other passages indicate that the ministry of prophets increased during this time (probably after the spiritual revival recorded in 1 Samuel 7). Quite a group of prophets gathered around Samuel, who was their God-appointed head (1 Samuel 19:20). Later references speak of schools of the prophets where men gathered to learn from the prophets. Teaching was an important part of their ministry. So was worship. Earlier, we saw how Miriam, under the prophetic inspiration of the Spirit used a tambourine (or tom-tom) as she led the women in worship. Under Samuel more music and more musical instruments were added, and these prophets learned to yield to the Spirit as they played their instruments and sang God's praises.

No doubt this helped prepare the way for the emphasis on musical instruments and song that David added to the official worship led by the priests and Levites. There does not seem to be any great precedent for this. It began as a spontaneous move of the Spirit of God. Thus, prophesying in song was not primarily concerned with foretelling the future. But neither was the prophecy of men like Moses and Samuel or even Isaiah and Jeremiah. Prophecy was speaking for God. Prophecy done with music and song was simply singing and playing for God under the inspiration of the Spirit.

David appreciated this so much that he set apart Levites for this Spirit-anointed ministry and encouraged the use of an even greater variety of musical instruments (1 Chronicles 25:1–7). Specifically, they prophesied "in thanking and praising the LORD" for they were "trained and skilled in music for the LORD" (1 Chronicles 25:3,7). This seems to mean they expected the Spirit to anoint the songs they learned from David.

Saul, as he joined the company of prophets, overflowed in song, not because of their enthusiasm, not because of an impulse from his own inner self, not because he had some dormant musical talent that their inspired music drew out of him, but because he himself was moved by the Spirit. By the Spirit he was thus equipped in a new way for the task that lay ahead of him. Though Israel was wrong in asking for a king, God gave them the kind of tall, handsome king they wanted. But He did more. He prepared him, changed him, and gave him His Spirit. They would not be able to say later that God had not done everything He could for them.

David Anointed

David's experience was different in that when Samuel anointed him, "from that day on the Spirit of the LORD came upon David in power" (1 Samuel 16:13). The same verb is used of the Spirit's coming here as is used of Samson and King Saul. It was the same rush of mighty power. But there is a slight difference in the preposition used and a great difference in David's experience. The Spirit came upon Samson and Saul. Their experiences were temporary and intermittent. It was almost as if the Spirit was not present with them in between (even though He was). The Spirit came to David (or, more probably, into David). David's case was different also in that there was no immediate outward reaction or sign. This mighty surge of power filled David's inner being and began the supernatural preparation for the leadership God was to give him. But the experience did not end after a few minutes. The next day that inner surge of the Spirit was still there. "From that day on" is literally "from that day upward." It was a rising experience, a growing experience.

It seems significant also that nothing is said about giving David a new heart or changing him into another man. Evidently, David already knew the Lord. The 23rd Psalm may have been written when David was older, but it certainly reflects the experience of his youth. As a shepherd boy on the hills of Bethlehem he looked out over his flock and said, "The LORD is my shepherd" (Psalm 23:1). In the long night watches under the glittering stars his heart cried out, "The heavens declare the glory of God; the skies proclaim the work of his hands" (Psalm 19:1). His heart was already changed, already open when the Spirit came. Then, songs poured out that gave us a great part of the sacred hymnbook of Israel and the Church, the Book of Psalms.

Only twice more does the Bible mention the Spirit's coming upon Saul after his initial experience. Saul was not accepted by everyone when he was first chosen king. So he went back to the farm. Then one day, news came of an Ammonite threat to gouge out all the right eyes of the men of Jabesh Gilead as the price of a treaty of peace. When Saul heard it, the Spirit came in a rush upon him and he led Israel to a great victory which established him on his throne (1 Samuel 11:6,15).

Saul, however, did not continue to trust the Lord. In fear and self-will, he offered a sacrifice that caused God to withdraw the right of succession from Saul's family. His sons would have no rights to the throne. A man after God's own heart would take Saul's place; one who would do all God's will (1 Samuel 13:14; Acts 13:22). A few years later, Saul again disobeyed, in spite of being reminded of the Lord's anointing. This time God took away Saul's right to be king. From then on Saul reigned without God's support and without authority (1 Samuel 15:1,19,26). He failed because he did not understand that the spiritual religion promoted in the Old Testament was not just a matter of seeing miracles and winning victories. It was one of obedience and faith.

After Samuel anointed David, the Spirit of the Lord departed from Saul (1 Samuel 16:14). Thus the Spirit was with him (available to him) between the mighty rushes of power; just as He was with Samson. It is evident from this also that when the Spirit of the Lord departs, the Lord himself departs as well. (See Judges 16:20.)

An Evil Spirit from the Lord

When the Spirit of the Lord departed, God did not simply leave Saul alone to go his own way. "An evil spirit from the LORD tormented [terrified] him" (1 Samuel 16:14; see also verses 16,23; 18:10; 19:9). This is difficult for us to understand. This spirit is not indicated to be a demon, for it was from the Lord. Some take this to mean it was from the Lord only in the sense that it was permitted by God. But the Hebrew text seems stronger than that. In 1 Samuel 18:10 the expression is literally "God's evil spirit," and in 19:9, "the LORD's [Jehovah's] evil spirit." It came quite frequently (1 Samuel 16:23), and on one occasion at least caused Saul to "prophesy" (1 Samuel 18:10).

Perhaps a key to understanding this may be found in Isaiah 45:7 where God says, "I form the light and create darkness, I bring prosperity and create disaster." "Disaster" here is the opposite of "prosperity" (including peace, well-being, health, and blessing) not the opposite of good. God is never the author of moral evil or sin. But He is a holy God who does send judgment on sinners, just as He did on Egypt (Exodus 12:12).

The word "disaster" is also translated adversity, affliction, and calamity. God often spoke of His judgments as bringing evil (1 Kings 21:20; 22:18; Jeremiah 4:6; 6:19). Later, Zephaniah (1:12) prophesied God's judgment on the careless people who were settled in their sins and who said, "The Lord will do nothing, either good or bad." The spirit sent by the Lord on Saul, then, was not an evil spirit or demon in the New Testament sense, but a spirit of judgment. Some compare this to 1 Kings 22:19–23. Others take it to be like an avenging angel.

The cause of this judgment on Saul was thus fully supernatural. His was no mere disease, sickness, or mental aberration. This spirit of judgment attacked him, rushed upon him, and into him. God's grace was withdrawn, but God's judgment was just as active.

Some take it that David's playing which quieted Saul shows that the natural affects the supernatural.[18] It is true that the Bible does not draw a sharp line between the two, nor can we in our experience. But we must remember that David was not an ordinary harpist. He was anointed by the Holy Spirit.

Saul's Prophesying

Saul's "prophesying" under the influence of this supernatural spirit of judgment is also hard to understand (1 Samuel 18:10). It was probably not normal prophesying. The same form of the verb is sometimes used of the raving and raging of the heathen prophets. Since this spirit of judgment terrified Saul (16:14), it may be that this "prophesying" also took the form of uncontrolled utterances.

We must also recognize that this "spirit of judgment" is not in a class with the Spirit of the Lord even though Saul did prophesy under its influence. This spirit that was sent out from the Lord was subject to His will. The Holy Spirit is God himself moving into the situation.[19]

An even stranger event is Saul's prophesying before Samuel when Saul was in pursuit of David (1 Samuel 19:20–24). Three times Saul sent messengers to arrest David. But when they came to Samuel, who was in Ramah at the head of a company of prophets, the prophets were prophesying. Each time the Spirit of the Lord came on the messengers and they also began to prophesy. Each time, the inspiration and blessing of the Lord made them forget their mission or change their minds about it.

Then Saul himself decided to go to Samuel and arrest David. Dressed in his royal robes, he expected to come down and overwhelm them. But the Spirit of the Lord came upon him before he found Samuel and he began to prophesy. Arriving before Samuel, he stripped off his royal robes and lay there prophesying all night, clothed only in his tunic.

The situation here is quite different from the time the Spirit first came upon him after his anointing. Here the Spirit came upon (not, "rushed upon") him before he met the prophets. He was resisting the Spirit. Instead of being prepared for kingship, he threw off his royal robes. Instead of prophesying among the prophets, he lay on the ground. There is no evidence that he did this because he wished to humble himself before God. Even his prophesying may have been more like ravings that came from his resisting the Spirit. God thus showed He was sovereign and David was allowed to escape.

David and the Psalms

That the Holy Spirit continued to indwell David is indicated in a negative way when David sought forgiveness after his great sin and cried out, "Do not . . . take your Holy Spirit from me" (Psalm 51:11). His truly repentant attitude here is in distinct contrast with King Saul, who sometimes admitted he had sinned when he was caught, but never showed genuine repentance. Instead, Saul went right back to doing the same thing.

David's recognition of the Spirit of God as the Holy Spirit is thus quite significant. He probably does not use the name in the full New Testament recognition of the Spirit's distinct personality. But he does see that the Spirit is personally active in relation to his needs.

The whole Psalm 51 is worth studying in this connection, especially the verses immediately preceding and following verse 11. "Create in [for] me a pure [unalloyed] heart" (v. 10). "Create" is a word used in the Bible only of God's unprecedented divine activity. It would have to be God. David could not do it himself. The same verse continues: "Renew [restore] a steadfast [firm, faithful, reliable] spirit within me [in my inner being]." This was his human spirit that sin had robbed of its fixed purpose to do God's will and to be ready to move with Him. "Do not cast me from your presence" (v. 11). God's presence is parallel to His Holy Spirit. Through the Spirit David was made aware of God's presence. The fact that the Holy Spirit was still dealing with him showed him that God had not yet cast him out or tossed him on the slag heap. (See 1 Corinthians 9:27.) "Restore [return] to me the joy of your salvation" (Psalm 51:12). For a year he thought he had covered his sin. But not until Nathan rebuked him did he wake up to the fact that the joy was gone. "Grant me a willing [generous] spirit, to sustain [uphold, assist, aid] me" (v. 12). The Spirit that is holy is also generous.[20] (The word "willing" is the same word that speaks of willing hearts and freewill offerings in Exodus 35:5,22.) David wanted the Spirit's help to uphold him, not merely to keep him from falling again, but so he could teach others and bring sinners to the Lord (Psalm 51:13).

David's prayer was answered. Not only did the Lord restore him, but at the end of his life he was able to say, "The Spirit of the LORD spoke through me [or, in me]; his word was on my tongue" (2 Samuel 23:2). He was "the man anointed by the God of Jacob, Israel's singer of songs [psalms]" (v. 1).

David had twice refused to kill King Saul because Saul was the Lord's anointed. Now David was God's anointed (Hebrew, *meshiach*, messiah) in a far better sense. As such he became a type pointing ahead to the greater David, who is the Messiah, God's anointed Prophet, Priest, and King.

There are only a few other brief mentions of the Spirit in relation to David. First Chronicles 28:12 indicates that the plan of the temple came to David by divine inspiration of the Spirit.[21]

In Psalm 139:7, David asked the question, "Where can I go from your Spirit? Where can I flee from your presence?" By this he does not mean he would ever want to do so. He is simply recognizing that the Spirit, power, and presence of God are everywhere.

Psalm 143:10 recognizes that God's Spirit is good. The verse might be translated, "Teach me [make me really learn] to do your will, for you are my God; may your good Spirit lead me on level land" (where there will be no stumbling, no hindrances to righteousness, no barriers to spiritual progress).

One further note: First Chronicles 12:18 indicates the Holy Spirit came upon (put on as clothes, filled) Amasai to give a word of encouragement to David. (The same Hebrew word is used of Amasai as was used of Gideon in Judges 6:34.)

Solomon

Though Solomon knew the inspiration and gift of wisdom that comes through the Spirit, he only speaks of the Spirit once. In Proverbs 1:23, Wisdom cries out, "I would have [freely] poured out my heart [Spirit] to [for] you and made my thoughts known [in your experience] to you." The wisdom here personified is divine wisdom or the wisdom from God. Pouring out is more often used of the pouring out of a torrent of words (as in Psalm 145:7). It is also used of the springing forth of a fountain. Thus, it intimates a greater pouring out of the Spirit to come, an outpouring connected with an outpouring of words through which the Spirit expresses himself.

Kings and Chronicles

The Spirit is mentioned in the rest of Kings and Chronicles only in connection with the prophets. When the kingdom was divided after Solomon's death, the kings of the northern ten tribes (which took the name of Israel) fell to a low spiritual level. All worshipped the golden calves Jeroboam set up at Bethel and Dan. Many fell into gross idolatry. Even in Judah, though there were revivals under Asa, Jehoshaphat, Hezekiah, and Josiah, the majority of the kings fell into idolatrous practices. Thus, though the kings carried on the history, the prophets spoke for God and laid the groundwork for the future.

This is seen in the very structure of the Books of Kings. The kings are introduced by a set formula. Another set formula gives the conclusion of their reign. The kings as a whole are only framework in the Books of Kings. But there is no set formula for introducing the prophets. Suddenly, they are there, as if the framework of Kings is pulled apart and they are injected into the situation. (See 1 Kings 17:1.)

All the true prophets, of course, were inspired and moved by the Spirit (2 Peter 1:21). One of the early prophets upon whom we are told the Spirit came was Azariah (2 Chronicles 15:1–8). He encouraged King Asa to put away idols and helped in his revival. His message reminded Asa of conditions in the times of the judges. As was so often the case, the messages of the prophets built on the Word of God already given.

Later, the Spirit of the Lord came upon Jahaziel to encourage Jehosphaphat to trust God, stand still, and let the Lord give them a victory. For once, it would not be necessary for Judah to fight (2 Chronicles 20:14–17).

About the same time, God was moving through Elijah in northern Israel to bring the people to a decision. When after three and one-half rainless years he met Obadiah, King Ahab's servant, Obadiah was afraid the Spirit of the Lord would catch Elijah up and take him away (1 Kings 18:12). This reminds us of how the Spirit of God later caught up Ezekiel (Ezekiel 37:1) and Philip (Acts 8:39). At least, Obadiah recognized the Spirit of God as a mighty power. (See also 2 Kings 2:16.) But the evidence that the Spirit was truly guiding Elijah came when fire from heaven consumed the sacrifice on Mount Carmel and the people said, "The LORD—he is God!" (1 Kings 18:39).

Elijah had a further lesson to learn, however (1 Kings 19). Miracles do not necessarily convince unbelievers. He expected that the fire from heaven would convert even Jezebel. When it did not, he became very discouraged and fled. In the strength of two supernatural meals, he went for forty days to the region of Mount Sinai. There, God let him know that the manifestations of His Spirit were not necessarily dramatic and external. A fire, an earthquake, and a mighty wind were without message to Elijah. But then in the silence that followed, a still, small voice let Elijah know that he was not alone, that seven thousand had not bowed the knee to Baal, and that God still had work for him to do. Let him quit his self-pity and get busy.

So much was Elijah characterized by the Spirit that Elisha, when he knew Elijah was to be taken from him, asked for a double portion of his Spirit (2 Kings 2:9). By this he did not mean Elijah's human spirit or enthusiasm, but the Spirit of God which was upon him. By asking for a double portion also, he was not asking for twice as much of the Spirit (though some point out that God worked twice as many recorded miracles through Elisha as through Elijah). Actually, the double portion was the portion of the heir. Many prophets and a number of schools of prophets were raised up through Elijah's ministry. Elisha asked for the privilege of being Elijah's successor in his ministry and in leadership of the schools of the prophets. This was granted, and the other prophets recognized that the Spirit of Elijah was upon him. (See 2 Kings 2:15.)

The people recognized Elisha as a holy man of God (2 Kings 4:9). So did the kings, as well as Naaman, the general of the Syrian army (2 Kings 5:14,15). On one occasion, however, he was so surrounded by unbelief that he asked for a minstrel to come and sing and play for him. As he worshipped the Lord, he created his own atmosphere of faith, and "the hand of the LORD came upon Elisha" (2 Kings 3:15). The phrase "hand of the LORD" is often used of the power of the Lord and often implies the move of the Spirit.

During Elijah's time God also used the prophet Micaiah to warn Ahab of the battle that brought his death (1 Kings 22:17–23). Other prophets had encouraged Ahab to believe he would return victorious. But Micaiah said they were moved by a lying spirit to bring God's judgment on Ahab. Zedekiah, one of the other prophets, then slapped Micaiah on the cheek and asked, "Which way did the spirit from the LORD go when he went from me to speak to you? (1 Kings 22:24). Obviously, Zedekiah thought he was the one truly inspired by the Spirit of God. Events proved Micaiah to be the true prophet. But Zedekiah's remark indicates people understood that true prophecy was inspired by the Spirit of God.

The Bible notes one more person in this period as specially filled with the Spirit (2 Chronicles 24:20). When King Joash and his people turned from the Lord, "the Spirit of God came upon [clothed himself with] Zechariah" and rebuked them. For this Joash had him stoned to death—a martyrdom to which Jesus drew attention as the last one recorded in the Hebrew Bible, which places Chronicles at the end (Matthew 23:35; Luke 11:51).

Job

Job is the only other early book that mentions the Spirit. In Job 26:13, "By his breath [*ruach*, Spirit] the skies became fair [brightened]," most take the brightening to be by the Spirit through the agency of the wind. "The breath [*ruach*, Spirit] of God in my nostrils" recognizes that man's life comes from the Spirit (Job 27:3). "The spirit in a man" (Job 32:8,18) is undoubtedly the human spirit, but the passage (along with Job 33:4, "The Spirit of God has made me") recognizes that man owes this spirit to the Spirit of God (as in Genesis 2:7).

Elihu (who begins speaking in Job 32:6) seems to feel that his own spirit has received a greater measure of wisdom and power by the Spirit than Job's three friends had. In this sense, Elihu suggests he has a charismatic gift.[22] This is ignored, however, in God's dealings with Job and his three friends in the rest of the book.

The Spirit in the Writing Prophets

The entire Old Testament looks on prophecy as the chief activity of the Spirit among His people. Moses' desire that all the Lord's people would be prophets is conditioned by the Lord's putting His Spirit upon them (Numbers 11:29). Joel's prophecy is "I [God] will pour out my Spirit on all people. Your sons and daughters will prophesy" (Joel 2:28). This was an important part of the assurance that God's covenant would finally be realized and the people would indeed be God's people. (See Exodus 6:7; 2 Samuel 7:24; Isaiah 32:15; 44:3–5; Jeremiah 31:31–34; Ezekiel 11:19; 36:25–28.)[1]

Joel, whose message fits in well with the boyhood of Joash when Jehoida the priest was in control, emphasizes a call to repentance (Joel 1:14; 2:12–17). After repentance, God promised restoration (v. 25) and revival (2:28,29).

Joel goes on to speak of signs that will not come until the end of the age (vv. 30,31) and promises judgment on the nations such as Egypt and Edom which were current enemies of Judah (3:19). For this reason some say that Joel's prophecy of the outpouring of the Spirit has only a future fulfillment and must be fulfilled only in relation to the Jews on the Day of the Lord.[2]

On All Flesh

Closer examination of what Joel has to say shows, however, that Joel himself may not have understood the full scope of God's promise here, and we cannot limit it to the Jews. Old

Testament prophets do not see the time gap between the first and second comings of Christ. "All people" clearly means more than just Jews; it means all people. (See Genesis 6:12,13; Deuteronomy 5:26; Job 12:10; 34:14,15; Psalms 65:2; 145:21; Isaiah 40:6; Jeremiah 25:31; Zechariah 2:13.)[3]

Nor does "your sons and daughters" restrict the outpouring to Israel. It simply shows there are no restrictions with regard to age or sex. The phrase is thus intended to be part of a removal of limitations and there is no intention of restricting the meaning to the Jews.[4]

Old men dreaming (prophetic) dreams and young men seeing (prophetic) visions is a further emphasis on the removal of limitations. The distinction between dreams and visions here is not significant, since the Old Testament often uses the two words interchangeably. But the cultural pattern that in those days gave age the precedence is no longer to be followed. All have equal opportunity for the ministry of the Spirit.

Social restrictions are also to be removed. The Spirit will be poured out in the same rich abundance on servants (slaves) and handmaidens (female slaves). This also was something unheard of in Old Testament times. Later Jews could not believe this. They interpreted it to mean God's servants instead of actual slaves. Pharisees despised the common people of Israel, to say nothing of slaves (John 7:49). One of their sayings was "Prophecy does not reside except on one wise and mighty and rich."[5]

Blessing for All

Actually, God's purpose has always been to bring blessing to all (Genesis 3:15; 12:3; 22:18; John 3:16). God did not choose Abraham to shut other people out. They were already cut off from God's blessing by their sin. God chose Abraham to begin a blood line that would lead down to the Messiah, the greater "seed" of Abraham (Galatians 3:16). The Jews are a chosen people, not for favoritism (Acts 10:34), but for service. God intended to use them to prepare the way for Christ to come so that others could be saved. In other words, God chose Abraham and Israel for the same reason He sent His Son, "For God so loved the world" (John 3:16).

The abundant outpouring of the Spirit is thus available for all, Jew or Gentile, rich or poor, young or old, educated or uneducated, regardless of race, color, or national origin. Nor would this outpouring be a one-time event. The Hebrew indicates progressive or repeated action, making the outpouring of the Spirit available to generation after generation. It can, of course, be rejected or disregarded, but it remains available.[6]

"Afterward" (Joel 2:28) may mean after repentance and restoration. It may also refer back to verse 23. The restoration that makes possible the coming of the Spirit must, in the light of the rest of the Bible, be a restoration to fellowship with God through the sacrifice of Christ on the cross. Thus, Calvary was necessary before Pentecost.

Some excellent Hebrew scholars see this indicated in Joel 2:23. The latter half of the verse may be translated, "For he will give you the Teacher for righteousness and will cause to come down for you rainfall, early rain, and latter rain first of all."[7] Thus, "afterward" makes the overflowing supply of the Spirit to be a "second and later consequence of the gift of the Teacher of righteousness."[8]

The sending of the literal rain in Joel's day not only fulfilled his prophecy of restoration after their repentance; it also guaranteed the further promise that God would pour out His Spirit after the Teacher of righteousness, the Messiah, came. The only limit would be our willingness to receive.

Micah, Filled with the Spirit

Micah and Isaiah alone, in what has been called Israel's "golden age of prophecy," mention the Holy Spirit. Hosea (9:7) does have a brief statement concerning the prophet who is "a fool" (stupid) and the man of the Spirit who is "a maniac" (acts crazy), but these refer to backsliders who had deeply corrupted themselves (9:9). Hosea himself was a man wholly dedicated to

God who learned from his own broken heart the love God feels for a backsliding people.

What Micah says about his call was undoubtedly true of all genuine prophets of God: "I am full of power, with [even] the Spirit of the LORD, and with justice [including right decisions] and might [courageous strength], to declare to Jacob his transgression [rebellion, guilt], to Israel his sin" (Micah 3:8). In the midst of a corrupt society, God filled him with His Spirit so he could see what was right before God and what was wrong. Then the Spirit gave him the power, courage, and strength to come to grips with the situation. (Compare John 16:8.) What a contrast he was with the false prophets who excused sin if the fee was right!

Micah also asks, "Is the Spirit of the LORD angry [shortened; that is, impatient, discontented]?" (2:7). His question calls for a negative answer. God is not impatient. He has not become discontented. That is, His acts of judgment on Israel are not the result of some change in His character. He is the same good God He has always been. The people had changed. They had risen up against God as an enemy (2:8). They did not really want to hear God's Word. In fact, "If a liar and deceiver comes and says, I will prophesy [drip words] for you plenty of [or, with reference to] wine and beer,' he would be just the prophet [preacher] for this people!" (v. 11). False prophets were ready to preach the kind of lust and pleasure the people wanted to hear. But they disregarded the fact that the Holy Spirit was given, not to promote fleshly enjoyment, but to deal with sin.

A Judgment Sign

Isaiah also had difficulty with drunken people and priests who mocked him. When he talked about judgment and future glories they said they were not babies (Isaiah 28:9). They had heard such prophecies before. To them Isaiah's prophecies were like ABCs or baby talk. (Isaiah 28:10 in Hebrew reads something like "zow l'zow, zow l'zow, cow l'cow, cow l'cow," as if he were repeating letters of the alphabet or talking gibberish.)

Isaiah's reply is that "with foreign lips and strange tongues [languages] God will speak to this people" (v. 11). By this he meant that if they did not learn the lesson from the Lord, they would learn it from the invading Assyrians, whose language might sound like gibberish to them (Isaiah 33:19). God intended the prophecies and the hope of the coming of the Messiah and the Spirit to be a rest and a refreshing. But, what they characterized as gibberish would become a judgment sign to them. They would hear it, and because they rejected Isaiah's message, they would "fall backward" (28:13) and be snared and captured (taken into captivity). This was fulfilled when Sennacherib took the cities of Judah (Isaiah 36:1) and, according to his records, sent two hundred thousand of them into captivity, probably in Babylon.

Isaiah's first mention of the Spirit is also in connection with dealing with sin. "Those who are left in Zion . . . will be called holy [that is, dedicated to God, consecrated to God] . . . The Lord will wash away the filth [excrement] of the women [inhabitants, men and women] of Zion; he will cleanse the bloodstains [pools of blood caused by murders] from Jerusalem by a spirit of judgment [justice] and a spirit of fire"—to prepare for the (Messianic) glory to come (Isaiah 4:3,4).

Some take this merely as a burning, cleansing wind,[9] but it is God who is doing the work. His Spirit brings the fire of divine wrath to punish evil and destroy the evildoers in order to bring in the time of the Messiah.

The Spirit on the Messiah

The climax of Isaiah's picture of the Messiah in both the early and latter parts of the book deals with the Spirit of God resting on him (11:1–5; 61:1–4). In the first part of the book Isaiah deals with the Messiah as King. He unfolds a wonderful picture beginning with 7:14.

At that time King Ahaz was planning to ask military help from Assyria. Isaiah wanted him to trust the Lord (7:11) and told him to ask for a supernatural "sign" (miracle) from the "deepest depths" (toward Sheol) or from the "highest heights" (heaven). But Ahaz had already made up his mind, so he pretended to be too pious to put God to the test. At that, Isaiah broke out with a condemnation not merely of Ahaz but of the "house [family, lineage] of David." They were all wearying God. "Therefore the Lord himself shall give you [plural, the whole house and line of David], a [supernatural, miraculous] sign: The virgin will be with child and will give birth to a son, and will call him Immanuel ['God with us']" (7:14).

The passage that follows is difficult, but it is clear that this verse refers to a miracle at least as great as the one offered King Ahaz. Virgin (Hebrew, *almah*) has sometimes been translated "young woman" because it is not the ordinary word for virgin. But the ordinary word *(bethulah)* means a virgin of any age, from a young girl to an old woman. The word Isaiah uses here narrows down the meaning to a virgin of marriageable age. (See Genesis 24:16 where the word is used of Rebekah.) The name Immanuel also makes the "with us" emphatic. He is the God with us, come to be with us in a special way.

To the Jews, the Holy Land was God's land, but in Isaiah 8:8 it is Immanuel's land. (See John 1:11 where He comes to His own, that is, to His own place, His own land, and His own people do not receive Him.)

The next step in Isaiah's unfolding picture shows that the virgin-born Child has the government on His shoulder (Isaiah 9:6, 7). His name is to be called Wonderful (a miraculous Wonder) Counselor (a name traditionally given both to God and to His Spirit), the mighty (heroic, courageous) God (implies the God who wins a great victory for His people), the everlasting Father (the Father or Author of eternity; see John 1:1,3), and the Prince of Peace (the Prince who will bring peace, blessing, and spiritual well-being; the Prince who will bring in the glorious age to come). He will establish David's throne and make it eternal. God himself is dedicated and full of zeal to carry this out.

The next chapter confirms that the "mighty God" indeed refers to the divine nature of the promised Son. In Isaiah 10:20,21, "the mighty God" is made parallel to "the Holy One of Israel."

The Sevenfold Spirit

Then, in Isaiah 11:1–5, this virgin-born Child is identified as a rod (a new shoot) from the stem (cut-off stump) of Jesse, and a branch (Hebrew *netser* or *nezer* from the same root as Nazareth and Nazarene) from his roots. In other words, by the time this virgin-born Son comes to be God with us, the glory of the Davidic kingdom will be gone and the family of David will be cut down and reduced to poverty. But when the Child grows up there will come something better than earthly glory upon Him. "The Spirit of the LORD will rest [continuously] on him— the Spirit of wisdom and of understanding, the Spirit of counsel and of power, the Spirit of knowledge and of the fear of the LORD" (11:2). As one Bible scholar has pointed out, the Spirit of the Lord is like the central shaft of a sevenfold lampstand. The other manifestations of the Spirit are in three groups: first, relating to the mind and intellect; second, relating to the practical life; and third, relating directly to God.[10]

Each aspect of this sevenfold Spirit is significant. As the Spirit of the Lord He is the Spirit of prophecy, the Spirit who works in redemption. Wisdom is insight able to see through a situation and see things as they are. (Compare John 2:24,25, where Jesus knows what is in man.) Understanding is the ability to discriminate between good and evil regardless of the external appearances. Counsel is the ability to weigh the facts and come to the right conclusions. Power is the courage and strength to carry out God's will. Knowledge is the personal knowledge of God that comes from fellowship with Him in love. The fear of the Lord is a reverence that exalts God and that is the beginning of all wisdom (Job 28:28; Psalm 111:10; Proverbs 1:7; 9:10). All this the virgin-born Child, the new David, will have as His permanent possession from the time the sevenfold Spirit descends upon

Him. (See Revelation 4:5; 5:6 where the sevenfold Spirit not only flames before the throne of God but is also active through the authority of the Lamb that was slain.)[11]

Because the Spirit is upon Him, "He will not judge by what he sees with his eyes, or decide by what he hears with his ears" (Isaiah 11:3). All ordinary men can do is decide on the basis of what they receive through their senses; thus judges and juries often make mistakes. But the Spirit-anointed Son will make no mistakes.

The next part of the chapter (11:6–9) jumps to millennial conditions. The prophets did not see the time gap between the first and second comings of Christ. But Isaiah's emphasis is on the fact that the ministry of the Spirit through the Messiah will continue and that the ideal conditions of the age to come will also be the work of the Spirit.

"In that day," Isaiah adds, "the LORD Almighty will be a glorious crown, a beautiful wreath for the remnant of his people. He will be a spirit of justice to him who sits in judgment, a source of strength [courageous strength, as in Isaiah 11:2] to those who turn back the battle at the gate" (Isaiah 28:5,6). From this we see that the same sevenfold Spirit that rests on the Messiah is made available to the people also.

The Anointed Servant

The latter part of Isaiah speaks often of the Servant of the Lord, the One who accomplishes His work. Israel was called as God's servant (Isaiah 41:8), but God had a work of salvation Israel could not do. Israel, too, needed to be saved. Out of Israel, then, comes One who is *the* Servant of the Lord, One who actually would do the whole work of the Lord and accomplish His salvation.

Isaiah 42:1 introduces Him as the chosen One in whom God delights. God has put His Spirit on Him, and by the Spirit He will bring forth justice (or God's decisions which are the basis of true and practical religion) to the Gentiles (all the nations of the world). This Servant will mediate God's new covenant, be a light to the Gentiles (42:6), open blind eyes, and bring prisoners (of sin) out to freedom (42:7).

In Isaiah 61:1 this same Servant of the Lord[12] says of himself, "The Spirit of the Sovereign LORD is on me, because the LORD hath anointed me to preach [bring] good news to the poor [meek, humble]. He has sent me to bind up the brokenhearted, to proclaim freedom for the captives [captives taken in war, that is, in the spiritual battles against sin and Satan] and release [a loosing, a deliverance] from darkness for the prisoners." He also proclaims "the year of the LORD's favor [the year or time of God's favor shown by His blessings] and the day of vengeance of our God" (61:2). Again, Isaiah, like Joel, does not see the time gap between the first and second comings of Christ.

The emphasis in this passage is, however, on the year of the Lord's favor, on the good news the anointed Servant brings. It may be that "the year of the LORD's favor" is a way of saying that the Messiah will bring a greater and deeper fulfillment of what the Year of Jubilee was supposed to bring to Israel. In the Year of Jubilee, lost inheritances were regained (Leviticus 25:10–13). The coming of the anointed Servant would mean a new entering into God's blessings and inheritance He has for His people.

All this implies the salvation He brings. This Servant of Isaiah 61:1 is not only the One of Isaiah 42:1; He is the Servant who bore our sicknesses and carried our pains and by whose stripes we are healed: the One who suffered and died in our place for our redemption (Isaiah 52:13 through 53:12).

He is the same One also who was sent by God with His Spirit in Isaiah 48:16 (where the Hebrew means "God has sent me and has sent His Spirit"). God commissioned and sent Him to carry out the divine purpose and be a Restorer of Israel and a light to the Gentiles (Isaiah 49:6). He is the One who has the tongue of the learned (because He is taught by God) to encourage the weary (those who are exhausted or ready to give up), and who also gives His back to the smiters (Isaiah 50:4,6). He rescues those who are hopelessly at the end of themselves (Isaiah 42:3), and He himself "will not falter [grow dim, as a light] or be discouraged [or, rush; or, be crushed], till he establishes justice [and practical religion] on earth. In his law [His teaching, or instruction about Him] the islands [including all distant lands] will put their hope" (42:4).

The Spirit in the Present and the Future

Isaiah has a way of jumping from the backsliding of Israel in his own day to the future glories and back again. We see this kind of alternation in the passages that deal with the relation of the Spirit of God to the people. Isaiah 30:1 deals with rejection of the guidance, power, and purity of God's Spirit by a rebellious people and unscrupulous leaders in Isaiah's day. Chapter 32:15 speaks of the future outpouring of the Spirit from heaven which will make the desert a fruitful field (like Carmel). Implied is a transformation of both land and people (32:16–18), with the whole world enjoying something better than it had ever known before.

Isaiah 34:16 ties the Word of the Lord and the Spirit together with assurance that the God who is the Creator will keep His promises just as He has made provision for all His creation. (See Psalm 33:6,9,11.) Isaiah 40:7,8 also deals with the Spirit and the Word, but in a very different way. It compares the Spirit of God bringing judgment on mankind to a drying wind that withers grass and flowers. Then he contrasts this with the Word of God which stands forever.

Another type of contrast may be seen between Isaiah 40:13 and 44:3. In the former passage, God's Spirit is recognized as sovereign, sharing in creation, needing no one to give Him counsel or wisdom, seeming almost unapproachable in His greatness. Then the same Spirit with all His blessing is poured out like water on a thirsty man or like floods on a dry ground (44:3). Outward restoration of the people and land is then linked directly with salvation and spiritual renewal (44:5,6).

Still another contrast is found in Isaiah 59:19–21. Verse 19 speaks of the mighty power of God sweeping everything before it. The meaning is similar to the usual translation, but the Hebrew is better taken to read, "And they shall fear the name of the Lord from the west and His glory from the rising of the sun for he [God] shall come like the river [the Euphrates] narrowed, the Spirit of the Lord driving it on."

The preceding passage has to do with God's judgment on His enemies. When He moves against them, no enemy will be able to stand before Him. Just as the Euphrates River coming to a narrow place between high banks redoubles its speed and sweeps everything before it, so the Spirit of God is the driving force against God's enemies and will sweep them all away.

In contrast to this, the Redeemer (Kinsman-Redeemer who restores the inheritance) will come to Zion, even to those in Jacob (the Jews) who turn back to God from their transgression (rebellion). To them, God's covenant is that His Spirit which is upon them (and has been upon them since they were restored to God) and His words which the Spirit puts in their mouth will not depart (be removed) forever (59:21).

Rebellion Grieves the Holy Spirit

One more passage in Isaiah refers to the Spirit (63:7–16). Isaiah first refers to the faithful love of God for His people and how "In all their distress he too was distressed, and the angel of his presence saved them. In his love and mercy he redeemed them; he lifted them up and carried them all the days of old. Yet they rebelled and grieved his Holy Spirit" (63:9,10). Significantly, the Holy Spirit is treated here as a Person who can be grieved (Ephesians 4:30), as most of the older Bible scholars and commentators agree.

This same Holy Spirit was in Moses (Isaiah 63:11). Many take this to mean that because the Spirit was in Moses, Miriam, the seventy elders, and Joshua, He was in the midst of the people of Israel. Thus, when they murmured, they grieved the Holy Spirit who was among them. The emphasis in verse 12 on the leadership of Moses, however, seems to mean that the Spirit was specifically in Moses. Thus, when Numbers 11:17 speaks of the Spirit upon Moses it does not deny that Moses was also filled with the Spirit.

Isaiah 63:14 goes on to compare a flock going down into a valley (led by a good shepherd into green grass and still waters) to the leading of Israel by the Spirit into the rest (of Canaan). Through Spirit-filled leaders they were brought into victory and blessing. But the real Guide was always the Spirit of the Lord.

God's Mighty Hand

Ezekiel's experiences are unusual, and he mentions the Spirit more than any of the remaining prophets. Jeremiah, in contrast, does not name the Spirit at all, though he does mention the hand of the Lord (Jeremiah 1:9; 6:12; 15:6; 16:21, for example). Then, in Ezekiel, the hand of the Lord is often parallel to the Spirit of the Lord (Ezekiel 1:3; 3:14,22,24; 8:1; 11:1).

This is little different from the interchange of "the Spirit of God" and the "finger of God" in Matthew 12:28 and Luke 11:20. The hand of the Lord and the arm of the Lord are often used as symbols of the power of the Lord. In our emphasis today on the gentleness of the Spirit, it is easy to forget that the Bible has much more to say about the power of the Spirit, as we have just seen in Isaiah's writings. Isaiah also shows that the Spirit means power when woe is pronounced on Israel for turning from God to seek help in Egypt, for "the Egyptians are men and not God; their horses are flesh and not spirit" (Isaiah 31:3).

Once again, we must keep in mind that these experiences of power do not imply frenzy, mysticism, or trance in the ordinary sense of the word. God's hand was on Elijah (1 Kings 18:46). Yet the simplicity of his faith and prayer are in strong contrast to the heathen frenzy and contortions of the yelling, screaming prophets of Baal (1 Kings 18:26,28,36,37). Ezekiel, too, though his experiences with the Spirit show much more variety than most, never fell into the kind of trance heathen prophets did. Through Ezekiel the Spirit brought edification, not confusion.

The first mention of the Spirit in the Book of Ezekiel is in connection with the cherubim that Ezekiel saw in his vision of God

(Ezekiel 1:12,20,21; 10:17). Each cherub had four faces representing all God's creation and thus indicating that God is over all His creation. Beside the cherubim were wheels at right angles to each other so they could go in any direction (indicating that God does not even have to turn around to get where you are). The wheels and the cherubim moved in harmony and unity when the Spirit moved.

Some take the Spirit here to be merely the breath of God, but the Hebrew is not "a spirit" but "the Spirit." (See also 1:20.) This is a symbolic picture then that not only is God over His creation, His Spirit is moving in His creation to accomplish His purposes.

Lifted by the Spirit

Another group of passages show how the Spirit moved on Ezekiel personally (Ezekiel 2:2; 3:12,14,24; 8:3; 11:1,5,24; 37:1; 43:5).

On the first occasion, the Spirit entered into him and caused him to stand on his feet so that he could hear the message God had for him (2:2). The same thing happened in 3:24, except this time God told Ezekiel to stay in his house. God would take away the power of speech from him except when he had a message from God for the people. In this way a rebellious people would be forced to see that Ezekiel only spoke when he spoke for God and that he was truly God's prophet.

On other occasions the Spirit lifted him up (3:12,14; 8:3; 11:1, 24; 43:5). Once (3:12,14), the Spirit then lifted him up (took hold of him), and he went in the bitterness and heat of his own spirit to the Jewish exiles at Tel Abib east of Babylon and sat among them. Later, the form of a hand seized him by a lock of hair and the Spirit lifted him up between earth and heaven, and brought him "in visions of God" to Jerusalem (Ezekiel 8:3). There, the Spirit again lifted him up and brought him to the east gate of the temple (11:1). Finally, the Spirit lifted him and brought him "in the vision given by the Spirit of God" into Chaldea (Babylonia). Then the vision was taken away from him (11:24).

Several years later, in a vision of the return of God's glory to the future millennial temple, he fell on his face in awe (43:3). Then the Spirit lifted him and brought him into the inner court where he could see that the glory filled the temple (vv. 4,5).

Two questions arise here. What is the nature of the Spirit? And what is the nature of the lifting and the visions?

Some writers say *Spirit* entered into Ezekiel, while *wind* carried him away.[13] Others, because the Hebrew says "Spirit" rather than "the Spirit" in several of these passages, take it that the emphasis is on power of energy and that only in a vague sense is the Spirit of God meant. However, the power comes from God. As Davidson says concerning Ezekiel 2:2, where the Spirit caused Ezekiel to stand on his feet, "While God desires man to stand erect before Him, it is only the Spirit from God that enables man to take this right place."[14]

We see further that in 11:5 the Spirit that fell upon Ezekiel is the Spirit of the Lord. Since the falling upon does not seem to have different effects than the entering in of 2:2 (both prepare him to hear the Word of the Lord), it seems obvious that the same Spirit is meant. Also in 11:24, Ezekiel is brought in a vision by the Spirit of God, and in 37:1, he is caused to go out by the Spirit of the Lord. These, too, are parallel to other passages where the Spirit is mentioned. All thus refer to the Spirit of God.

God-Given Visions

The question of the nature of the visions and how the Spirit lifted Ezekiel is more difficult. When he goes to the exiles at Tel Abib, he is impelled into action and actually goes from one place to another. However, when the Spirit takes him to Jerusalem it is in "visions of God" (8:3). Because "what looked like a hand" (something shaped like a hand) seized him by a lock of his hair and because he is brought to various parts of the temple and its courts, many take it that Ezekiel was physically transported to Jerusalem. It is also said he dug in the wall of the temple and went through a door (8:7–9).

Vision, also, is not the common word for a prophetic vision. In some cases it is translated "appearance" (10:1; 41:21) and it could mean something seen, a sight. (Ezekiel 23:15 speaks of princes *to look to*, the same word.) Thus, "visions of God" could simply mean actual appearances or manifestations of God.

There are problems with this view, however. No one in Jerusalem could see Ezekiel while he was watching what was going on there. Nor were they aware of the glory which Ezekiel saw departing from the temple and the city. Later, the hand of the Lord caused him to go out in the Spirit and deposited him in a great, broad, flat valley full of dry bones (37:1). These bones are stated to represent the whole house of Israel (all twelve tribes) scattered among the nations (37:11–14). Thus, the valley is not intended to be an actual valley but a picture of mankind as a whole. Ezekiel is lifted spiritually to a place where God can show him this vision.

Again, the Spirit lifts him up and brings him to the inner court of the future millennial temple (43:5). The appearance of the glory there is the same as in the visions he saw before (43:3). Since the millennial temple is not yet in existence, it is clear that what Ezekiel saw here was also a vision and that he was lifted to a higher spiritual level to see it, but was not physically transported into it. But perhaps all we can say about Ezekiel's transport to Jerusalem in chapter 8 is to compare it to Paul's experience of his vision of Paradise and the third heaven, "whether in the body or apart from of the body, I do not know, but God knows" (2 Corinthians 12:3). We can be sure, however, that Ezekiel experienced the power of the Spirit in a mighty way.

A New Spirit in God's People

The remainder of the references to the Spirit in Ezekiel deal with the time of Israel's future restoration (Ezekiel 11:19,20; 18:31,32; 36:26,27; 37:14; 39:29). The repeated emphasis in these passages is the new heart and spirit God puts in His people. Then God puts His Spirit in them.

First, He talks about giving them one [undivided] heart as well as a new spirit (11:19). The new spirit will make possible a new unity among God's people beyond anything they ever had before. God will also take out the heart of stone that was insensitive and hardened to the Word and the Spirit of the Lord. It will be replaced by a heart of flesh; that is, a mind tender and responsive to the things of God.[15] (A heart of flesh here simply means one that is functioning properly as God originally intended it to; but as is usual in the Old Testament, the heart includes the mind.) Then as they walk in obedience and faith, they will truly be God's people, and He will be their God (11:20).

God really wanted Israel to enjoy this new heart and new spirit in Ezekiel's day. Judgment would soon be necessary the way the people were going. But God still called them to repent, get rid of their rebellious sins, and make for themselves a new heart and a new spirit. He did not take any pleasure in bringing judgment and death, so why did they not turn back to Him and live (18:30–32)? That is, they could make a new heart and spirit for themselves by coming back to God and letting Him renew them by His Spirit.

Ezekiel 36:25–27 goes a step farther. It speaks of the cleansing that God will give after bringing Israel back to their own land. There God will give them the new heart and new spirit and replace their stony heart, as He promised them. Then also, He will put His Spirit within them to make it possible for them to live in obedience and faith in the land as His people. This He will do, not because Israel deserves it, but so that all shall know He is the Lord, the God who keeps His promises (36:32–38).

Exactly the same is pictured dramatically in the vision of the valley of dry bones. God asked Ezekiel if these bones could live. Ezekiel did not want to say that it looked impossible, so he said, "O Sovereign LORD, you alone know" (37:3). Then God told him to prophesy over the bones, and by the power of the prophetic Word, the bones came together and there was a physical restoration: "But there was no breath in them" (37:8). God then commanded Ezekiel to prophesy a second time and speak for God to the wind, calling for breath to come from the four winds to "breathe into these slain, that they may live" (37:9). By the power of the prophetic Word, the breath came into them and they stood up alive. After explaining that the bones represented the twelve tribes of Israel scattered among the nations with no hope of returning, God also explained that the breath represented His Spirit (37:14). That is, as in chapter 36, the promise was that Israel would first be restored to the land in unbelief. Then God would do a work of cleansing, change them, and give them His Spirit.

In Ezekiel 39:28,29, God again explains that this return of Israel will cause Him to be sanctified among many nations. They will know that He is the Lord (they will see that He is the kind of God He says He is) when the restoration is complete. The language of *knowing* the Lord is similar to that of the Book of Exodus, and Ezekiel seems to treat this final return as a second exodus. Then God adds that He will never hide His face from them again (as He did after the first exodus), "for I will pour out my Spirit on the house of Israel."

Before leaving Ezekiel, the river of Ezekiel 47:1–12 might be worth noting. Because water is often a type or symbol of the Holy Spirit, many take this as a picture of a revival stream where we move more and more out into the life of the Spirit. No doubt there are spiritual lessons to be drawn from this passage, but Ezekiel presents it as a real river bringing life to the Dead Sea and changing the desert of Judea into a pleasant land.[16] This will take place in the Millennium.

In Daniel, the Babylonians speak of "the spirit of the holy gods" in him (4:8,9,18; 5:11,14). This is just their heathen way of recognizing Daniel's prophetic gifts as well as his knowledge and wisdom. Otherwise, Daniel does not mention the Spirit.

Haggai also has only a brief statement, but it is very significant. He says that as God covenanted with Israel when they came out of Egypt, so His "Spirit remains" (taking His stand) among them (2:5). Thus, they could quit being afraid. This is one of the clearest statements in the Old Testament that the Spirit is eternal and that He is divine and unchanging.[17]

Not by Might Nor by Power

Zechariah gives us another very significant passage concerning the Spirit. It is the fifth vision of a series of eight, all given to encourage those who were rebuilding the temple after its destruction by the Babylonians. These visions look beyond the events surrounding the building of the temple, however. All eight have the work and times of the Messiah in view. God wanted Zerubbabel the prince and his people who had returned from Babylon to know that what they were doing was of more than local significance. It was part of a great plan that would find its consummation in the work of the Messiah. A brief survey of these visions will help place the fifth vision in its proper context.

The first vision (Zechariah 1:8–11) is of a company of horsemen among myrtle trees in a deep valley (perhaps suggesting the lowliness and security of God's people). Through them the world is at rest, indicating assurance of the victory of God's people. The horsemen are led by One on a red horse, One who is more than either man or angel, One who is the Messiah revealed as the Protector and restorer of His people.

The second vision (1:18–21) is of four horns, representing four world powers, and four smiths (workers in wood or metal). The four horns probably represent Babylon, Medo-Persia, Greece, and Rome (as in Daniel 2 and 7), though some see them as Assyria, Egypt, Babylon, and Medo-Persia.[18] The four smiths represent the same world powers which in turn bring God's judgment on the ones preceding them.

The third vision (2:1–13) pictures a surveyor (the Messiah) with a measuring line, indicating that through Him will come the fulfillment of God's promises of enlargement, peace, and glory for Jerusalem. Through Him also, many nations (Gentiles) will be joined to Jerusalem and God's people (2:11).

The fourth vision (Zechariah 3:1–10) shows Joshua, the then-current high priest (Ezra 2:2; 3:2), clothed in filthy (excrement-covered) garments representing the sins of the people. Though the adversary accuses him, the filthy garments are taken away, the sin is forgiven, and clean, beautiful garments are put upon him. This is then said to picture the work of the Messiah, the "Branch," that is, the new shoot from the rootstock of David (as in Isaiah 11:1; 53:2; Jeremiah 23:5).

Significantly, the fifth vision (Zechariah 4:1–14) emphasizing the Spirit of God as the Giver of power (Acts 1:8) follows immediately on this picture of the forgiveness of sin. The remaining visions give further pictures of sinners being destroyed and sin removed. They show, however, that the agencies that will bring this about at the end of the age were, in Zechariah's day, being held in check.

The fifth vision clearly takes a definite step beyond the fourth one. This is indicated by the fact that the angelic messenger had to rouse Zechariah to a higher, more acute stage of spiritual consciousness or awareness in order to receive the vision. (Note that Zechariah was not actually asleep in 4:1.) It is also seen by the fact that Zechariah found the vision very hard to understand.[19] Many modern commentators seem to have even more difficulty understanding it than Zechariah did, and there is much disagreement about the interpretation of details.[20]

Forty-Nine Lights

One difficulty is that the vision itself is hard to picture. Zechariah sees a solid gold lampstand. (Tallow or wax candles were not used in Old Testament times.) The lampstand held seven lamps. Above there was a large reservoir bowl from which seven "channels" led to the seven lamps. The Hebrew reads, "seven seven channels to the lamps." These repeated sevens have been interpreted as one channel to each lamp, seven in all; two channels to each lamp, fourteen in all; or seven channels to each lamp, forty-nine in all. The last interpretation seems best, for the phrase "seven seven" according to Hebrew usage is best taken distributively. Most commentators who take it this way see in the seven channels to each of the seven lamps a picture of fullness of supply.

Another difficulty in picturing this is that the Bible does not say how the lamps are arranged. The lamps were probably not in a line as they were in the lampstand in Herod's temple. More likely, they were in a circle under the bowl "on arms of equal length branching at regular intervals from the central shaft."[21] Thus the lamps would give light in all directions.

It seems, however, that the beauty of the golden lampstands is marred by picturing seven "channels" to each lamp. *Channels* actually means a place for pouring, a lip or spout. Archaeological discoveries show that such lamps were very simple. They were just small, shallow, shell-shaped bowls with lips pinched into the rims where the wicks were placed.

A better understanding of this picture would take the phrase "seven seven" to mean that the large reservoir bowl at the top had seven lips. From these a continuous supply of oil poured into the lamps, which were so arranged that one lamp was underneath each of these lips. Then, the distributive sense would apply to the lamps so that each lamp had seven lips for wicks, giving forty-nine lights in all. This would picture not only fullness of supply but a fullness of light spreading to all the world. (Compare Acts 1:8 and Matthew 24:14.) The light given by the Spirit and the Word must continue to spread toward the uttermost parts of the world until the consummation of this age.

God's Word to Zerubbabel from this was, " 'Not by might nor by power, but by my Spirit,' says the LORD Almighty" (Zechariah 4:6). Might and power are used somewhat interchangeably in the Old Testament. Sometimes they denote the inherent power, bravery, courage, fortitude; sometimes, the power of armies, riches, organization, and other external means. All sorts of human might and power are never enough to do God's work.

This was not an indication of any change in God's way of doing things. His Spirit has been the means of carrying out His plan at every stage, from Creation on. Even where God used armies, the victory was always the Lord's. (Compare Exodus 17:9–15, where Joshua moved forward only as long as Moses held up the rod of God toward heaven.) "By my Spirit" is a fundamental principle that all who are fellow laborers with the Lord must keep in mind.

There can be no doubt, therefore, that the oil is a type or symbol of the Holy Spirit and the lamps represent those through whom the Spirit gives light to the world.[22] But again, there is little agreement among commentators concerning what the lampstand represents. Some modern interpreters arbitrarily cut out the passage between Zechariah 4:6 and 10 and make the seven lamps the seven eyes of God.[23] This would make the lampstand represent God or Christ and the lamps symbols of the Spirit. But this hardly fits the context, though Calvin took the lamps to represent the "graces or the various gifts of His Spirit," and the number seven to indicate perfection.[24]

Some Jewish commentators and most modern dispensationalists take the lampstand to be Israel or Israel restored during the Millennium. The latter see a contrast here between the one lamp of this vision and the seven separate lampstands which the Book of Revelation uses to represent the seven churches of Asia, and through them the Church as a whole (Revelation 1:12).[25]

Most, however, agree with Keil in taking the burning lamps as "a symbol of the church or the nation of God which causes the light of its spirit or of its knowledge of God to shine before God and stream out into the night of a world estranged from God."[26] Certainly, the New Testament often refers to disciples or the Church as lights (Matthew 5:14; Luke 12:35; Revelation 1:20).

In the picture also are two olive trees, one on each side of the lampstand. Each has a golden pipe through which oil empties. "Pipes" in Zechariah 4:12 is a completely different word from that in verse 2, however. Here the meaning is *conduit*. Yet the Hebrew can mean either that the oil in the bowl is supplied by the olive trees or that the oil in the bowl actually supplies the trees (called anointed ones, sons of oil, in verse 14) with their oil.

If the bowl supplies the trees, this may be taken to teach that the light is maintained by God, not by the prince, Zerubbabel, or his civil administration, and not by the priest, Joshua, or his religious establishment.

If, on the other hand, the trees supply the bowl, it must be recognized that the "two who are anointed" means more than Zerubbabel and Joshua, more than the church and state. Rather, they picture the princely and priestly ministry which God's spirit ordains, a ministry that finds its fullness in the Messiah.[27] But however we take the direction of the flow of oil, we can see the Messiah as the real source, the Giver of the Holy Spirit.

The latter part of the Book of Zechariah looks ahead also to both the first and second comings of Christ. In connection with the final victories and future restoration God promises, "I will pour out [abundantly] on the house of David and the inhabitants of Jerusalem a spirit of grace and supplication [for favor]. They will look on me, the one they have pierced, and they will mourn for him, as one mourns for an only child" (12:10).

The Holy Spirit as the Spirit of grace pours out the grace (unmerited favor) of God in full measure. As the Spirit of supplications, He moves on the people to respond to that grace and seek the favor God offers them. Grace, too, must be interpreted with respect to the One who was pierced, that is with respect to the redeeming love of God manifest in the death of Christ on Calvary. Surely, there is no greater love, and there will be no greater sorrow than that of Israel when they discover who it was they pierced.

Saturating Rains

Looking back over the Old Testament, it is striking that Hosea promises God will "come to us like the winter rains, like the spring rains that water the earth" (Hosea 6:3). "Spring rain" is best taken as a verb form meaning "saturating." That is, God will come as the winter rains, saturating the earth.

This is parallel to the Old Testament promises of the pouring out of His Spirit (Isaiah 32:15; 44:3; Ezekiel 39:29; Joel 2:28;

Zechariah 12:10). But the context here is possibly connected with the death and resurrection of Christ (Hosea 6:1,2). At least, it is immediately preceded by restoration to the knowledge of (and personal fellowship with) God. In fact, Hosea calls for a following on to know the Lord that reminds us of the words of Jesus, "If you hold to my teaching, you are really my disciples. Then you will know the truth, and the truth will set you free" (John 8:31,32). The outpouring of the Spirit following Christ's death and resurrection can therefore be characterized as the spring rain.

Palestine has a long, rainless summer. In the fall, the former rains come in connection with plowing and planting. In the spring the latter rains come to prepare the crop for harvest. In this sense, God's coming and pouring out His Spirit beginning with Pentecost is as the spring rain. The harvest began with three thousand converted and it has continued through the Church Age. The current outpouring of the Spirit and His gifts is bringing many more thousands to Christ all over the world.

In contrast, the Spirit coming upon people here and there through Old Testament times may be called winter rain. The Spirit's work in the Old Testament was preparatory, as in times of plowing and planting. Few of the prophets had many converts. Jeremiah only had one that we know of (his secretary, Baruch). Ezekiel compared the revelation of God and His will to a lovely song that the people heard, sometimes seemed to enjoy, but did nothing about (Ezekiel 33:31,32).

Nevertheless, the Old Testament gives us considerable understanding of the work of the Spirit as well as a broad foundation for the outpouring of the Spirit in the New Testament.[28]

The Spirit and the Word

One of the most important themes brought out in the Old Testament is the close relationship between the Spirit and the Word (Proverbs 1:23; 2 Samuel 23:2; Micah 3:8). The prophets who spoke God's Word were regarded as His chief agents. As Amos says (3:7), "Surely the Sovereign LORD does nothing without revealing his plan to his servants the prophets." It is true there were false prophets who claimed inspiration (1 Kings 22:24; 2 Chronicles 18:23; Jeremiah 28:1–4). But they followed their own spirits (Ezekiel 13:3) and the Lord had not sent them. Events as well as the judgment of God showed they were false. But the Word of God continued to burn in the hearts of the true prophets even in the face of severe opposition and indifference (Jeremiah 20:9).

The prophets as men of the Spirit were also the chief writers of Scripture (recognizing that Moses was a prophet as well as David). The statement that the Spirit "spoke through" David indicates that the Spirit was also the Inspirer of the psalms he wrote (2 Samuel 23:2). This is also true of the Spirit's inspiration of Isaiah's words and writings (Isaiah 59:21). Jesus recognized the same thing when He quoted Psalm 110:1 as spoken by David through the Spirit (Matthew 22:42,43). So did Peter in reference to Psalm 41:9 (Acts 1:16). Then, Paul attributes Isaiah's words and writings to the Spirit in the same way (Acts 28:25, referring to Isaiah 6:9,10).

Nehemiah, near the end of the Old Testament period, gives more attention to the reading and teaching of the Word, as does Ezra (Nehemiah 8:1,8,9; Ezra 7:10). Nehemiah, in his prayer, recognized that God gave His good Spirit to instruct the Israelites in the wilderness (9:20). He also mentions the Spirit in the prophets as warning the later Israelites, but implies that later generations can learn from this (9:30).

God did raise up Malachi about the same time as Nehemiah's second visit (432 BC). But Malachi was the last of the writing prophets. Teaching seems to have predominated in the ministry of priests, rabbis, and scribes from then until New Testament times. But the Spirit continued to be recognized as the source of power, strength, miracles, and help, as well as of divine revelation. The Old Testament kept before them that wisdom and right training could not be had except through the Spirit. The prophecies of future outpourings kept before them the fact that there was still something ahead. What they had was not all God had for them. There was more.

The Spirit in the Life and Ministry of Jesus

What happened to spiritual religion during the four hundred years after Malachi? The common view is that it degenerated to the observance of empty forms and ceremonies. To a large extent that was true. The Pharisees made many requirements of the Law meaningless by the traditions they developed (Matthew 15:3,6; Mark 7:8–13). The Sadducees also had their traditions. So did the Qumran community which copied the Dead Sea Scrolls.

Luke, however, from the beginning of his Gospel, makes it clear that the Jews had not entirely lost either the concept or the experience of the Holy Spirit. The Spirit was active in the events preceding and surrounding the birth of Jesus as well as in His birth and in His life and ministry. In fact, though the references to the Holy Spirit in Christ's ministry are very significant, Luke's Gospel mentions the Spirit more often in the first two chapters than in all the rest of the Book.

Spirit-Filled and Expecting the Messiah

That a considerable segment of the Jews still held to the life and hope taught by the prophets is reflected throughout the story of Christ's birth. Among the priestly class Zechariah and Elizabeth, the parents of John the Baptist, are outstanding examples. Among the common people Simeon and Anna are representative of many who "were waiting for the "consolation [comfort, encouragement] of Israel" (Luke 2:25) and looked with expectation for "the redemption of Jerusalem" (Luke 2:38). That is, they looked for the salvation and restoration the prophets promised would come in the Messianic age. (Jews sometimes called the Messiah "the Consoler.")

It was undoubtedly for the "consolation of Israel" that Zechariah was praying as he burned incense on the golden altar before the entrance to the Holy of Holies in the temple. (It is not likely that he was praying for a son. He was there as a representative of the people.) But like so many of the day, he longed for the day of Israel's redemption. When the angel Gabriel appeared, he brought the promise of a son, but not just a son. This son would "make ready a people prepared for the Lord" (Luke 1:17).

The angel Gabriel also promised that John would be great in God's eyes, would not drink wine or other alcoholic beverages, but would be filled with the Holy Spirit (see Ephesians 5:18) even from his mother's womb. The Greek can also mean he would be filled with the Spirit while still in his mother's womb (see Luke 1:41,44).

John was thus to combine the best in all the Old Testament saints and prophets. He was to be a Nazirite expressing and testifying to total dedication to God all his life. He was to be guided, taught, prepared, and moved by the Holy Spirit in his own personal life and in his ministry. He was also to "go on before the Lord in the spirit and power of Elijah" (v. 17). When this was said of Elisha (2 Kings 2:15) it meant the other prophets recognized that Elisha was the God-appointed successor of Elijah. John the Baptist would be the heir and successor of Elijah (and all the prophets) in an even greater sense. Jesus himself recognized John as the Elijah who was to come (Matthew 17:10–13). In this context Jesus was really telling His disciples that if they would listen to His interpretation instead of that of the Pharisees, they would know that John the Baptist was the true fulfillment of Malachi 4:5,6.

The same thing is implied in the angel's words of Luke 1:16, which is a reference to Malachi 4:6. Jesus further declared that John was more than a prophet. He was the promised messenger of Malachi 3:1. As such, none was greater than he. Yet he remained an Old Testament prophet, never entering for himself the fellowship for which he prepared the way (Matthew 11:9–11).

Both of John's parents shared in the blessing of the Holy Spirit that came to John. When Mary came down to visit Elizabeth, Mary's salutation or greeting caused the baby to leap in Elizabeth's womb, through the influence of the Spirit (Luke 1:41,44). At this, the Holy Spirit filled Elizabeth and she cried out loudly and pronounced God's blessing on Mary and on her child who would be Elizabeth's Lord.

After John was born, Zechariah also was filled with the Holy Spirit (Luke 1:67). Under the anointing of the Spirit he prophesied and gave thanks for the salvation God was about to provide. It would fulfill the promises given to Abraham and make it possible for God's people to serve Him without fear. John the Baptist would be called a prophet of the Highest and would fulfill Isaiah's prophecy of the voice in the wilderness preparing the way of the Lord (Isaiah 40:3).

The activity of the Holy Spirit is seen in an even more striking way when Mary and Joseph took Baby Jesus to the temple (Luke 2:25–35). At the same time, the godly Simeon came in and met them there. But this was no accident. The Holy Spirit was continually upon this humble man of God. The Spirit also prepared him by promising he would not die before he would see the Lord's Christ (Messiah, the anointed Prophet, Priest, and King to come). Then he came by the Spirit (led, directed by the Spirit) into the temple at just the right time. By the Spirit also he recognized this Child whose mother came offering the offering of the poor as the One he hoped for. Then, he too gave an inspired prophetic utterance that identified Jesus as the Light prophesied for the Gentiles (the nations) and the glory of God's people Israel. He also foretold the heartbreak that would come to Mary (fulfilled at the Cross).

Immediately after that came Anna, a godly woman of the tribe of Asher (one of the northern ten tribes). She was a prophet and was, therefore, moved by the Spirit as she too came in at just the right time and added her thanks to the Lord (Luke 2:36–38). As a prophet also she spread the good news to others who were looking for the redemption of Jerusalem.

Jesus, the Son of God

Mark, who gives no details of the birth of Jesus, begins his Gospel by calling Jesus the Son of God. Luke, who gives many details, makes the same statement (Luke 1:35). Matthew implies the same thing, but only later makes it clear (Matthew 2:15; 16:16).

Matthew tells the story from the standpoint of Joseph, through whom Jesus was the legal heir of the throne of David. (Legal inheritance was just as important to the Jews as natural inheritance. Matthew emphasizes how Jesus fulfilled the Law as well as the promises. Thus the Messiah must have the legal right to the throne. That is also why Matthew draws attention to the fact that Joseph took Mary as his wife and the marriage ceremony was performed in Nazareth before Jesus was born.) Matthew is careful to make it very clear, however, that Joseph was not the father of Jesus. Joseph was surprised and shocked by the fact that Mary was to have a child. (Engaged couples did not see each other between the betrothal and the marriage ceremony.) Twice it is stated that the child was "through [out of, from, by] the Holy Spirit" (Matthew 1:18,20). It is also identified as the fulfillment of Isaiah's prophecy of the Virgin Birth and the child Immanuel (which the Greek gives as "with us is *the* God").

Luke's account is told from Mary's viewpoint and is the record of what Mary carefully remembered (Luke 2:51). It emphasizes even more strongly that Jesus was born of the Holy Spirit.

When the angel Gabriel told Mary she would have a Son who would be "called the Son of the Most High [that is, of God]" and "The Lord God will give him the throne of his father David"

(Luke 1:32), she expressed surprise. How could this be, since she did not have a husband. But Gabriel said, "The Holy Spirit will come upon you, and the power of the Most High [that is, of God] will overshadow you [cover you like a cloud]. So the holy one to be born will be called the Son of God" (Luke 1:35).

The idea of the overshadowing is reminiscent of the cloud of God's presence that enveloped Moses on Mount Sinai and that covered the tabernacle (Exodus 24:18; 40:34,35). It also suggests the creative Spirit hovering over the waters of the earth in the beginning (Genesis 1:2). However, even though the birth of Jesus was by the Holy Spirit, there is no suggestion that the Holy Spirit contributed anything of himself. As Alford points out, the world was not created by the Holy Spirit, but by God through the Son (John 1:3). So the creative act that made possible the Virgin Birth was by God through the Holy Spirit.[1] Jesus was and is the Son of God not only because by His very nature He is the eternal Son (John 3:16; 8:58; Hebrews 1:2,3), but because His birth was the result of a direct supernatural creative act by the Father.

Not until later is the theology of this developed. (See Romans 8:3 where the Bible says God sent His own Son in the likeness of sinful flesh, and Galatians 4:4 which says, "God sent his Son, born of a woman." See also Romans 1:3; Hebrews 10:5.)[2] All that is emphasized here is the fact of the Virgin Birth and the supernatural power that made it possible.

The Virgin Birth and the direct agency of the Holy Spirit in it is an important part of the gospel, however. It was good news that God himself was stepping down once again into the stream of human life and history to perform specific acts that would carry forward His plan and bring salvation. Those who deny the Virgin Birth or say it is not important only give themselves away as anti-supernaturalists. They usually try to explain away the miracles of Jesus and His resurrection and second coming as well.

The fact that Jesus was miraculously conceived in Mary's womb by the power of the Spirit is probably an indication also that the Spirit was with Him and indwelt Him from that time on. There is and has always been perfect fellowship between the members of the Trinity. Jesus said He was and is in the Father and the Father in Him (John 14:10,20). By His very nature, then, the Holy Spirit must have been in Him. But this does not exclude Jesus from having a distinct experience with the Holy Spirit when the Spirit came upon Him after His baptism by John.

The Mighty Baptizer

John the Baptist came to the very desert prophesied by Isaiah (Matthew 3:1; Isaiah 40:3). "Desert" in the Hebrew is *arabah*, the name of the lower Jordan-Dead Sea valley. As the prophesied voice, John the Baptist called for repentance and baptized those who came confessing their sins. But he refused to baptize anyone until after they truly repented (Matthew 3:1–12). When Pharisees and Sadducees came, as a Spirit-filled prophet he recognized that there was no change in their attitudes. He demanded that they bring fruit or evidence of their repentance before he would baptize them. They were self-satisfied, feeling secure in the fact that they were children of Abraham. But John showed that this would not protect them from the coming judgment. Then John went on to say, "I baptize you with [in] water for repentance [that is, because of repentance, since he had already indicated that his baptism could not produce repentance]. But after me will come one who is more powerful than I, whose sandals I am not fit to carry. He will baptize you with [in] the Holy Spirit and with [in] fire" (v. 11).

Baptized in the Holy Spirit and in Fire

All four Gospels record John's prophecy that the coming One will baptize in the Holy Spirit (Matthew 3:11; Mark 1:8; Luke 3:16; John 1:33). Matthew and Luke add that He will also baptize in fire.

The baptism in the Holy Spirit is, of course, the fulfillment of the promises to pour out the Spirit (Isaiah 44:3; Ezekiel 36:26;

39:29; Joel 2:28). But John adds a new thought not mentioned in the Old Testament. The Spirit is not only to be poured out upon them; they are to be immersed in Him, saturated with Him. As Barclay says, if life is drab, inadequate, futile, earth-bound, it is because believers have neglected the Holy Spirit and failed to enter into the sphere of life dominated by the Spirit through this baptism which Christ alone has the power to give.[3]

The baptism in fire has been interpreted in a number of ways. Most critics who deny the inspiration and integrity of the Bible say John prophesied only one baptism, a baptism of fire, and that the idea of a baptism in the Holy Spirit was added later on. Others say that by *Spirit* John meant breath or wind and that John's proclamation was of one baptism that would bring a breath of fiery judgment or that would be like a wind of judgment clearing the threshing floor.[4]

It is clear, however, that John's message is not one of judgment only. He has come to prepare the way of the Lord. But it was still possible to flee from the wrath to come. It was still possible to bear good fruit. Only the chaff would be burned (Matthew 3:7, 10,12). Basically, John's message was good news. The kingdom (rule) of God was about to be manifest. There is no good reason for the critics to take John's promise as one of a baptism of judgment only.[5]

Those who see a twofold baptism in the Holy Spirit and fire are also divided in their interpretation. Some say it is one baptism with two elements or aspects, Holy Spirit and fire at the same time. Others say it is a twofold baptism: in the Spirit for the righteous, and in fire for the wicked.

Those who hold that the baptism in the Holy Spirit and fire is one work with two elements acting at the same time draw attention to the fact that the preposition "in" is actually used before "the Spirit" but not before "fire." They also point out that John expected the Coming One to baptize the people he was preaching to in both the Holy Spirit and fire. From this they say that the Messiah baptizes everyone in the same Holy Spirit and fire experience. To those who truly repent, it will be a blessing and salvation or sanctification. To the wicked it will be judgment.

There are several difficulties with this view. First, it is true that when a preposition is not repeated before a second noun this usually puts the two nouns in the same category. But there are exceptions.[6] Some authorities do recognize that John proclaimed that the One to come would bring "not only the Holy Spirit but also the fire of divine judgment"[7]

It is also true that John the Baptist addressed the people as if the judgment were going to take place in their own day. Obviously, he did not see any time difference between the baptism in the Holy Spirit and the baptism in fire. But John was still in the company of the Old Testament prophets to whom the time interval between the first and second comings of Christ was not revealed. They often spoke of events connected with the two comings in the same breath. But there are hints, however, that the Messiah must first suffer before He would reign. He must first make His soul (His whole person) an offering for sin, before the pleasure of the Lord would prosper in His hand (Isaiah 53:10). Zechariah had multiple crowns placed on the high priest Joshua in a symbolic action to show that the Messiah must first do His priestly work before He would reign as a priest on His throne (Zechariah 6:11-13; see also Luke 24:25,26; Philippians 2:8-11).

This was hard for Jesus' own disciples to understand. He gave them a parable to show that it would be a long time before he would return to establish the Kingdom (Luke 19:11,12, "a distant country"). Yet before His ascension they still asked, "Lord, are you at this time going to restore the kingdom to Israel?" His reply was that it was not for them to know the times and dates. These the Father keeps under His own authority (Acts 1:6,7). In other words, they are none of our business. (However, Acts 1:8 is our business.)

It is not strange, then, that John fails to distinguish between the time of the baptism in the Spirit and the baptism in fire. But Jesus clearly did. To the disciples just before His ascension, He said, "John baptized with [in] water, but in a few days you will be baptized with [in] the Holy Spirit" (v. 5). Thus he identified the baptism in the Spirit with the outpouring that took place at Pentecost. But He recognized the fire of judgment would be at the end, as does Paul (2 Thessalonians 1:8).

The Purpose of the Fire

The purpose of the baptism in fire is also a point at issue. Many who hold to a single baptism of Holy Spirit and fire, with the fire and the Spirit acting together to affect the one baptized, take the fire to mean purification or sanctification of the believer. But the work of the baptism in the Holy Spirit does not seem to be primarily sanctification. Paul still has to tell believers who have been filled with the Spirit to count themselves to be dead to sin and alive to God. They must not permit sin to reign in their bodies (Romans 6:11,12). It is true that through the Spirit we are to "put to death the misdeeds of the body" that we may live (8:13). But this is a continuous present tense in the Greek. We must keep on putting to death the evil deeds of the body and then we shall keep on living. It is true also that we are dead and our life "is now hidden with Christ in God" (Colossians 3:3). But the very fact that we have this standing in Christ means we have a responsibility ourselves to put to death (by definite action) our members on the earth (that is, what is earthly in us), which Paul identifies with lusts of the flesh or sinful nature (v. 5).

Jesus himself connects the baptism in the Spirit with power for service rather than with purification or sanctification (Acts 1:8). Sanctification (dedication, consecration to God and His will) must come through both definite acts of self-discipline and through continued cooperation with the Holy Spirit as He applies the Word (as we shall see later).

Fiery Zeal

Others who take the Spirit and fire to be one experience identify the fire with zeal or enthusiasm with enlightenment and gifts of the Spirit.[8] Many of them do indeed have the "fire" in that sense. Romans 12:11 speaks of a fervency, a boiling, or a burning zeal of the Spirit. First Thessalonians 5:19 commands people to stop trying to put out the fire of the Spirit. The same fire is implied in speaking "the word of God boldly" that came as the result of the Spirit's filling (Acts 4:31). This boldness is a wonderful, joyous confidence, freedom, courage, and fiery zeal. Truly, we have a right to ask God to send this fire!

The Bible does not talk about a baptism of fire when speaking to believers, however. John's Gospel, addressed to Christians, mentions only baptism in the Holy Spirit (John 1:33). In John, water is the chief symbol of the Spirit, not fire. Jesus also, in speaking to His own disciples, mentions only baptism in the Holy Spirit (Acts 1:5).

Many do identify the tongues of fire on the Day of Pentecost with a baptism of fire.[9] These tongues of fire preceded the Pentecostal baptism, however, and had nothing directly to do with it. When the one hundred twenty were filled with the Holy Spirit, the sign was speaking in other tongues, not fire (Acts 2:4). At the house of Cornelius, the gift of the Spirit received by the Gentiles there is identified with the baptism in the Holy Spirit. It is called the "same" (identical) gift. But there is no mention of fire (Acts 10:44,45,47; 11:15-17). In Acts also, Stephen and Barnabas are said to be full of the Holy Spirit and faith, but nothing is said about fire (Acts 6:5; 11:24). In fact, nothing is ever said in the Book of Acts about believers being filled with fire. The terminology is always simply that they were filled with the Holy Spirit.

The Fire of Judgment

When Jesus talks about fire, it is always the fire of judgment or destruction, especially of the hell *(gehenna)* of fire, which really refers to the lake of fire (Matthew 5:22; 18:8,9). The same thing is usually true in the Epistles (1 Corinthians 3:13; 2 Thessalonians 1:8; Hebrews 12:29; 2 Peter 3:7).

Going back to the context of John's prophecy of the baptism in the Holy Spirit and in fire, the Bible shows that John had just been warning of the wrath to come (Matthew 3:7). The verses just preceding and following this promise of this baptism speak of trees cut down and cast into fire and of chaff burned with unquenchable fire (fire that by its very nature can never be put out; in other words, the lake of fire). It would seem strange if the fire in Matthew 3:10 and 12 means one thing and then, without any explanation, it means something different in verse 11.[10] From early times, many have recognized that the baptism in fire does mean judgment,[11] although the idea has often aroused controversy.

Again, we must keep in mind that John failed to see the time difference between the baptism in the Holy Spirit and the fire. When John was put in prison, this is probably what bothered him. Jesus was healing the sick and forgiving sins, but He was not bringing any judgment. In fact, Herod and Herodias who deserved judgment were the ones who held John in prison. So John sent two disciples to ask if Jesus really was the One to come, or was He just another forerunner like himself. Jesus sent John's disciples back with a report that Jesus was indeed doing the prophesied works of the Promised One (Matthew 11:1–6; see also Isaiah 29:18,19; 35:5,6; 61:1).

Actually, Jesus had already made it clear that He did not come at this time to condemn the world but to save it (John 3:17). At Nazareth as He read from Isaiah 61:1,2, He deliberately closed the book before coming to "the day of vengeance of our God" (Luke 4:19,20). The sword Jesus brought was to draw a line of division between those who accepted Him and those who did not. It was not the sword of judgment or destruction (Matthew 10:34; Luke 12:51).

The Spirit Like a Dove

By being baptized by John in the Jordan, Jesus identified himself with mankind. Then God proclaimed Him as His Son by sending the Holy Spirit upon Him like a dove and by a voice from heaven saying, "This is my Son, whom I love; with him I am well pleased" (Matthew 3:17). The name "David" means "beloved." Thus, this may also have at least hinted that Jesus is the greater David, God's David. The phrase "whom I love" (Greek *agápetòs)* is also closely tied with "one and only" (Greek *monogenê,* implying unique, one of a kind; John 3:16). There is a parallel to this in Abraham's relation to Isaac. In Abraham's great test God told him to take his son, his only son, whom he loved, and offer him for a sacrifice (Genesis 22:2). The New Testament, in referring to this, calls Isaac Abraham's "one and only" (*monogenê,* Hebrews 11:17).

All four Gospels record this descent of the Spirit like a dove (Matthew 3:16,17; Mark 1:10,11; Luke 3:21,22; John 1:32–34). Luke adds that the Holy Spirit descended in a bodily shape or form like a dove. That is, there was an actual, visible appearance that looked like a dove and that everyone could see. Matthew and Luke state that the Spirit as a dove came upon Him. John says it remained on him. But some ancient manuscripts of Mark and at least one of Luke say the Spirit as a dove descended into Him. This, of course, is just another way of emphasizing that the Spirit did not leave Jesus after coming upon Him.

The phrase "with him I am well pleased" (Matthew 3:17) indicates that the descent of the Spirit was also a visible sign of the Father's acceptance and approval of the Son in the ministry He was about to begin. The phrase might also be translated, "in whom I take delight." (Mark 1:11 and Luke 4:22 show that the voice was primarily addressed to Jesus.) But this expression of active delight may have foreshadowed the Cross. Isaiah 53:10 says, "It was the LORD's will to crush him," referring to His sacrificial (substitutionary) death. This may also be a reason why the descent of the dove in John is followed shortly after by a recognition of Jesus as the Lamb of God who takes away the sin of the world (John 1:36). The dove to the Jews was more than a symbol of gentleness and peace. It was also the sin offering which the poor substituted for the lamb (Leviticus 5:7). Jesus is God's own Lamb provided as a substitute for the poor, the needy, the sinful of this world, which includes us all (Romans 3:23).

Identifying the Baptizer

In addition to this, the descent of the Spirit was a specific sign to John the Baptist that Jesus would be the One baptizing in the Holy Spirit. John did not know this at the time Jesus came to the Jordan to be baptized in water. Thus, when John suggested he needed to be baptized by Jesus, he meant baptized in water, not in the Spirit. John had known the moving and guidance of the Spirit all his life. Through the Spirit and the Word, he challenged the people to repent. Through the Spirit he sensed the hypocrisy of those who came to be seen but had no intention of repenting. Yet when Jesus came to the Jordan, John sensed his own need.

Isaiah, confronted with a vision of the majesty, glory, and holiness of God, suddenly felt he was the man with unclean lips (Isaiah 6:3,5). Peter, when confronted with the power of Jesus in something he as a fisherman knew had to be a miracle, suddenly realized he was a sinful man (Luke 5:8). But the One who came to be baptized by John the Baptist had emptied himself of the glory He once shared with His Father (Philippians 2:6,7). There was no halo or anything external to distinguish Him from any other man from Nazareth. Nor had Jesus done any miracles. Yet the person of Jesus caused this Spirit-filled man to realize he still fell short (Matthew 3:14). He needed a baptism of repentance, just as did the others who came to him. Not until afterward did the Spirit come upon Jesus as a dove. Then John's attention was drawn to another baptism, which he contrasts with his own.

The words of John 1:31–33 draw a very clear line of distinction between water baptism and the baptism in the Spirit. Luke also indicates a clear distinction between the baptism by Jesus and the descent of the Spirit upon Him. The Greek reads literally, "Jesus, having been baptized, and continuing to pray, the heavens opened, and the Holy Spirit descended" (Luke 3:21,22). That is, it was not until after the baptism in water was over and Jesus was praying that the Spirit came. Matthew indicates further that Jesus went up from (away from) the water (Matthew 3:16). Mark says "out of the water" (Mark 1:10). Thus, Jesus was at least up on the bank.

Those who picture Jesus still standing in the water with the dove coming upon Him are missing an important point.

Distinct from Water Baptism

Luke's emphasis on the fact that Jesus was continuing to pray after He left the water is also important. Prayer and praise often preceded the coming of the Holy Spirit on believers in the New Testament. (See Luke 24:53; Acts 1:14; 4:24,31; 8:15; 10:30.) It is interesting to see some recognize this who otherwise do not want to see any parallel between the experience of Jesus here and that of the disciples at Pentecost and after.[12]

It is true that the coming of the Spirit on Jesus was in some ways unique. His experience went beyond that of anyone before or since, for God did not give Him the Spirit "without limit" (John 3:34). The Spirit coming upon Jesus was also a specific fulfillment of prophecies given long before (Isaiah 11:2; 42:1; 61:1). But we must not overlook some similarities. The Spirit has also come on us to stay (John 14:16). Even though Jesus is the Baptizer in the Spirit, the Spirit still comes upon us from the Father (vv. 16,26).

Identified with Mankind

We must keep in mind also that the Holy Spirit came upon Jesus after Jesus had declared His identification with mankind in water baptism. Later, when Satan tempted Him to make the stones bread, He refused. To do so would have broken that identification with us. Had He made the stones bread, then it would have been easy for Him to continue using His divine power to keep Him from feeling hunger, pain, or weariness. Even His sufferings on the cross would not have been real. But He took His place among us as a real Man, so He could be touched by the feeling of our infirmities and be able to sympathize with us (Hebrews 4:15).

Certainly, then, there was no intention on the part of the Father to break that identification with humanity when He sent the Spirit on Jesus. What happened to Jesus was necessary, not because He was God, but because He was also man. As a man He had to minister in the power of the Spirit. As a man He had to suffer and die. When the Father said, "This is my Son, whom I love," He was simply reinforcing the fact that the humanity of Jesus in no way detracts from His deity. Somehow Jesus held within His one person the full complement of human qualities as well as the full complement of divine qualities without their interfering with one another. He was the God-Man, but not in the sense of being half God and half man. He was fully God, one hundred percent God. He was also fully human, one hundred percent man.

Upon the God-Man, Jesus, the Spirit came to prepare Him for a ministry among men as well as to identify Him as the Baptizer in the Spirit. Thus, even though the experiences are not exactly parallel, it is a fact that Jesus did not begin His earthly ministry until the Father sent the Spirit. Similarly, Jesus commanded the disciples to sit or stay in Jerusalem and not to begin their ministry until the Holy Spirit came (Luke 24:49; Acts 1:4).

Led by the Spirit

In view of the full humanity of Jesus and His identification with us, it is noteworthy that as soon as the Spirit came upon Jesus, He submitted to the Spirit's leading (Matthew 4:1; Luke 4:1). First, He was led up by the Spirit into the desert (that is, up from the Jordan River into the barren hills to the west) to be tempted by the devil. Mark uses an even stronger word. The Spirit drove Him ("sent him out," drove Him out violently). This was not going to be a pleasant experience. Jesus was going to feel the pressure of temptation the way we feel it. Thus, a mighty surge of the Spirit's power brought Him from the Jordan into those desert hills. He was already full of the Spirit, but in this experience the Spirit moved Him, almost lifted Him. For forty days the Spirit continued to guide Him. So full of the Spirit was He that He did not even feel hunger until after the forty days were over (Matthew 4:2).

In His temptation, Jesus did not use His divine power to defeat the devil. Still identifying himself with us as a Spirit-filled human, He defeated Satan by the same means that are available to us—the Word, anointed by the Spirit. Eve, tempted in exactly the same areas—the lust of the flesh (appetite), the lust of the eyes (desire), and the pride of life—failed (Genesis 3:6; 1 John 2:16). In these areas, which John says together comprise the things of the world or worldliness (1 John 2:15), Jesus won a complete victory for us. He has truly overcome the world (John 16:33). We can do the same by our faith (1 John 5:4).

In this victory there is also a parallel with the calling and ministry of some of the Old Testament prophets. As the Spirit filled Micah so he could warn against sin (Micah 3:8), so the Holy Spirit filled Jesus and sent Him immediately into the battle against sin and Satan. Jesus was not filled with the Spirit just to do miracles, but to prepare Him to do all God's work. He was given the Spirit without measure because He was sent to speak the words of God and because the Father, in love for Him, has given Him all things (John 3:34,35). This can only mean that the carrying out of all God's plan is in His hands.

Matthew, Mark, and Luke skip over the remainder of Jesus' first year of ministry (which was mostly in Judea). They jump ahead to the great year of popularity in Galilee. Matthew says it was after the arrest of John the Baptist that Jesus departed ("withdrew") into Galilee (Matthew 14:13). But this was not because of a desire to escape the fate that overtook John. Jesus was in Judea, which was under the Roman governor or procurator, Pilate. Galilee was Herod's territory. Luke makes it clear. Jesus was still led by the Spirit. He went by the power of the Spirit into Galilee (Luke 4:14).

John introduces another factor. The Pharisees heard that Jesus was making and baptizing more disciples than John the Baptist. This indicates opposition was rising among the synagogue leaders in Jerusalem. It was the part of wisdom for Jesus to withdraw. In fact, throughout the Gospels we see Jesus avoiding anything that might bring an arrest or death before God's time. He even spoke in parables, not to clarify the message, but to obscure it to His enemies. They would be hardened further, while His disciples could ask questions and learn the truth from His explanations (Matthew 13:10–12; Luke 8:10). By this also, His enemies were frustrated in their hopes of arresting Him. They could hardly use parables as evidence in court against Him.

John's Gospel also goes on to show that Jesus did not withdraw merely to escape the opposition of the Pharisees. Even though John does not say so at this point, Jesus was definitely led by the Spirit. This is shown by the route He picked for the return to Galilee. Jews usually avoided the shorter, more direct route through Samaria and went through the Jordan Valley and Perea. But Jesus "had to go through Samaria" (John 4:4). This speaks of an inner urging, the voice of the Spirit laying a divine necessity upon Him. God had an appointment arranged for Jesus to be at Jacob's well when a certain Samaritan woman of ill-repute would come, find the water of life, and spread the good news (John 4:14,15,28,29).

Ministering through the Spirit

Not only was Jesus led by the Spirit; His ministry was accomplished through the Spirit. Not much is actually said in the Gospels about the Holy Spirit empowering Jesus for ministry. But once it was made clear, there was no need for constant repetition.

When Jesus returned in the power of the Spirit to Galilee, the power was first manifest in His teaching and then in His healing ministry. At Capernaum, before any miracles were performed, the people were struck with amazement at His teaching. The anointing of the Spirit on His teaching made them feel His authority, something they had never felt during all the years they had been listening to the scribes (who claimed to be authorities on the meaning of the Scriptures).

The news of this ministry quickly spread. At Nazareth Jesus read from Isaiah 61:1,2 and declared openly that this prophecy of the Spirit upon the Servant of God and on His ministry was being fulfilled in and through Him (Luke 4:18,21).

Later, when the Pharisees began to plot against Him, seeking some way to destroy Him, Jesus again withdrew. But this did not stop His ministry. The crowds followed Him, and He healed them all (Matthew 12:15). The Bible specifies this as a fulfillment of Isaiah 42:1–4, which prophesies the Holy Spirit's coming and resting on God's Anointed Servant to bring God's mercies and His victory.

Rejoicing in the Spirit

After the return of the seventy disciples whom Jesus sent out in Perea, Jesus rejoiced "full of joy through the Holy Spirit" (Luke 10:21). Some ancient manuscripts have "in spirit" here. But it really makes little difference which is correct. Whether Luke uses the phrase "in the Spirit" or "in spirit," he usually means the Holy Spirit, and it is evident that he does here.[13] (Note also that the ancient Greek did not distinguish between capital and small letters the way we do.)

This rejoicing is another indication of the continuous working of the Spirit in Jesus' life and ministry. We never read of Jesus telling jokes. There is a sense of humor expressed in some of His sayings and parables. But there is never any frivolity, never any humor at the expense of others. He was too much taken up with His Father's work. There was a harvest that needed to be brought in before it was too late (John 4:32–36). But the Holy Spirit gave Him something better than what the world calls happiness. He gave Him joy, real joy that only those led by the Spirit know.

This expression of joy in Luke 10:21 was more than a good feeling. He rejoiced because of what God was doing through the seventy. The wise and prudent (the skilled interpreters of the Law, the religious leaders and chief priests) looked down on such humble folk as Jesus chose to send out. But through them God revealed His grace, power, and salvation. Already, their names were written down in heaven (Luke 10:20). Moreover, everyone would have to recognize that what the seventy accomplished was not through any power, authority, or official position of their own. The power had to be God's.

All through the life of Jesus there is an underlying note of joy, even as He faced the Cross (Hebrews 12:2). Part of this was in anticipation of the future. But a great part was because of the life He lived in the Spirit. Through the Spirit He knew peace and joy. Through the Spirit He also imparts them to us (John 14:27; 15:11; Galatians 5:22).

Blasphemy against the Holy Spirit

The passages that deal with the sin against the Holy Spirit give us further evidence from Jesus himself that His ministry was accomplished through the power of the Spirit (Matthew 12:24–32; Mark 3:22–30; Luke 11:15–20; 12:10).

From the beginning of Jesus' ministry, His casting out of demons caught the attention of the people and filled them with amazement (Mark 1:27,28). On this occasion, a demon-possessed person who was blind and deaf was brought to Jesus and He healed him (Matthew 12:22–28). When the astonished people asked, "Could this be the Son of David?" the Pharisees were upset. In a very derogatory manner, they proclaimed that this fellow Jesus was casting out demons by the power of Beelzebub (Satan), the prince of demons.

Jesus first pointed out the foolishness of their statement. A kingdom divided against itself (disunited) is laid waste. A divided or disunited city or house will not stand. If Satan casts out Satan he is disunited and working against himself, so how can his kingdom stand? Furthermore, if Jesus was casting out demons by Beelzebub, it followed that any children (disciples) of the Pharisees who would cast out a demon would have to do it the same way. But if Jesus was casting out demons by the Spirit of God, then the kingdom (royal rule and power) of God "has come upon you." That is, the Kingdom is actually in operation on your behalf (Matthew 12:28).

Mark (3:23) adds that these Pharisees were not local Galileans, but scribes (experts in the Law of Moses), sent down from Jerusalem (to watch Jesus and try to trip Him up or discredit Him). Luke uses a different expression, substituting "the finger of God" (11:20) for the Spirit of God. This is similar to the Old Testament references which used the hand of God to express the power of God. Undoubtedly, Jesus used both expressions to represent the power of the Spirit as well.

The accusation that Jesus cast out demons by the power of Satan was too serious simply to explain this way and leave, however. The people needed a warning lest they listen to these scribes of the Pharisees and lose their own hope of eternal salvation. Jesus made it clear also that they could not simply remain neutral. "He who is not with me is against me, and he who does not gather with me scatters" (Matthew 12:30).

A Severe Warning

The warning against blasphemy of the Holy Spirit is difficult to interpret. Matthew 12:31,32 says, "Every sin and blasphemy [abusive speech, slander] will be forgiven men, but the blasphemy against the Spirit will not be forgiven. Anyone who speaks a word [makes a blasphemous assertion] against the Son of Man will be forgiven, but anyone who speaks against the Holy Spirit, will not be forgiven, either in this age or in the age to come." This is followed by another exhortation to make their decision between Jesus and the Pharisees who were trying to turn the people away from Him. "Make a tree good and its fruit will be good, or make a tree bad [corrupt, rotten] and its fruit will be bad, for a tree [a person] is recognized by its fruit" (v. 33).

Mark 3:29 emphasizes the same thing in a slightly different way, "Whoever blasphemes against the Holy Spirit will never be forgiven; he is guilty of an eternal sin." "An eternal sin" indicates that those who blaspheme against the Spirit either are guilty of or are involved in an eternal sin. Mark then draws attention to the reason Jesus had for giving this warning. His enemies were saying He had an unclean (impure, vicious, evil) spirit.

Luke does not bring this warning in immediately after what the Pharisees said. But he shows Jesus repeated the warning after saying, "Whoever acknowledges me [publicly] before men, the Son of Man will also acknowledge him before the angels of God. But he who disowns [repudiates, denies] me before men will be disowned before the angels of God" (Luke 12:8,9). This is a theme frequently found in the New Testament (John 9:22; 12:42,43; Romans 10:9,10; 2 Timothy 2:12; 1 John 4:2,15; 2 John 7). Then Jesus added, "And everyone who speaks a word against the Son of Man will be forgiven, but anyone who blasphemes against the Holy Spirit will not be forgiven" (Luke 12:10).

An Important Distinction

All these passages distinguish clearly between the person of Jesus and the person of the Holy Spirit. They also distinguish between blasphemous statements against Jesus as the Son of Man and against the Holy Spirit. Most commentators take the blasphemy against the Son of Man to be a failure to recognize the humble Jesus as the One fulfilling the glorious prophecies of the coming Messiah.

After the healing of the lame man at the Beautiful Gate of the temple, Peter reminded the crowd that in the presence of Pilate they denied "the Holy and Righteous One," and asked for a murderer, and "killed the author of life, but God raised him from the dead." But Peter adds that he knew they did it through ignorance, as did their rulers. Therefore, repentance was available to them (Acts 3:13–19). Their sin had been enormous, but it was not unpardonable.

Paul also, regretting that he "was once a blasphemer and a persecutor and a violent man [insolent, arrogant, shaming, mistreating, and insulting the Christians]," recognized that he obtained mercy because he did it ignorantly in unbelief (1 Timothy 1:13). Thus, even though in a sense he not only blasphemed Christ, he also blasphemed the work of the Spirit in and through the Church, yet he did not commit an unpardonable sin.

The blasphemy against the Holy Spirit is distinguished then from things said against Jesus or His body, the Church, when these statements come from an unbelief that arises from ignorance. That is, things people say because they have been taught wrong can be repented of and forgiven.

A Total Rejection

Clearly, the blasphemy of the Spirit is something willful and involves a sin against knowledge. Matthew relates it to willfully attributing the works of Jesus to the power of Satan. These works were the Spirit's witness to Jesus as Messiah and Savior. The Pharisees, who knew the Scriptures, were absolutely refusing to recognize the salvation that comes through Jesus alone. "For there is no other name under heaven given to men by which we must be saved" (Acts 4:12). The total rejection of the Spirit's work in bringing us to Jesus thus closes the door on salvation in this age. Nor will there be a second chance in the age to come. After death, there is nothing left for the unbeliever but judgment (Hebrews 9:27). It is either now or never.

Mark relates the blasphemy of the Spirit to the further blasphemy which said Jesus had an unclean spirit. In other words, they were saying that the Holy Spirit in Him was an evil spirit. By this also they were refusing to recognize that the Spirit given after His baptism was from God. They were also repudiating the Father's witness to His Son. As in Matthew, to treat the Holy Spirit as an evil spirit was to resist His influences intending to lead us to salvation. To call Him injurious and impure is to cut ourselves off from all hope.

Luke, by making the blasphemy of the Spirit parallel to the total denial and repudiation of Jesus before men, also indicates that the blasphemy of the Spirit is something willful. In fact, it is a final rejection of the witness of the Spirit to Jesus, a witness that prompts us to confess Christ as Savior and Lord. Thus, the only result can be Christ's denial of us in the judgment without any further chance of forgiveness.

The possible translation of Mark 3:29 as "involved in an eternal sin" causes some to take it to mean that the blasphemy of the Spirit is unforgivable only as long as a person is still involved in it. That is, only as long as he resists the Spirit's witness to Jesus as Lord and Savior is there no possibility of his being saved. Those involved in this sin in this passage were Pharisees. Later we do read of a group of Pharisees who believed (Acts 15:5). But not all Pharisees repudiated Jesus during His ministry. (Nicodemus is an example; John 3:1). Others, like Paul, opposed Him only because of ignorance.

It should be recognized further that this blasphemy of the Spirit was not something said in a moment of anger, discouragement, or even rebellion. Neither was it something that arose from unbelief that came from wrong teaching or a misunderstanding of the Scriptures. It was the willful rejection of the Holy Spirit as something evil and from the pit of hell. Behind it also was a settled determination to turn others away from Jesus.

Once a person is hardened to that state they are like the determined rebels of Old Testament times who called evil good and good evil, who put darkness for light and light for darkness (Isaiah 5:20). These have lost all power to distinguish evil from good. They actually hate the good and love evil (Micah 3:2). As Jesus said, they prefer darkness to light because their deeds are evil (John 3:19,20). Thus, they shut the door on God and on the message of salvation.[14]

Jesus' statement that "If I drive out demons by the Spirit of God, then the kingdom of God has come upon you" (Matthew 12:28) adds another aspect to the seriousness of the blasphemy of the Spirit. By attributing the work of the Spirit in and through Jesus to Satan, they were really rejecting the whole promised rule and reign of God they professed to be waiting for. It was already in operation because the King was in their midst. But they were putting themselves in opposition to God's kingdom or rule and, thus, outside the promised blessing and salvation.

Like the chief priests and Pharisees of the Sanhedrin who plotted Christ's death, they did not want God to bring any changes. They were satisfied with the status quo (John 11:47, 48). In view of this, one of the reasons they would not have forgiveness in this age is that they would never ask for it.[15] This could have an application today where men totally reject the demonstration of the rule of Christ which operates through the Spirit in and through the Church. They put themselves in the same category as these Pharisees. In this sense, blasphemy against the Holy Spirit would involve total apostasy. (See Hebrews 6:4–6,8; 10:26–31.)[16] We must keep in mind, however, that Matthew, Mark, and Luke all indicate that this sin is directly blaspheming the Spirit as He works through Jesus.[17] Moreover, only God knows whether in any particular case this comes from willfulness or from ignorance. We have known, for example, some who have attributed the Pentecostal experience to the devil. Later, the Lord has opened their hearts and minds and they have been baptized in the Spirit and found the gift of tongues edifying.

The Spirit in the Teaching of Jesus

Jesus gave very little teaching about the Holy Spirit to the crowds. Most of it was given in privacy to His disciples, especially during the last hours before going to Gethsemane, as recorded in the Gospel of John. The other Gospels do have some significant statements, however.

As we have already seen, Jesus recognized the Spirit's inspiration of the Old Testament writers (Mark 12:36; Matthew 13:14; Luke 20:42) as well as the work of the Spirit with respect to the Messiah. But He gave specific teaching to His disciples in these Gospels with respect to four things about the Spirit. First, He recognized the Spirit as God's gift, the key to all God has for us (Matthew 7:7–11; Luke 11:9–13). Second, He promised that the Spirit would be with His disciples to help them in ministry and to anoint them even in the midst of persecution (Matthew 10:16–20; Mark 13:9–11; Luke 12:11,12; 21:12–15). Third, He commanded them to baptize believers in the name of the Father, Son, and Holy Spirit (Matthew 28:19). Fourth, He commanded them to wait in Jerusalem until they were clothed with power from on high (Luke 24:49), the power of the Spirit which would make them witnesses (Acts 1:8). In addition, there are references to such things as the oil in the virgins' lamps (Matthew 25:3,4, 8), which is usually taken as a type of the Holy Spirit actively present in the heart of the believer.[1]

The Giver of Good Gifts

Luke 11:13, "If you then, though you are evil [evildoers, weak people who do not always have the best intentions], know how to give good [useful, beneficial] gifts to your children, how much more will your Father in heaven give the Holy Spirit to those who ask him!" comes as a climax to Jesus' teaching on prayer. The disciples came asking Him to teach them how to pray. He gave them the Lord's Prayer (really, the disciples' prayer, a model prayer showing them things for which they always ought to join together in prayer). Then, to keep them from making this a form or a ceremony, He gave them a parable to show them our prayers should involve real needs and that we should come to God with persistent faith.

To emphasize this, Jesus said plainly, "Ask [keep asking] and it will be given to you; seek [keep on seeking] and you will find; knock [keep knocking] and the door will be opened to you. For everyone who asks [who keeps on asking, who is an 'asker'] receives [keeps on receiving]; he who seeks [who keeps on seeking, who is a seeker] finds [keeps on finding]; and to him who knocks [who makes it his practice to knock on doors], the door will be opened" (vv. 9,10). There is nothing wrong with bringing all our needs to the Lord. Nor is there anything wrong with bringing the same need to the Lord again and again. We show persistent faith, not by asking once and quitting, but by continuing to ask.

Next, Jesus made several comparisons to show we can come freely and boldly (vv. 11–13). We need not be afraid to ask God for our needs. Any earthly father would not give a stone to a son who asks for bread, a poisonous snake if he asks for a fish, or a scorpion if he asks for an egg. If earthly fathers who fall so far short of the goodness of God know how to give good gifts, then surely we do not have to be afraid to ask the Father for the best of all gifts, the gift of the Holy Spirit. Moreover, we can depend on Him to give the Spirit. If we come persistently asking Him, He will give us what we ask for, not something bad, not something less than the best, but the Holy Spirit himself.

Matthew 7:11, instead of mentioning the Holy Spirit, follows the same line of reasoning and then records that Jesus said, "How much more will your Father in heaven give good gifts to those who ask him!" Jesus, in His comparison, thus included all the good, useful, beneficial gifts that come from God. The emphasis again is that God can be depended on to give these gifts. As James 1:17 says, "Every good and every perfect gift is from above, coming down from the Father of the heavenly lights, who does not change like shifting shadows." That is, God does not have phases like the moon, sometimes bright, sometimes dark. He is always the same bright Source of light and blessing. His good gifts include the supply of material needs, for He knows our need for such things as food and clothes (Matthew 6:25–33). The good gifts also include everything necessary to see us all the way through to glory (Romans 8:32). Thus, Luke quotes the words of Jesus who gives the emphasis to the Holy Spirit as the gift which sums up and in a sense includes all the good gifts.[2] Or to put it another way, the Father sent the Son as the Living Word to reveal His nature and character and to do His work of salvation on our behalf. The Father then sent the Holy Spirit to bring gifts to us and to continue His work in and through us.[3]

Asking for the Gift of the Spirit

Some writers today say we do not need to ask for the Spirit since the Holy Spirit already dwells in all true born-again believers. They take this promise of the gift of the Spirit as one already fulfilled.[4] Others recognize that we must keep asking and when we pray, if we keep on believing that we will receive God's good things we are asking for, we shall have them (Mark 11:24). It cannot be denied that the one hundred twenty prayed (Luke 24:53; Acts 1:14) or that Peter prayed for others to receive the Holy Spirit (Acts 8:15). Yet some say all we need to do now is follow the example of the Galatians and accept through faith (Galatians 3:13,14).[5]

It is not likely, however, that the faith of the Galatians was passive. Nor is there any way of proving that they did not ask as they heard the promise. After Pentecost, Peter told the Sanhedrin, "We are witnesses of these things (especially of the resurrection), and so is the Holy Spirit, whom God has given to them who obey him" (Acts 5:32). Most probably, that obedience included asking in faith.

There is a sense also in which we must keep on asking for the Spirit if we are to keep being filled with His presence and power. God gives some blessings, like the sun and the rain, on the evil and the good without discrimination (Matthew 5:45), but the gifts of the Spirit need eager desire that comes from a prepared heart (1 Corinthians 12:31; 14:1). How much more is this true of the Holy Spirit himself![6] Our desire for Him, our hunger for God, our heart cry to know Christ better, ought to underlie all our prayer (Psalm 42:1; Philippians 3:10).[7]

It should be noted that although prayer for the gift of the Spirit is primarily addressed to the Father, Jesus as the Baptizer in the Spirit also shares in the giving of this gift. Though the Old Testament indicates the Father pours out the Spirit, not only on men and women, but also on the Messiah, the New Testament shows that one reason the Messiah was filled was to mark Him out as sharing in the giving (John 1:33). Luke also indicates that Jesus shares in giving special fillings for special needs. (Compare Luke 12:11,12 with Acts 4:8 where the Greek indicates Peter had a new, special filling of the Holy Spirit as he faced the Sanhedrin. Then note Luke 21:15 where Jesus promised that He himself will give the words and wisdom that believers need under the same circumstances. Thus, we may take it that Jesus does this by filling us with the Spirit.) We pray, therefore, to the Father and the Son for the Spirit.[8] On the other hand, nothing in the Bible forbids us to address prayer to the Holy Spirit. We are richer for the hymns and songs that call on Him to come and to fall on us afresh or fill us again.

Sent Forth with the Spirit

In sending forth His disciples, Jesus did not promise them an easy time. He warned them also that they could not expect everyone to welcome the gospel, no matter in how much power it was preached. This was not pessimism; it was realism. Their ministry was not to be an expression of shallow optimism but of the promises of God, promises that guaranteed victory in spite of and in the midst of continuing opposition. The gates of hell will not prevail against the Church, which includes all true believers, all who belong to Jesus (Matthew 16:18). Yet the Church (that is, the people of God) will have to face the powers of hell and be sure they have the armor of God on (Ephesians 6:11–18). Nor can we expect the opposition to decrease as we approach the end of the age, for "there will be terrible times in the last days" (2 Timothy 3:1).

Both the warnings and encouragements Jesus gave to His disciples are therefore especially appropriate today. He sent them out (after Pentecost) as sheep among wolves (Matthew 10:16). But they had the assurance that Jesus was the One sending them out, so they could expect Him to be with them (John 15:16; 16:2; Matthew 28:20).

As they went out, they would need all the wisdom and all the gentleness they could get (Matthew 10:16). Even then, men would arrest them and turn them over to religious councils (such as the Sanhedrin) and whip them in their synagogues. But the result would not be defeat. Even when they were brought before governors and kings because of Jesus, the result would be a testimony to them (rather than against them) and to the Gentiles.

The way their arrests and court trials would become opportunities for witness is through obedience to Matthew 10:19. When believers are arrested because of their faithfulness in spreading the good news about Jesus, they are not to worry or become anxious about what they are to say or how to say it. At the time it is needed, it will be given to them what to say: "for it will not be you speaking, but the Spirit of your Father speaking through you" (Matthew 10:20). That is, they will be filled with the Spirit who will give both wisdom and the words to bring a testimony that will glorify Jesus.

Jesus repeated this warning on the Mount of Olives after the disciples asked Him about the signs of the end. He warned them first that too much attention to signs could deceive them: first, because many deceivers would come (Mark 13:5,6); and second, because wars and rumors of wars would characterize the whole age. People would be alarmed, thinking the end was near, when actually they should simply be more concerned about spreading the gospel (v. 8). During the course of this age also, as Jesus said before, they would be brought before rulers for Jesus' sake so they could be a witness to them. This would be an important part of the spread of the gospel to all nations (v. 10). Then once again, Jesus warned the disciples not to worry ahead of time, but to expect the Holy Spirit to give them what they should say when the opportunity came to speak.

Luke 12:11,12 is a parallel to Matthew 10:17–20, adding the thought that the Holy Spirit would teach (instruct) them concerning what would be necessary to say. Luke 21:12–15 is parallel to Mark 13:9–11, adding that they must "make up [their] mind not to worry beforehand" how they would make a defense. Jesus (by the Spirit) would give them "words and wisdom that none of [their] adversaries will be able to resist or contradict" (Luke 21:14,15).

This began to be fulfilled almost immediately after Pentecost. When the healing of the lame man brought opportunity to teach the crowd in the temple (Acts 3:1–26), the religious leaders arrested Peter and John and put them in jail overnight. This was a test. Would they worry all night about what they were going to say, or would they remember the words of Jesus and have a good sleep? I believe they slept. The next day when they faced the Sanhedrin, Peter had no prepared reply. Instead, in fulfillment of Jesus' promise, the Holy Spirit gave him a new filling (as the Greek indicates) and the words to say. As a result, instead of defending himself, which he probably would have done if he had worried about it, he gave witness to Jesus, to His resurrection, and to the salvation which is ours through Him alone. Peter's boldness and clear, plain, free way of presenting the truth amazed the Sanhedrin members. And with the man who was healed there with them, "there was nothing they could say" (or they could not contradict anything, Acts 4:14; the same Greek word used in Luke 21:15). Note also, the Spirit gave only what was *necessary* to say (Luke 12:12). If they had prepared their own defense, they probably would have said too much.

This shows also that the Spirit is more concerned about the spreading of the gospel than about the safety of those who spread it.[9] Proclaiming the gospel in the Spirit's wisdom and power will still get people into dangerous situations. Stephen, full of the Holy Spirit, gave the witness of Jesus that was necessary at that time. Because the Sanhedrin was not able to withstand or contradict it, they were overcome with rage and killed him (Acts 7:54,55,57). Paul also, after many wonderful opportunities to testify before rulers and kings, finally poured out his life's blood under a Roman sword (2 Timothy 4:6). Paul did not seek martyrdom, for he often left secretly when persecution arose. Yet martyrdoms like his continued, not only in the early centuries, but through all of Church history. In multitudes of cases, the words of Jesus have proven true. Revivals have broken out in prisons. Jailers have been converted. Those who died for their faith have inspired a host of others.

Sent Forth with Power

The Great Commission as Matthew records it emphasizes the authority of Jesus. "All authority in heaven and on earth has been given to me" (Matthew 28:18). By this authority, Jesus promised them power (mighty power) which became theirs through the Holy Spirit (Acts 1:8). The primary purpose of the power is to teach (make disciples, real students who are anxious to learn more about Jesus and the Word). The emphasis is not on going. "Therefore go and make" is better translated "having gone therefore, make." The Lord assumes that they will go. He would see to that through persecution and various other means. But the command is that wherever they find themselves, they are to make disciples.

Nor is the command to baptize. Rather, as they are obeying the command to teach or make disciples, they will be baptizing them into the name (into the service and worship) of the Father, and of the Son, and of the Holy Spirit.

The word "name" is singular here because it means one name (or title) each. The repetition of the phrase "and of" also makes it clear that each is respected as a distinct Person within the One God. This, of course, refers to baptism in water. The disciples did all the baptizing in water for Jesus (John 4:2). He is the Baptizer in the Spirit. Thus, the Early Church as a whole recognized that it took no special qualifications to baptize in water. Any believer might do it. (See 1 Corinthians 1:14–17.)

Jesus did not give a great deal of attention to baptizing here. Quickly, He went on to emphasize that making disciples was primarily a matter of teaching them to observe everything He had commanded them, which would certainly emphasize the command to love (John 15:12,17). Then He would be with them—and with us—to the end of the age.

Mark's account is similar to Matthew's. Again, the idea of going is not emphasized. The command is that wherever they are they are to "preach [proclaim publicly] the good news to all creation [every person]. Whoever believes and is baptized will be saved [not merely converted, but ultimately receiving their eternal salvation, their inheritance through Christ], but whoever does not believe will be condemned [to eternal judgment]" (Mark 16:15,16). By this, Mark is not making baptism a means of receiving the grace of salvation. That would go against Romans 10:9,10 and Ephesians 2:8,9,13. Baptism is simply a part of obedience to Christ that brings a witness to Him. As Peter brings out (1 Peter 3:20,21), water baptism does not save us any more than the water of the Flood saved Noah. But the fact that Noah came through the Flood was a witness to the faith that believed God before the Flood. So water baptism does not wash us from any of the filthiness of the flesh. We are washed in the blood of Jesus (Revelation 1:5; 7:14) and through the water by (in) the Word (Ephesians 5:26). Thus, water baptism is the answer or testimony of a good conscience that has already been cleansed before baptism.

These Signs Shall Follow

Mark goes on to say, "These signs will accompany those who believe: In my name [by my authority] they will drive out demons; they will speak in new tongues; they will pick up snakes with their hands; and when they drink deadly poison, it will not hurt them at all; they will place their hands on sick people, and they will get well" (Mark 16:17,18). Then after the ascension of Jesus, once they went out, they preached everywhere, the Lord working with them, confirming the Word with (miraculous) signs following (just as He had promised).

Unfortunately, some have misunderstood the phrase "pick up snakes with their hands" to be a command to handle poisonous snakes to prove their faith. The phrase is not a command but a simple statement of fact. Then, though "pick up" is one of the meanings of the Greek word, it is not the only meaning. Other legitimate meanings are "take away, remove, sweep away, conquer," all without any suggesting of lifting up or picking up. (See Matthew 24:39, which uses it of the Flood sweeping everyone away; John 10:18, where it is used of taking away life; John 11:48, of conquering a city; and Colossians 2:14, where it speaks of taking the handwriting of ordinances out of the way.) Certainly, early Christians did not make a practice of picking up snakes. When Paul picked one up accidentally, he shook it off into the fire (Acts 28:5). More importantly, the whole passage in Mark 16:15–20 indicates victory over the works of the devil, and the serpent was symbolic of evil and of Satan (Revelation 12:9; 20:2).

Speaking in tongues and sweeping away Satan's "snakes" are normal activities of believers. On the other hand, the next phrase has an "if" (KJV; "when," NIV) that indicates the drinking of poison is considered extremely unlikely. Nevertheless, God will protect believers who unintentionally do so in the course of spreading the gospel. None of these things are intended as a way of testing or proving our faith, not even speaking in tongues. They are all simply signs that will follow believers who believe enough to obey the command to preach the gospel to every creature, as Mark 16:20 indicates. (We are not overlooking the fact that modern critics cast doubt on the last twelve verses of Mark. There is, however, evidence that they are very old and there is no reason Mark himself could not have written them. In any case, everything these verses say is in line with the rest of the New Testament. See Appendix: Is Mark 16:9–20 Inspired? p. 284.)

Luke's account of the Great Commission calls for the good news of repentance and forgiveness of sins to be proclaimed among all nations (Luke 24:47). Jesus stated that this should begin at Jerusalem. But first He would send the promise of the Father (the Holy Spirit) upon them. They must therefore wait in Jerusalem until they are clothed with power. This is brought out further in Luke's second volume, the Book of Acts.

Born of the Spirit

John's Gospel gives more teaching about the Spirit and His work than do the other three Gospels. The major emphasis is found in John 14 through 16 which speaks of the Spirit as the Counselor (Paraclete) and the Spirit of Truth. But the earlier teachings are basic.

When Nicodemus came by night, Jesus went right to the heart of his need by telling him, "No one can see the kingdom of God unless he is born again [from above]," (John 3:3). Jesus explained this new birth further as "born of water and the Spirit" (v. 5), "the Spirit gives birth to spirit" (v. 6) and "born of the Spirit" (v. 8).

The emphasis is clearly on the work of the Spirit in bringing new life to the believer; life from above, life from heaven, from God. But the phrase "born of water and the Spirit" is difficult to interpret. There are four common views of the meaning of the water. Some take it as water baptism. Others take it as the water of natural birth, others as the Word, and still others as the Spirit himself.

Churches who claim that spiritual life comes through the sacraments universally take the water to be water baptism. Some take the water of baptism to represent death, with the water receiving the body as into a tomb. Thus the water effects death and the Holy Spirit brings new life.[10] Others refer to baptism as a rite of initiation which is the gateway to new life and carries with it all the gifts of the Spirit.[11] Or, they refer to baptism as a sacramental washing that is the sign and means of the new birth and of a new life brought about by the gift of the Spirit. That is, the sacramentalist treats the water of baptism as a necessary channel for salvation, the gift of the Spirit, and the gifts of the Spirit. He says a person gets it all when he is baptized.[12] Most, however, do emphasize that the sacraments as such are not the source of the new life. The real source of spiritual life is the Holy Spirit, even to the sacramentalist.[13] However, as has already been noted, the water of baptism, rather than being the agency or channel of the Spirit's life and cleansing, is a *symbolic* act by which we bear testimony to a cleansing and life already received.

Among those who do not identify the water of John 3:5 with water baptism, some take it as an explanation of what it means to be born again, with the emphasis on *again*. They take water as symbolic of the first birth, physical birth (which is accompanied by the "breaking of the water"). The Spirit thus brings the second birth. However, though "born again" is a legitimate meaning of the Greek and the idea is certainly included in John 3:3, the more common meaning is "born from above." In this same chapter the same word that is translated "again" is used to describe Jesus as the One coming "from above" (John 3:31). In the same verse this is explained as "from heaven." James 1:17 also translates it "from above."

Furthermore, John 1:12,13 makes a strong contrast between natural birth and spiritual birth. Those who are given the right to become sons of God are those who believe on His (Jesus') name, and the birth that makes them heirs of God is not of blood (not based on human blood lines), nor of the will of the flesh (our attempts to satisfy God by weak, human efforts), or of the will of man (of a husband), but of God. Thus, the new birth is purely and completely of God, and both water and the Spirit must refer to what comes from God.

In view of this, some take the water as symbolic of the Word (as in Ephesians 5:26). This is a strong possibility, for the Bible speaks of being born again by the Word of God, specifically, the gospel as preached by the apostles (1 Peter 1:23,25). James also states, "He [God] chose to give us birth through [by] the a truth" (James 1:18).[14] Then, Jesus himself said His disciples were washed (they had a full bath, spiritually speaking) before the Last Supper (John 13:10). Then He explained that they were clean through the word (the gospel) that He had spoken to them (John 15:3); that is, the Word that came through the Spirit and was anointed by the Spirit in Jesus (John 3:34; 6:63).[15]

Others simply take the water to symbolize cleansing in general or relate it to the cleansing by the blood.[16]

The Spirit Himself

As we go through the Gospel of John, however, it becomes obvious that water more often symbolizes the Spirit himself, especially in His life-giving power (John 4:14; 7:38). It is also true that the word *and* can also mean *even*, so that John 3:5 could be translated "born of water even of the Spirit." Nicodemus put a wrong interpretation on Jesus' meaning when He told of the necessity of being born again (or from above). Jesus may have decided to give him the explanation this time. If we take the water as the Spirit, then there is no problem. The water, even the Spirit, is from above, from heaven, and is completely outside the realm of earthly things.[17]

John 3:6-8 shows even more strongly that neither the water nor the Spirit can be tied to water baptism. The new birth is from above. Jesus then goes on to emphasize again the contrast with natural birth. Natural birth was what Nicodemus was depending on. Like Paul, he was a Pharisee of the Pharisees, proud that he was a son of Abraham. He trusted in his position before God as a Jew and his obedience to the Law to save him. But even in the Old Testament no one was ever saved just because he was a Jew or because he offered the right sacrifices. Faith and faithfulness were necessary. Thus, natural birth could only produce something natural. It would take the Holy Spirit to bring the life from above.

To explain further the birth from above, Jesus compares it to the action of the wind. "The wind blows wherever it pleases [where it wills]. You hear its sound, but you cannot tell where it comes from and where it is going. So it is with everyone born of the Spirit" (John 3:8). Since the Spirit, like the wind, cannot be limited to one place or one direction, this makes it impossible to suppose that water baptism is the channel for His operation.[18] Actually, the Spirit and the Word are both needed. The Spirit takes the Word and applies it to the heart to bring repentance and faith, and through this, life. But we cannot limit His operation to any prescribed channels. That wind has a way of blowing in the most unexpected, wonderful, and mysterious ways.

Living in the Spirit

Being born from above is not an end in itself. It is only the first step toward living in the Spirit. To the woman at the well Jesus presented himself as the Giver of water that will become in a person a well of water springing up into everlasting life (John 4:10,14). Thus, He goes beyond the promise of a new birth to the promise of a life in the Spirit, bringing not a few drops of water merely but a spring or artesian well continually flowing because it comes from a higher source.[19]

Though Jesus did not explain the nature of the water to the Samaritan woman, the meaning is made clear in John 7:37–39. There, on the last great day at the conclusion of the Feast of Tabernacles, Jesus called the people to come to Him and drink. The Feast of Tabernacles was a memorial of the forty years Israel spent in the wilderness. It was intended to remind them that they were still just as much dependent on God as their ancestors were in the days when God fed them with manna from heaven and gave them water out of the rock. As part of its ceremonies the High Priest would pour water out of a golden pitcher to symbolize the water given by God. But Jesus called the people to Him. He had the Spirit without measure (John 3:34). The overflow of the Spirit from Him was available to satisfy the thirst of their souls.

Then, Jesus did more than offer them what He at that moment could give. He promised that the one who "believes (keeps believing, is a believer) in me, as the Scripture has said, streams of living water will flow from within him (his innermost being). By this he meant the Spirit, whom those who believed in him [by a definite act of faith] were later to receive [receive actively, take]. Up to that time the Spirit had not been given, since Jesus had not yet been glorified" (John 7:38,39).

This clearly refers to what would happen beginning at Pentecost. During His ministry, the disciples depended directly on Jesus. The Holy Spirit did His work in and through Jesus on their behalf. Thus, the Holy Spirit was only with the disciples, not yet in them (John 14:17). They were living in a transitional period where the Holy Spirit was not yet given to everyone, just as was the case in the Old Testament. However, since the word "given" is not in most of the ancient Greek manuscripts, they read, "the Spirit was not yet," or, "it was not yet Spirit." The meaning seems to be that the age of the Spirit (as prophesied by Joel and the other Old Testament prophets) had not yet come.

This adds a new dimension to the promise of the outpouring of the Spirit upon all flesh (Joel 2:28). It also draws attention to another important distinction between the experience of Old Testament believers and that which has been available since Pentecost. Even when the Old Testament says the Spirit came upon people, there are often indications that He was also in them. (See 1 Samuel 16:13 through 2 Samuel 23:2.) But here Jesus promised that the Holy Spirit would give more than an inner filling. There is an outward flow, a pouring forth as well as a pouring upon. This goes beyond any Old Testament experience. Nor is it limited to priests, kings, prophets, or people with special abilities as was so often the case in the Old Testament. The promise is available to every believer. We need only exercise an act of faith and receive the promised gift (better, take it).

Worshipping in Spirit and in Truth

To the Samaritan woman at the well (John 4:4–42), Jesus gave still further explanation about life in the Spirit. Worshipping in the Spirit is a very important part of it. Mankind failed first at the point of worship (Romans 1:21), and this is still the place where backsliding begins.

The woman herself brought up the question of whether it was right to worship in Mount Gerizim or in Jerusalem (which was the chief difference between Jews and Samaritans at the time). The question was off the subject, but Jesus did not ignore it. He answered it in such a way as to get back to the subject, which was the need of the Spirit and the life which Jesus alone could give her.

Soon, in fact, already, neither place would be necessary for the worship of the Father. "A time is coming and has now come when the true worshipers will worship the Father in spirit and truth, for they are the kind of worshipers the Father seeks. God is spirit, and his worshipers must worship in spirit and in truth" (John 4:23,24).

True worshipers, genuine worshipers, are not those who go to the right places and say the right prayers. They are those who recognize the nature of God. By His very nature He is Spirit, and if we worship in truth we must not only recognize His nature, we must conform our worship to His nature. Therefore, we must worship "in spirit," for this is the chief emphasis in this passage.[20] "In spirit," however, as is so often the case, really means "in the Spirit." Our own spirits do not conform to God's nature as Spirit. But the Holy Spirit's does. Thus, we need to open our hearts to the Spirit and let Him worship through us if we are to be genuine worshipers of God. Paul sees the same thing in his epistles. (This will be discussed later.)

In answer to the woman's question, Jesus is also saying that since God is Spirit, He is everywhere. The Old Testament believers really knew this. They were able to worship God in Babylon and Shushan (Susa), just as well as in Jerusalem. Even Solomon at the dedication of the temple recognized that God could not be limited to the temple, for the heaven of heavens cannot contain Him (1 Kings 8:27). Thus, it does not really matter about the place or the form of the worship as long as it is moved and inspired by the Spirit.[21] This is always worship in truth.

Partaking of Christ's Life through the Spirit

Another passage that shows that ceremonies and sacraments do not confer the Spirit or spiritual life is John 6:63,64: "The Spirit gives life; the flesh counts for nothing [is of no value, accomplishes nothing]. The words I have spoken to you are spirit and they are life. Yet there are some of you who do not believe."

Behind this is a long passage that emphasizes Jesus as the bread of God, the true manna from heaven that gives eternal life to the world. Those who come to Him will never hunger and those who believe on Him will never thirst (vv. 32–35). Believing on Him is the key. "He who believes [is a believer, keeps on believing] has [keeps on having] everlasting [eternal] life" (v. 47). Eternal life is already defined as the kind of life the Father has and which He has given to the Son to have by His own right and nature (5:25). Thus, eternal life is Christ's life in us, which we have only as we believe. (Compare John 15:1–6.)

The problem is in the believing. Many had seen Jesus and His miracles but refused the work of the Spirit and still did not believe (6:29,30,36). Believing is more than accepting the fact there is a Jesus or even the facts of His death and resurrection. Jesus went on to compare believing to eating and drinking His flesh and His blood, His life made available through Calvary (vv. 51,53–57). He even used a word for noisy eating, or munching, to indicate enjoyment, eating with delight. Those who eat (keep eating with enjoyment) His flesh and keep drinking His blood, keep on having eternal life. This means they keep on dwelling (living, abiding) in Christ and He in them (vv. 54,56).

The idea of continually eating Jesus' flesh and drinking His blood caused the Jews to grumble in displeasure. Their eyes were on the physical body of Jesus (v. 42) and His actual flesh and blood (v. 52). When they complained, Jesus suggested that He would ascend to heaven, thus making His actual body no longer available on earth (v. 62). The Holy Spirit is, therefore, the One who makes it possible for us to keep munching His flesh and drinking His blood (v. 63). He does it by taking the words of Jesus and making them the means of sharing the outpoured life of Jesus.[22]

He does this also, not in some mystical way, but in His function as the Teacher Spirit, the One guiding us into all truth (John 16:13). This prepares us to regard the Lord's Supper as a memorial feast, just as the Passover was. Only the first Passover was an effective sacrifice in that it protected from death. Similarly, the sacrifice of Christ on the Cross was the once-for-all offering of His body and blood on our behalf (Hebrews 10:12). Jesus said of the Lord's Supper, "Do this in remembrance [in memory] of me" (1 Corinthians 11:24). By eating the bread and drinking the wine, "you proclaim the Lord's death until he comes [returns]" (v. 26). By this it is clear that the bread and wine are symbols, object lessons, by which we testify to our faith and by which we proclaim our continual appropriation of the benefits of His life which was outpoured for us at Calvary. As 1 John 1:7 puts it, "If we walk [keep walking] in the light, as he is in the light, we [continue to] have fellowship with one another [between us and God], and the blood of Jesus, his Son, purifies [keeps purifying] us from all sin."

Discernment from the Holy Spirit is necessary also if the Lord's Supper is to give a witness that will really glorify Christ. Some Corinthians became sick and died, not because they failed to perform the Lord's Supper correctly, but because of the unworthy attitude that showed they were not appropriating the benefits of the Cross nor the help of the Spirit to show His fruits. Gross fleshly appetite put them in a condition unworthy of witnesses for Christ. By ignoring the needs of hungry brothers, they ignored the love outpoured on Calvary and were thus unable to proclaim its true meaning in the Lord's Supper. (See Romans 5:8; John 15:12,17.) In this also, they did not discern the Lord's body (the body of Christ) in their brothers. They needed to judge themselves and wait for one another (1 Corinthians 11:29–33; 10:16,17).[23]

The Counselor Who Comes to Stay

After the Last Supper Jesus began to give teaching to His disciples to help prepare them for His death, resurrection, and ascension. Important in this is His teaching concerning the Holy Spirit. Jesus would be leaving them. But He would not forget these who loved Him. He would pray (ask) the Father, and the Father would give them another Counselor (Paraclete) who would never leave them (John 14:16).

The Counselor is immediately identified by Jesus as the Spirit of Truth, literally, the Truth (John 14:17; 15:26; 16:13; 1 John 4:6). The truth is what Jesus proclaims from God (John 1:17; 8:40,45,46; 18:37), and He is the Truth (14:6). God's Word is also the truth (17:17). The Spirit guides into all the truth (16:13), and the Spirit is also the Truth (1 John 5:6).

The Counselor is further identified as the Holy Spirit, sent by the Father in Jesus' name (that is, by calling on His name). As the Spirit of the Truth also, He will teach the disciples all things and bring everything Jesus said to their remembrance (John 14:26). He will also testify (bear witness) concerning Jesus to the world and enable the believers to do so (John 15:26,27; illustrated in Acts 5:32). As the Counselor and Guide into all truth He will also convince the world with respect to sin, show things to come (things related to Christ's coming and to the consummation of the age), and glorify Jesus by taking the things of Christ (which are of God) and showing them to His disciples (John 16:13–15).

As Jesus came to declare (explain, reveal, interpret, make known, unfold the nature and will of) the Father, so the Holy Spirit comes to explain, reveal, interpret, make known, and unfold the nature and will of Jesus (vv. 12,13).[24] He is thus the Bearer and Teacher of the truth that is in Jesus. He shows Jesus to be the Revealer of the Father, the Savior, the Forgiver of Sins, the risen Lord, the Baptizer in the Spirit, and the Coming King and final Judge. Specifically, to the disciples, His teaching, His unfolding or exegesis of the truth in Jesus, and His reminding them of the words of Jesus guaranteed the accuracy of their preaching and the correctness of their theology, thus giving us assurance of the inerrancy of the New Testament with respect to both facts and doctrine.[25]

The same Teacher also continues His teaching work in us, not by bringing new revelation, but by bringing new understanding, new comprehension, new illumination. But He does more than show us the truth. He brings us into the truth, helping us put it into action, making it real and effective in our lives, so that Christ dwells within us and we carry on the work of Christ in a way that glorifies Him.[26]

John also speaks of the Spirit's teaching work in the believer as an anointing, an unction that gives us insights and instructs us how to put the truth into action in a way no mere human teacher could possibly do (1 John 2:20,27). The real test of this anointing, however, is not the zeal, enthusiasm, or any outward evidences but the way the Holy Spirit exalts Jesus through it.[27] Human teachers who are not anointed by the Spirit tend to strip Jesus of the glories and power that belong to Him. They cut Him down and emasculate Him until He is not even the shadow of the God-Man who is revealed in the Bible. Actually, they make their humanistic philosophies the mold and try to force Him through it. But the Holy Spirit always reveals Jesus as all the Bible says He is.

The Counselor: Helper or Counsel for the Defense

There has considerable controversy over the meaning of the word *Comforter* from the King James Version, which is also translated "advocate" when applied to the ascended Christ (1 John 2:1, KJV; "one who speaks . . . in our defense," NIV).[28] The translation "Comforter" came into our English in Wycliffe's version (AD 1380), but in the old sense of *Strengthener*. Wycliffe, for example, translated Philippians 4:13, "I may all thingis in him that comfortith me"[29] However, in contemporary translations, this controversy has been eliminated.

The Greek word *parakletos* is derived from *para,* "to the side of," and *kaleo,* "to call or summon." It is passive in form and its oldest meaning (long before New Testament times) was "one called to help, aid, advise, or counsel someone."[30] This was taken by most of the early Roman Catholic scholars to mean an advocate, lawyer, counsel for the defense (that is, giving counsel rather than pleading a case).[31] Some today also insist that the meaning "advocate" is the only proper one, especially in John 15:26 and 1 John 2:1.[32]

The Holy Spirit in John is not an attorney, however, nor even primarily an intercessor. Even in John 16:8–11, He is not an advocate and especially not a prosecuting attorney seeking to gain a conviction that will send people to hell. Rather, He is the Teacher, the Representative of Christ seeking to convince men and women of the truth and bring them to repentance. Nor is He primarily an advocate or counsel for the defense when the disciples are brought before rulers and kings. He is the One who teaches them what to say so they will glorify Christ and give Him witness, instead of defending themselves (Luke 12:12). In fact, He is in no way an Advocate or legal Counselor to the disciples, but the Teacher who speaks for Christ and completes His revelation.[33]

This recognition of the Counselor as the Spokesman and Interpreter of Jesus in the present age has an interesting parallel in the Hebrew word translated "interpreter" in Genesis 42:23, where Joseph spoke through an interpreter to his brothers, and in Job 33:23, where it speaks of an angelic messenger who is a "mediator." The same word is translated "spokesmen" (Isaiah 43:27) and "envoys" (2 Chronicles 32:31). The Jewish Targums translate the word by a form of *parakletos* which they also use to translate the witness in heaven (Job 16:19) and the Kinsman-Redeemer (19:25). This indicates that the idea of spokesman and interpreter was a common meaning of *parakletos* in the first century among the Jews.[34]

Actually, a *parakletos* in its original meaning was not a lawyer or a professional man at all. Rather, he was a friend who appeared on someone's behalf or who acted as a mediator, intercessor, adviser, or helper. This was recognized by the Early Greek Fathers of the Church, who saw that the usage of the word called for an active meaning as Helper or Counselor.[35]

By translating *parakletos* as "Comforter" in the King James Version, however, they did not mean Comforter in the modern sense of consoling someone in grief or loss. The New Testament does promise comfort for mourners (Matthew 5:4), healing for the brokenhearted (Luke 4:18), joy for sorrow (John 16:20), consolation for those who partake of the sufferings of Christ (2 Corinthians 1:5,7), and a future day when God will wipe away all tears from our eyes (Revelation 7:17, 21:4). But what the Holy Spirit does for us is much more than that.

One biblical illustration is in Acts 9:31, where we find that the church "was strengthened; and encouraged by the Holy Spirit, it grew in numbers, living in the fear of the Lord." The context shows that the Spirit brought about this multiplication by anointing the Word and by quickening, empowering, sanctifying, encouraging, and emboldening the believers. Thus, we see in the Counselor the combination of the ideas of a Teacher and Helper who mediates the truth of Christ and gives power for the spread of the gospel and the growth of the Church.

In this sense also, the Holy Spirit is truly "another Counselor" as Jesus promised He would be (John 14:16). In another sense, without detracting from the promise of a future Second Coming, Jesus in the Gospel of John indicated that He himself comes to us in the Holy Spirit, for the Holy Spirit mediates both the Father and the Son to us (John 14:18,20,23).[36] When Jesus says, "I will not leave you as orphans; I will come to you" (John 14:18), He means He will come to you *by* the Holy Spirit. Yet by calling the Spirit another Counselor, Jesus sharply distinguishes between himself and the Holy Spirit as a distinct Person. Jesus is not the Spirit. As the risen Lord, Jesus sends the Spirit (John 15:26; 16:7).

By "another," the Greek means another of the same kind. That is, the Spirit comes to do for us everything Jesus did for His disciples and more. He was their Counselor. They called Him Rabbi, Teacher. When they did not know how to pray, He taught them. When they could not answer the questions or objections of the scribes and Pharisees, He was right there to teach them. When they needed to understand what the Bible had to say about Him and His place in God's plan, He opened their minds and warmed their hearts (Luke 24:32,45). When they could not still the storm or cast out a demon, He was there with the power to help them. The Spirit as another Counselor is a Teacher and Helper of the same kind.

Reprove, Convict, Convince

Most of what Jesus taught about the Spirit had to do with His relationship to the believer. John 16:8–11 is the chief passage that deals with the Spirit's relationship to the world (humanity in general). He comes to "convict the world of guilt in regard to sin and righteousness and judgment." Some take "convict" to mean simply to announce the verdict or pronounce the world guilty with respect to these things.[37] "Convict," however, is translated more correctly "convince" or "refute" as in Titus 1:9, where the bishop (overseer, superintendent, as we would say, "pastor" or a local church) "can encourage others by sound doctrine [correct, healthy, scriptural teaching] and refute ["both to exhort and to convince" KJV] those who oppose it [those who contradict the gospel]." The clear meaning of the word is seen also in 1 Corinthians 14:24,25, where the gift of prophecy will convince the unbeliever so that he worships God and recognizes God's presence in the midst.

The world wants to ignore or deny sin, righteousness, and judgment. They either set up their own standards of right and wrong and ignore the principles of the gospel by which they will be judged (Romans 2:5–12,16), or they exalt sin or else make everything a matter of personal preference, blurring the distinction between right and wrong altogether. Few today want to think of hell and judgment. Thus, they blind themselves to their need of the gospel. The Holy Spirit has to do more than just proclaim the facts of the gospel. He presents them in such a way that people will be convinced with regard to these things and begin to feel their need of the salvation offered through Christ. (Notice how most of the first three chapters of Romans is taken up with showing that everyone, whether Jew or Gentile, needs the gospel.)

All of this work of convincing the world and causing a conviction that will bring men and women to repentance is done in relation to Christ and His victory at the Cross. It will also be done in such a way as to show the essence of what each really is.[38]

The first subject about which the world needs convincing from the Spirit is sin—not just sins, but sin. The world may admit that some things are sins. Things harmful to society or to health may be condemned. But the things recognized as sins will vary from place to place, culture to culture, and individual to individual. The Bible does deal with specific sins. It calls for repentance and the confession of sins. Sins must be cleansed and washed away. But sin itself is the real problem, and sin in its essence is unbelief.

Unbelievers may not think of their unbelief as of any consequence. But unbelief was at the root of Eve's sin when she listened to the serpent's "Did God really say" (Genesis 3:1) and "You will not surely [really] die" (v. 4). Unbelief kept Israel out of the Promised Land (Numbers 14:11; Hebrews 3:17,19). Unbelief caused Moses to take honor to himself instead of giving it to God, so that he too failed to reach that land (Numbers 20:10,12).

When Jesus came, people did not have to do anything to be condemned. By their unbelief in Him they were condemned already (John 3:18). Sins kept them from coming to Christ, but the real sin was unbelief (vv. 19,20). Through Christ forgiveness has been made available to all who believe. Now the only reason for people to die in their sins is unbelief (v. 24). By Jesus' death also we see the enormity of sin and by the Spirit we are made to realize that our unbelief is indeed sin. He who knew no sin was made sin for us (2 Corinthians 5:21). Thus, at the Cross, we are convinced of what sin really is. Then, once unbelief is out of the way, the cleansing blood of the Savior can take care of all other sins.

Along with conviction of sin, the world needs to be convinced by the Spirit with respect to righteousness—not their own righteousness or lack of it, but of what righteousness really is as it is seen in Jesus. His righteousness includes an uprightness that is always honest, fair, and just, that always does what is right before God. Once we are convinced of sin, we need to know "we have one who speaks to the Father in our defense—Jesus Christ, the Righteous One. He is the atoning sacrifice [or sin offering] for our sins, and not only for ours but also for the sins of the whole world" (1 John 2:1,2).

What the Spirit uses to convince us of His uprightness is the fact that death could not hold Him and, that by His resurrection and ascension, He is now at the Father's right hand interceding for us (Hebrews 7:25; Romans 1:4,16).

Finally, the world needs to be convinced by the Spirit with respect to judgment. John's Gospel shows a continuing conflict between belief and unbelief. But it will not go on forever. There is an end, a judgment day coming. The world imagines that all things remain as they were (or are always continuing on) since the beginning of Creation (2 Peter 3:4). The philosophy of uniformitarianism that dominates much of modern science is nothing new, nor is it limited to scientists. Human thinking tries to avoid the idea of a real beginning or a real end to the present universe. It takes the Holy Spirit to make people see the truth.

The world must be convinced of judgment by recognizing who the prince of this world is and that judgment was never really meant for people, for the lake of fire was prepared for the devil and his angels (Matthew 25:41). It must recognize that judgment in essence is Satan's judgment and that he has already been judged. Christ's victory over death at the Cross sealed his doom (Hebrews 2:14) and assures us that the world will also be judged in righteousness (Acts 17:31). From this, it appears also that the world must be convinced by the Spirit that it is under the domination of Satan, as Jesus brings out by calling him the prince of this world (John 12:31; 14:30; 16:11; see also 1 John 5:19; Ephesians 2:2).

The Book of Acts is full of examples of how the Holy Spirit carried out this convincing through the preaching of the apostles. On the Day of Pentecost as Peter spoke in prophetic utterance, there was conviction of sin through what their unbelief did to Jesus (Acts 2:22,23); of righteousness through the recognition that God did not allow His Holy One to see corruption but raised Him to sit on His throne (vv. 27,30–33,36); and conviction of judgment (v. 40). By this conviction the people were first brought to despair (v. 37) and then to surrender and glad acceptance of the truth (v. 41).[39] It was the same when Peter preached in the temple (Acts 3:14,15,19,21), before the Sanhedrin (4:10–12), and in the house of Cornelius (10:39–42). So it was also with Paul (13:27–30,37,41).

A New Creation

Jesus gave many promises of the Spirit during His ministry. Then on the Resurrection Day in the evening, Jesus appeared in the midst of His disciples, and said, "As the Father has sent me, I am sending you" (John 20:21), then He breathed on them and said, "Receive the Holy Spirit. If you forgive anyone his sins, they are forgiven; if you do not forgive them, they are not forgiven" (vv. 22,23).

There are a number of ways in which this command to receive (take) the Holy Spirit is interpreted. Liberal critics often call this the Johannine Pentecost, as if John had never heard of Pentecost and thought this was the fulfillment of the promised baptism in the Holy Spirit. The Book of Acts is too specific in the way it names John in connection with Pentecost for this to be true. Nor would it be likely to be true of anyone else living in Ephesus at the time John's Gospel was written.

Others take it that, since the Greek has no "the" here and reads only "receive Holy Spirit," Jesus did not mean the personal Holy Spirit but the breath of God, symbolic of power. Jesus breathed on them and they received power.[40] It seems quite evident, however, that in John, as in Luke, the presence or absence of the article is not significant. (See John 4:23,24.) Receiving the Holy Spirit here is just as much receiving a Person as is receiving Jesus.

Still others say the disciples did not receive anything at this time. The breathing is taken as only a symbolic action to let them know that when the Spirit came at Pentecost it would be the Spirit of Jesus. In other words the breathing was prophetic, but though the command was given, the Spirit was neither given nor received.[41]

The chief difficulty with taking this as an actual receiving of the Spirit is that John previously indicated that the age of the Spirit would not begin until after Jesus was glorified (John 7:39). Peter at Pentecost makes it clear also that the pouring out of the Spirit was evidence that Jesus was "exalted to the right hand of God" (Acts 2:33). Then, Paul indicates that God did not give Jesus His place as Head to His body, the Church, until after He was glorified (Ephesians 1:20–23). As Christians today we have a position in Christ seated with Him in heavenly places, which was not possible until after the Ascension. Most important, Jesus said it would be expedient (beneficial) for the disciples for Him to go away: "Unless I go away, the Counselor will not come to you; but if I go, I will send him to you," in order to convince the world of "sin and righteousness and judgment" (John 16:7,8). Forty days later, Jesus made it clear before He ascended that the disciples had not yet received the promise of the Father, had not yet been baptized in the Spirit, and the Holy Spirit had not yet come upon them (Acts 1:4–8).[42] Incidentally, some wonder why Jesus gave the command when Thomas was not present and why the Bible does not go on and actually say that the disciples did receive the Spirit at the time.[43] Nor is there any evidence that they did anything as a result.

An Actual Impartation

The language used in John 20:21–23 does not fit the idea that nothing happened, however. The act of breathing is parallel to the breathing of God in Genesis 2:7. When God breathed, something happened. When God called for breath to come on the corpses in Ezekiel's vision (37:8–10), life came into them. When Jesus touched people or spoke the word they were healed. It seems ridiculous to suppose that Jesus could breathe on them or give a command and have nothing happen. The authority of Jesus was such that all He had to do was speak the word and it would be done, as even a Roman centurion recognized (Matthew 8:8). Further, the use of the word *receive* is used later of actual receiving of the Spirit (Acts 8:15,17; Romans 8:15; 1 Corinthians 2:12). The form of the Greek word here also indicates that the Spirit was not merely promised and that the breathing was more than a bit of typology. The command to receive indicates that the Spirit was actually then being given.[44]

The other difficulties can be explained. The fact that Jesus said, "I am sending you" (John 20:21), and they did not go until after Pentecost is only parallel to the other expressions of the Great Commission (which Jesus found necessary to repeat more than once). He is simply stating here, "In the same manner as the Father sent me, so I am sending you." This was a statement of the authority He was giving them, as verse 23 indicates. (The meaning there is that for all of the disciples, divine authority would back up their preaching. When they gave the gospel promise of remission or forgiveness of sins, those who believed would indeed be forgiven. Those who did not believe would indeed remain under judgment.)

Some have tried to meet the objection that Jesus must ascend before the Spirit could be poured out by saying that there were two ascensions, one where Jesus ascended immediately after death to present His blood once for all before the Father (Hebrews 9:12,14), and another after the forty days of Resurrection appearances. Some even take it that Paul means that the Resurrection appearances took place after an ascension (1 Corinthians 15:5–7).[45]

Though this is possible, Hebrews 9:24 does not make a clear distinction between the presenting of His blood and Christ's entering His present work of intercession for us. Some have argued that Jesus' command to Mary not to "hold on to" (John 20:17) Him for He had not yet ascended implies an ascension between verses 17 and 19 or at least before verse 27. However, the word translated "hold on to" in verse 17 means "grasp, take hold of," and the form of the Greek word indicates a command to stop doing something one is already doing. Evidently, Mary did the same thing the other women did who met Jesus on the road and "clasped his feet" (Matthew 28:9); something that probably happened before Jesus appeared to Mary. In other words, Jesus told Mary to stop hanging onto Him. He had not gone yet. But He had something for her to do. She had to go and tell the disciples there would be an ascension coming (from the Mount of Olives).

The only more positive indication of an ascension before John 20:19 is in John 16:16–22. This is a discussion about Jesus' going away and coming back to the disciples. It is connected with His going to the Father, as John 16:7 is. But in a little while when they would see Jesus again they would rejoice. In John 20:20 we read, "The disciples were overjoyed when they saw the Lord." "Were overjoyed" is the same verb translated "rejoice" in 16:22. The parallel seems too close to be accidental. This would also mean that John 16:7 cannot be used against an actual impartation of the Spirit in 20:22; though the primary emphasis of 16:7 is on the sending of the Counselor in His work of convincing the world. This sending did come at Pentecost, but it still does not preclude a direct impartation by Jesus before Pentecost.

A Measure of the Spirit Given

The majority of those who recognize that John 20:22 is an actual impartation of the Spirit take it as a bestowal of a measure of the Spirit. In response, some argue that since the Holy Spirit is a Person, it is impossible to split Him up. They take it that to receive the Spirit is to receive all there is of Him so that we cannot receive more of Him; we can only give more of ourselves to Him. But we too are persons. If we can give more of ourselves to Him, He can give more of himself to us. Paul said, "For to me, to live is Christ and to die is gain" (Philippians 1:21). By "gain" he meant "gain in Christ." That is, to live meant Christ (in him), and to die meant more of Christ. Certainly it was possible to receive a measure of the Spirit on the Resurrection Day and an overflowing experience on the Day of Pentecost.

In view of this, John 7:39 and Acts 1:4–8 do not rule out the possibility of a previous bestowal of a measure of the Spirit. John 7:39 clearly refers to that overflowing experience. The rivers of living waters would not and could not flow until Christ was ascended and the age of the Spirit begun. Peter also identifies the baptism in the Spirit at Pentecost with the outpouring on all flesh promised by Joel (Acts 2:16–18). The fulfillment of Joel's prophecy obviously could not take place in connection with a breathing done on a few disciples in a locked room. But neither does it rule out the receiving of a measure of the Spirit prior to Pentecost.

Acts 1:4–8 also indicates that power (Greek, *dynamis,* mighty power) would come on them after the Pentecostal baptism. The emphasis in John 20:21–23 is on authority, rather than active power. Obviously, what the disciples received on that first Easter was not the baptism in the Holy Spirit, nor the outpouring of the Holy Spirit, but it was the Holy Spirit.

Some who recognize this say that what the disciples received was a measure of the Spirit which was still within the bounds of the Old Covenant. That is, the disciples received only what the Old Testament saints did when the Spirit came on them for some particular purpose or function. Those who say this do so because they believe the Spirit given at Pentecost brought regeneration and because they identify the baptism in the Holy Spirit with regeneration or the new birth.[46] However, the Old Covenant was abolished at Calvary (Ephesians 2:15) and the death of Christ put the New Covenant into effect (Hebrews 9:15–17). The emphasis of Acts 1:8 is also power for service, not regeneration.

Some beg the question by saying that perhaps the disciples received a large supply of the Spirit for some purpose which the Bible does not reveal.[47]

Still others take it that the impartation of the Holy Spirit either effected regeneration or at least corresponds to what the present believer receives when he is born again.[48]

It is true that the Church as the body of Christ was not constituted as we now know it until after the Ascension (Ephesians 1:19,

22; 2:6; 4:15,16), that is, on the Day of Pentecost. But it is also true that Jesus said of the disciples earlier that their names were written in heaven (Luke 10:20). They were clean before God, having had a spiritual bath through Christ's Word (John 13:10; 15:3). But the disciples were also in a special situation. Their faith was quickened, their cleansing through the Word was accomplished by the Spirit in Jesus, the Spirit who was thus with them but not in them (John 14:17). They were therefore already in right relation to the Lord. When they saw the Lord and believed the benefits of Calvary, the Spirit came to dwell in them as He does in all who are now regenerated under the New Covenant. As Paul said, "If anyone does not have the Spirit of Christ, he does not belong to Christ" (Romans 8:9). Paul was making a contrast between those who are in the flesh, living on a carnal human level without the Spirit indwelling at all and those in whom the Spirit is life, that is, in whom He has brought regeneration (Romans 8:10).

An illustration may be seen when God sent Moses to Egypt to tell Pharaoh to let Israel go, for Israel was God's "firstborn," that is, the heir to His promises. But Moses' own firstborn was not circumcised; he did not bear the sign of the Covenant. So God had to nearly kill Moses before his wife was willing to circumcise her son (Exodus 4:22–26). Under the New Covenant, all believers are heirs of God and the new birth (regeneration by the Spirit) has taken the place of circumcision (Galatians 6:15). But Jesus' own disciples, who were already heirs through His death (Hebrews 9:15–17), did not have the Spirit in them. He was accepting them as His. He could not have said, "I am sending you" (John 20:21), if He were not. But they did not yet have the witness of the Spirit that they were the children and heirs of God (Romans 8:16,17; Galatians 4:6,7). Galatians 4:5 also indicates relationship, as does John 20:21. Jesus could not let even the Resurrection Day pass without making this new relationship to Him real in their own experience through the Spirit.

This was, in a sense, a special situation. After this, all who believed received the Holy Spirit as we do in regeneration; and had His witness to their sonship and to the fact that they were Christ's. Jesus' disciples did not have to wait until Pentecost to receive this assurance. Even though it is not specifically stated, we can be sure that Thomas received the same impartation of the Spirit when he cried out to Jesus, "My Lord and my God!" (John 20:28).

Not Limited to the Eleven

Nor can we say that the impartation was limited to the eleven apostles. The identification of Thomas as one of the Twelve (John 20:24) seems to imply that there were other disciples there in the room with them. This is confirmed in Luke 24:33, where the two from Emmaus, whose hearts were already warmed by the presence and words of Jesus, came back to find the Eleven, "and those with them." This may have included a considerable portion of the one hundred twenty who were later present at Pentecost.

Very definitely, Pentecost was not the first communication of the Spirit. The same blessing that came on Thomas when he saw and believed comes to all who believe even though they do not see. In other words, by believing, they have life through His name. They are regenerated and share this same breath that came on all these disciples.

The Spirit
in the
Book of Acts

The Book of Acts begins by drawing attention to the fact that the work of Jesus was continued by the Spirit first through the apostles. But the apostles are not really dominant in the Book of Acts. The Holy Spirit is.[1]

Jesus dominates the Gospels, and in comparison, little is said about the Spirit. But in the Book of Acts, the Holy Spirit is indeed another Counselor, Helper, Teacher. Everything in the lives and preaching of the apostles and early believers still centered in Jesus as their living Savior and exalted Lord. The program to extend the gospel to the uttermost part of the earth is Christ's program (1:8). The power to do it is the power of the Spirit, and this is not different from the power of Christ.[2] Yet there is running throughout the Book a new awareness of the Holy Spirit. It came, not only from their initial Pentecostal experience, but from a daily consciousness of the presence, guidance, and fellowship of the Spirit and from many special manifestations of His power. Their baptism in the Spirit never became a mere memory of something that happened in the distant past. It was an ever-present reality.[3]

Jesus did begin by giving special commands through the Spirit to His chosen apostles. This does not mean, however, that the Spirit could not work through others or that the direction of the Church was to be given over to the apostles. The Spirit was in charge. He could and did use whomever He willed. Ordinary believers carried the gospel in all directions after the death of Stephen, while the apostles stayed in Jerusalem (Acts 8:1,4;

11:19–21). An ordinary believer was sent to lay hands on Saul of Tarsus (9:10,17). James, the brother of Jesus, who was not an apostle, gave the message of wisdom at the Jerusalem Council and otherwise took a pastoral leadership in the church at Jerusalem as time went on (Acts 15:13; Galatians 2:12).

Acts shows, however, that the apostles were the primary witnesses to the Resurrection and the teachings of Jesus. The conditions laid down for the selection of a successor for Judas make this clear. He had to be one of those who customarily assembled with and traveled with the Twelve all the time Jesus went about during His earthly ministry so that he could be a witness to the teachings of Jesus. He also had to be a witness of the Resurrection and the post-Resurrection teaching of Jesus (Acts 1:21–25). The apostle Paul bases his claim to apostleship not only on the fact that he was sent by Christ (an apostle is one sent with a commission), but on the fact that he was a firsthand witness to both the Resurrection and the sayings of Jesus. He did not get the gospel he preached from men, but directly from the Lord Jesus himself (Galatians 1:11,12,16–19; 2:2,9,10). In fact, he often draws attention to the fact that he could back up what he was teaching with actual sayings of Jesus (1 Corinthians 7:10).

The visits of the apostles also were not primarily a matter of supervision or of giving apostolic sanction, but of establishing the churches. Thus, Peter and John went up to help Philip (Acts 8:14). But they did not tell Philip what to do next. First an angel and then the Spirit gave him direction (8:26,29). When unnamed believers spread the gospel to Gentiles in Antioch, Barnabas was sent to help them. Barnabas was also an apostle (14:14); yet the emphasis is that he was a good man and full of the Holy Spirit and faith (11:24). Thus, the Holy Spirit, not the apostles, gave direction. From this we are justified in referring to the Book of Acts as the Acts of the Holy Spirit.

From the beginning, the Holy Spirit's prominence is seen. Not only were the final commands of Jesus given through the Spirit in Him; they had to do with the Holy Spirit.

First, He told them not to leave Jerusalem (Acts 1:4). The out-pouring on the Day of Pentecost would never have had the effect or gained the attention it did if only five or six people had stayed. Jesus wanted the Church to have a good start. Moreover, the Book of Acts goes on to emphasize again and again a unity, being in "one accord" (1:14; 2:1, KJV) by which the Spirit was fulfilling the prayer of Jesus in John 17 (vv. 1–26). It was impor-tant for the believers to be together in one place for this unity to be fostered and for its blessings to be realized.

The Promise of the Father

Next, Jesus told them to "wait for the gift my Father prom-ised" (Acts 1:4), which He identified as the baptism in the Holy Spirit. Jesus referred to it as "the gift my Father promised" because the Father is the One from whom the promised out-pouring comes, as Jesus had already taught them. He would ask the Father, and the Father would send the Spirit.

It is called a baptism to remind them of John the Baptist's prophecy, recorded in all four Gospels, that Jesus would baptize them in the Holy Spirit (Matthew 3:11; Mark 1:8; Luke 3:16; John 1:33). Though the Father indeed sends the Spirit, the Son shares in this, as we have seen, and He is the Baptizer. It is called a baptism also to compare it with John's baptism and at the same time distinguish it from it. John baptized in water. Jesus baptizes in the Holy Spirit. The believer must submit or yield to Jesus before he can be baptized. But the contrast between water and Spirit is very strong in all these passages. Emphatically, Jesus' baptism has nothing to do with water.

John's baptism was only a preparation for the new age of the Spirit, while Jesus' baptism is actually a part of it. Some point out that the term "baptism in the Holy Spirit" is not used of believers in the Epistles and try to limit the baptism in the Spirit to the actual inauguration of the new age on the Day of Pentecost. They suppose also that other references to baptism in the Spirit in Acts are just an extension of that inauguration, first to the Samaritans (where it is implied in Acts 8:15,16), and then to the Gentiles at the house of Cornelius (11:16).[4]

From this many take it that the baptism in the Holy Spirit was given once and that there were no further baptisms, only fillings. They suppose God gave the Church a big supply of the Spirit all at once, from which they have been drawing ever since. Taking it this way, the Church would now be the source from which we receive fillings of the Spirit.[5]

God, however, did not give the Holy Spirit in the sense of putting Him in the Church as if separated off from heaven or in the sense of giving Him away. When we receive the Spirit, there is no less of Him in heaven. He is in heaven, in the Church, and in our hearts all at the same time. But God is still the Giver and Jesus the Baptizer. The Church is not a reservoir that received one donation of the Spirit forever.[6] Jesus still asks the Father as the believer comes, and the Father still sends the Spirit.

It is important to remember also that the baptism in the Spirit is immersion into a relationship with a divine Person, not into a fluid or an influence. It is a relationship that can continue to grow and enlarge. Thus the Baptism is only a beginning, but it is like a baptism in that it involves a distinct act of obedience and faith on our part.

But what happened on the Day of Pentecost was not only called a baptism. Many other terms are used. Since the Holy Spirit is a Person, baptism can only picture one aspect of the experience. The Bible often uses a variety of figures of speech to bring out various aspects of experience and relationship. The Church is a Bride, a Wife, a Body, a building, a temple, a vineyard, a vine, a pillar, and an assembly of citizens. No one figure of speech can bring out all that it is. Christians are sons, heirs, adopted, born-again, new creations, servants, friends, brothers. Again, no one term can bring out all aspects of our relationships. So no one term can bring out all aspects of what happened on the Day of Pentecost.[7]

It was indeed a baptism, but the Bible also says it was a filling. "All of them were filled with the Holy Spirit" (Acts 2:4). It was a pouring out of the Spirit upon them, as Joel prophesied (Joel 2:28–32). It was a receiving (an active taking) of a gift (Acts 2:38); a falling upon (8:16; 10:44; 11:15); a pouring out of the Gift (10:45); and a coming upon (19:6). With all these terms used, it is thus impossible to suppose that *baptism* refers to something different from *filling,* or that the Pentecostal experience was limited to the Day of Pentecost. Nor need we suppose that the lack of use of the term "baptism in the Spirit" in the Epistles is significant.

It may be possible to see in the term *baptism,* however, another comparison with John. He continued to baptize in water as long as people came to him for baptism. We should recognize that baptism is something that happens to individuals. Though all were filled at the same moment on the Day of Pentecost, the filling itself was an individual experience. We should expect, therefore, that Jesus, in view of John the Baptist's prophecy, will continue to baptize individual believers in the Holy Spirit as long as they keep coming to Him to receive.

Waiting

Jesus' command to wait (Acts 1:4) and not depart from Jerusalem was necessary for this occasion only. There was no necessary waiting after the Day of Pentecost. But Pentecost with its symbolism of harvest was important in that the purpose of the baptism in the Spirit was power for service, especially in the harvest fields of the world (1:8).

Was this a time of preparation? Some take it that way. But the evidence is that the preparation was done during the forty days by Jesus himself. He taught them, dealt with Peter, recommissioned them, and then told them not to start their ministry until they were clothed with power (Luke 24:49). This was to be no mere human enterprise. They were not to use their own ingenuity to figure out ways to spread the gospel. They were to be led by the Spirit. He would be in charge.

They spent the time of waiting in prayer and supplication, joining together in one accord. They were already united with one another in Christ (Acts 1:14). They were all still filled with great joy and (especially at the times of morning and evening prayer) were continually in the temple, praising and blessing (thanking) God (Luke 24:52). The Spirit was already working in their lives, but they were waiting for the Baptism, the enduement with power (Luke 24:49).

They also gave time to the Word, and the Spirit who spoke through David directed their attention to the prophecies concerning Judas (Acts 1:16). When the Spirit draws attention to the Word, He expects a response; therefore, they did something about it and chose Matthias to take Judas's place. (Some argue that this choice was a mistake since Matthias is not mentioned by name again. But neither are most of the other disciples, and Matthias is certainly included as part of the Twelve in Acts 6:2.)

Wind and Fire

We must not overdo the distinction between the Old and New Testament fillings any more than the distinction between an initial baptism and fillings that follow. Though the Pentecostal experience was a distinct advance, neither the Book of Acts nor Paul's epistles contain any suggestion that the Spirit they experienced was different from the Spirit of God who filled the Old Testament saints.[8]

The signs preceding the Pentecostal outpouring connect it with the Old Testament experiences as well as with the Old Testament promises. The Day of Pentecost was an Old Testament harvest festival. For the Church, it marked the day when the long-awaited spiritual harvest would begin. But before the outpouring of the Spirit came, two unusual signs gave further connection with Old Testament symbolism. First, a sound "like the blowing of a violent wind came from heaven" (Acts 2:2). Though there was no actual wind, the sound filled the house. Wind was a frequent symbol of the Spirit in the Old Testament. The fact that it was the sound of a violent wind, a wind with carrying power, also suggests that this was more than the breathing of the Spirit in regeneration that brings new life. Again, it speaks of power for service.

Then appeared "tongues of fire that separated and came to rest on each of them" (v. 3). "Separated" means "distributed." What happened was that something appeared that looked like a mass of flame over the whole group. Then it broke up and a single tongue like a flame settled on the head of each.

This in no sense was a baptism of fire. Nor was it judgment or cleansing, as some suppose.[9] These were people whose hearts and minds had already been opened to the teachings of the resurrected Jesus, people filled with joy and praise to God, people who were already cleansed, already responsive to His Word, already united. The fire here must be connected, not with judgment or cleansing, but with another aspect of Old Testament symbolism.

The Old Testament records a progressive development with regard to worship. First, it was simply at an altar, as with Abraham. Then God commanded His people to build a sanctuary in the wilderness, the tabernacle. Fire from heaven came down on a sacrifice there to indicate God's acceptance of this new sanctuary. But it happened only once. The next change came when Solomon built a temple. Again, fire came down and consumed the sacrifice, indicating God's acceptance of the sanctuary. But it happened only once. The temples built by Zerubbabel and by Herod were just rebuildings of the same temple, so the sign was not repeated.

Now the old temple was about to be destroyed. (God allowed a forty-year overlap until AD 70.) The believers, united together as the Body, were living sacrifices (Romans 12:1) as well as priests and living stones for the temple (1 Peter 2:5). But in another sense, the new temple is twofold. The Body of believers united together is the temple (sanctuary) for the dwelling of God by His Spirit (Ephesians 2:21,22; 1 Corinthians 3:16). In addition, the bodies of the individual believers are each a temple or sanctuary of the Holy Spirit (1 Corinthians 6:19). The appearance of fire came over the whole group to indicate God's acceptance of the whole Body as a temple. Then it broke up with the single tongue on the head of each to show God's acceptance of the body of each as a temple of the Spirit.

These signs were not part of the Pentecostal baptism or the gift of the Spirit. They were not repeated, just as the fire came only once on each new sanctuary in Old Testament times. At the house of Cornelius they were not present, though Peter identified the experience there with Jesus' promise that they would be baptized in the Spirit and called it "the same [identical] gift," identical with what the one hundred twenty received when the Spirit was poured out on the Day of Pentecost (Acts 11:15–17). But the tongues of fire do show that before the Spirit was outpoured, the believers were acknowledged by God as the temple, the body of Christ. The Church was now in full-fledged existence with the glorified Christ as the Head of the Body. The members of the Body were now ready for the Promise to be outpoured.

They Were All Filled

Among certain denominations many suppose the baptism in the Spirit at Pentecost and the speaking in tongues were limited to the twelve apostles. However, more than twelve languages were spoken.[10] The emphasis on the outpouring on all flesh also precludes this. All one hundred twenty present were filled, all spoke in tongues, and "God-fearing Jews from every nation under heaven . . . heard this sound" of the tongues (Acts 2:5,6). Peter also, speaking before a large group in Jerusalem after the experience at the house of Cornelius, said that "God gave them the same gift as he gave us, who believed in the Lord Jesus Christ" (11:17). This suggests that the Spirit fell in the same way, not only on the apostles and the rest of the one hundred twenty, but on the three thousand who believed after the message Peter gave at Pentecost. Clearly, this experience was not just for the favored few.[11]

Other Languages

Only one sign was a part of the Pentecostal baptism. All who were filled with the Holy Spirit began to speak with other tongues as the Spirit enabled them. That is, they used their tongues, their muscles. They spoke. But the words did not come from their minds or their thinking. The Spirit gave them the words, which were expressed boldly, loudly, and with obvious anointing and power.

This is interpreted in various ways. Some take Acts 2:8 ("How is it that each of us hears them in his own native language?") and suppose that the disciples were all really speaking in their native Aramaic and that this was a miracle of hearing rather than of speaking. But the preceding two verses are too specific for that. Each man heard them speak in his own language without any of the usual Galilean accent.

Others compromise by taking it that the disciples spoke in unknown tongues, which the Spirit interpreted in the ears of each of the hearers in their own language. But Acts 2:6,7 rules that out too. The one hundred twenty spoke in real languages that were actually understood by a variety of people from a variety of places. This brought a witness to the universality of the Gift and to both the universality and unity of the Church.

Another common misconception is the supposition that these tongues were a gift of languages for preaching and teaching the gospel in order to hasten its spread. But there is no evidence of any such use. It would have been helpful to Paul at Lystra, where he did not understand the language and had to preach and try to explain in Greek (14:11–18).

On the Day of Pentecost, the sound of the tongues did gather the crowd, but what they heard was not discourse or preaching. Rather it was the wonderful works (the mighty, magnificent, sublime deeds) of God. This may have been in the form of shouts of praise, speaking unto God. It was certainly worship, not preaching. If it were preaching, it should have brought the salvation of at least some (1 Corinthians 1:21). But no one was saved as a result of the tongues.

Instead, people were amazed (astounded) and in doubt (perplexed, at a loss), completely unable to understand what this was all about (Acts 2:12). They understood the meaning of the words, but not the purpose. They were confused by what they heard.

Others began to mock saying these men (these people, both men and women) were full of new wine (not grape juice here, but a different word meaning a specially intoxicating wine made from a sweet grape). What they heard was primarily what they mocked. Some drinkers become loud and talkative. Yet we must not suppose that there was any sign of the kind of frenzy that marked heathen drunken debauchery. The one hundred twenty were still in control of their faculties. Their chief emotion was still joy. And they all quit speaking immediately when the apostles stood up.

Evidently, as the one hundred twenty continued speaking in tongues, the mocking increased, for this is all that Peter takes note of when he begins to speak (2:14). It may be that as the crowd grew it was harder to pick out the individual languages. Perhaps also, many joined the crowd who were not close enough to anyone who was speaking a language they could understand. With the confusion, it was time for the tongues to stop. They had blessed the believer, been a sign to the unbelieving crowd, but did not and could not do the Spirit's work of convincing the world of sin, righteousness, and judgment. Only the believers really received anything from the experience up to this point. They were filled. The Spirit who caused them to glorify God in other languages must also have revealed the same truths to their own hearts, so that their joy and emotion rose out of new appreciation of God and Christ.[12]

The Spirit's work of convincing the world began when Peter stood up and began to speak. What he gave was not a sermon. He did not study or prepare for it or try to figure out three points. The word "addressed" in verse 14 is the same Greek verb used in verse 4 of the one hundred twenty speaking in tongues as the Spirit "enabled" them. But this time the Spirit gave words in Peter's own language, Aramaic, a language the whole crowd understood. In other words, instead of a sermon, it was a manifestation of the gift of prophecy (1 Corinthians 12:10; 14:3). In the tongues, the one hundred twenty spoke to God of His wonderful works. Now Peter was speaking to men for edification, and later in exhortation (Acts 2:40) which the Spirit gave.

Joel's Prophecy Fulfilled

After showing the unreasonableness of the idea that the one hundred twenty were drunk, Peter began by declaring that what they saw and heard (2:33) was the fulfillment of Joel 2:28–32. The first part of the prophecy obviously explains what was happening to the one hundred twenty. Joel's prophecy of the outpouring of the Spirit was taking place before their eyes. Sons and daughters of Israel were prophesying, filled with the Spirit and speaking under His anointing. (Tongues that were understood are here taken as the equivalent of prophecy.)

The fact that Peter quotes the part about the signs of blood, fire, smoke, and darkness bothers some. Many interpret these symbolically.[13] Others suppose they were somehow fulfilled during the three hours of darkness while Jesus hung on the cross. It seems rather that the signs are mentioned as a means of connecting the Pentecostal outpouring with the end-time. This gift of the Spirit was the firstfruits of the age to come (Romans 8:23).

The unregenerate human heart has no conception of the things that God has prepared for those who love Him. But God has "revealed it to us by his Spirit" (1 Corinthians 2:10). The joys that will be fully ours when we see Jesus are no mystery to us. We have already experienced them, at least in a measure. In a limited way, we have "tasted [really experienced] the heavenly gift, . . . have shared in the Holy Spirit, . . . have [already] tasted the goodness of the word of God and the powers [mighty powers, miracles] of the coming age (Hebrews 6:4,5).[14] The context in Joel goes on to say more about the judgment and the end of the age. It will reach a climax with multitudes in the valley of decision (God's decision, not theirs).

In view of this, some say that Joel's prophecy was not fulfilled at all on the Day of Pentecost. Joel, they say, expected the outpouring to come in connection with the restoration of Israel and the judgments on the Day of the Lord. One writer goes so far as to say that Peter did not really mean, "This is what was spoken by the prophet Joel" (Acts 2:16). What he meant was "This is something like that." In other words, the outpouring on the Day of Pentecost was only similar to what will happen at the end of the age.[15]

Peter, however, did say, "This is what was spoken by the prophet Joel." Joel, like the other Old Testament prophets, does not see the time gap between the first and second comings of Christ. He puts it all in the same context of deliverance and judgment, just as John the Baptist did. Peter now recognized that there is a difference. But he, along with the other disciples, did not have any idea that the time would be so long. Nor did Jesus tell them (1:6).

To Peter it seemed as if the coming Messianic Age was just ahead. Nor did it bother him that all of Joel's prophecy which he quoted was not yet fulfilled at the time he quoted it. The one hundred twenty did not dream any dreams at nine o'clock in the morning. Nor is anything said about their seeing visions while they were speaking in tongues (though that is not impossible). It is not likely either that any slaves were among the one hundred twenty. But this was just the beginning. The rest would come in due time, including the signs and judgments Joel prophesied.

To bring this out, Peter, under the inspiration of the Spirit, specified what the word "afterward" in Joel 2:28 means. The outpouring is "in the last days" (Acts 2:17). Thus, the last days had actually begun with the ascension of Jesus (3:19–21). In other words, the Bible recognizes here that the whole Church Age is "last days." It is the last age before the restoration of Israel and Christ's reign on earth, the last age before He comes in flaming fire to take vengeance on those who know not God and reject the gospel (2 Thessalonians 1:7–10).

Even after years had passed, the early Christians still looked forward to this hope with anticipation. The cry of the apostle Paul toward the end of his missionary journeys was: "The hour has come for you to wake up from your slumber, because our salvation [including our eternal inheritance] is nearer now than when we first believed. The night is nearly over; the day is almost here" (Romans 13:11,12).

Peter saw, too, that the "last days" bring opportunity for times of refreshing. Acts 3:19 could be translated, "Repent therefore and turn to God for the blotting out of your sins so that times of refreshing [or revival] may come from the presence of the Lord and He may send Jesus Christ who was appointed for you [or appointed as your Messiah]."

The way Peter looked at Joel's prophecy shows he expected a continuing fulfillment of the prophecy to the end of the "last days." This means also that Joel's outpouring is available to the end of this age. As long as God keeps calling people to salvation, He wants to pour out His Spirit upon them. "The promise [that is, the Old Testament promise in Joel] is for you and your children and for all who are far off—for all whom the Lord our God will call" (Acts 2:39).

In view of this, and in view of Jesus' own promise that the disciples would be baptized in the Holy Spirit, the baptizing work must continue. Thus, we are justified in calling subsequent fulfillments of the promise "baptisms in the Holy Spirit" as well. Acts 2:38 does refer to what was promised as the "gift of the Holy Spirit." But as we have already seen, the terminology is interchangeable. Clearly, the fulfillment of Joel's prophecy cannot be limited to the Day of Pentecost or any one occasion.

What Shall We Do?

When the Spirit convinced and convicted Peter's hearers, they asked, "What shall we do?" Peter's answer was also part of the Spirit's prophetic utterance in the form of exhortation: "Repent [change your minds and your basic attitudes toward sin, righteousness, and judgment] and be baptized every one of you, in the name [upon the authority] of Jesus Christ [as expressed in Matthew 28:19] for [because of] the forgiveness of your sins. And you will receive [take] the gift of the Holy Spirit" (Acts 2:38). Keep in mind that baptism in water is a testimony, a declaration of what has already happened within. It does not produce or mediate the forgiveness of sins. The expression in Greek is parallel to John's baptism "of repentance," which means "because of repentance," as the context shows.

Peter's call, then, was for them first to repent, which meant they changed their minds from unbelief to belief. Because they believed they were then cleansed and forgiven. Water baptism declared their identification with Christ in His death (Romans 6:3). Then, the next thing in the normal sequence is receiving (really, actively taking) the gift of or baptism in the Holy Spirit.

Making Disciples

From the Day of Pentecost on we see the Holy Spirit active in the life of the Church—in teaching, in miracles, in further fillings, and new baptizings, but above all in the work of spreading the gospel and establishing the Church.

The first evidence of the continuing work of the Spirit is that He enabled the apostles to make disciples, real students, out of the three thousand who were converted. This discipleship was developed through several kinds of learning experiences. They spent much time in the teaching of the apostles; second, in the fellowship; third, in the breaking of bread; and fourth, in the prayers (Acts 2:42).

Part of this was in the temple, for the believers spent much time together in the temple (v. 46), and the apostles were there daily teaching and telling the good news of the Christ (the Messiah), Jesus (3:1,12–26; 5:42). But the apostles did the same thing daily from house to house (5:42).

The teaching of the apostles was not just theoretical, however. The Holy Spirit was the real Teacher. He used the teaching of the truth to bring them all into increasing fellowship, not merely with one another, but first of all with the Father and the Son (1 John 1:3,7; 1 Corinthians 1:9). This fellowship was also a spiritual sharing, a fellowship of the Holy Spirit (2 Corinthians 13:14; Philippians 2:1). This may have included sharing the Lord's Supper. But the emphasis here is not on ritual. The result of the work of the Spirit was a bringing of the people into a new unity where they were of one heart and one soul (Acts 4:32). As Ezekiel 11:19 indicates, the one heart, the unity of mind and purpose, goes with the new experience in the Spirit.[16]

This fellowship, this unity in the Spirit gave them a faith, love, and concern for one another that made them share what they had with brothers and sisters who were in need. (See James 2:15,16; 1 John 3:16–18; 4:7,8,11,20.) In this sense, they "had everything in common" (Acts 2:44,45). This was not communism. "Common" simply means "shared." No one said, "This is mine. You cannot have any of it." Whenever they saw a brother in need, they shared what they had (4:32). Some did sell property and bring the money to the apostles to distribute (2:44; 4:37). But they were under no compulsion to do so (Acts 5:4).

Much of this sharing was in table fellowship. As they broke bread around the table in their homes, they shared their food with a fullness of overflowing joy and in simplicity of heart, "praising God and enjoying the favor of all the people," that is, with the mass of the Jews in Jerusalem (Acts 2:46,47). No wonder the Lord kept adding daily "those who were being saved"!

Times of prayer also marked their discipleship. They were in the temple regularly for the morning and evening prayer. Time, often extended time, was spent in prayer when they faced opposition and danger (2:42; 4:24–30; 12:5,12).

The miracles, as signs pointing to the nature and power of Jesus and as wonders drawing attention to Christ in their midst, strengthened the believers. They also caused a fear, a spirit of awe and reverence, to come upon the people around them (2:43). But the power of the Spirit expressed in the teaching and sharing, and the power of the Spirit shown in the miracles was part of the one life in the Spirit. The people did not see themselves living on two levels, one spiritual and one natural. The Holy Spirit pervaded their whole lives. Worship, fellowship with God, sharing in a practical way, evangelism, and miracles were all part of a unified experience in the Spirit.[17]

The moving of the Spirit in the larger group thus encouraged the move of the Spirit in the smaller groups in the various homes. But the common needs and dangers brought them back together in the larger group. The witness in the temple was needed. So was the witness in the groups that met in homes. From the beginning, the Holy Spirit helped them to maintain a balance without falling into empty form or ritual.

Fresh Fillings

A marked evidence of the Holy Spirit's superintendence of the work of the Church was the way He continued to give fresh fillings to meet new needs and new challenges. The Book of Acts gives two examples of such fillings of individuals and one of the whole group at once. Because of limitations of space, Acts often gives only a few examples of things that must have taken place often. The healing of the lame man at the Gate Beautiful is, for instance, only one example of the many wonders and signs done by the apostles (Acts 2:43; 3:1–10).

The first example of a fresh filling is of Peter before the Sanhedrin (council), the same Sanhedrin that condemned Jesus to death. For fear of it Peter earlier had denied his Lord. This time, as Peter stood up, he was filled anew with the Spirit and gave an answer that proclaimed the truth and glorified Jesus (4:8,10–12). The form of the Greek verb clearly indicates that this was indeed a new filling. Ervin supposes this could not be because Peter was already filled and full.[18] But the idea is not that he had lost anything from the previous filling. God just increased his capacity and poured out the Spirit anew upon him in all His wisdom and power.

The same form of the verb is used in Acts 13:9, when Paul, "filled with the Holy Spirit," faced Elymas the sorcerer and rebuked him. Paul did not ordinarily go around rebuking people in this manner. But the rebuke given here was the Spirit's rebuke in a special way. The judgment upon Elymas was therefore God's hand, God's power, and became the Spirit's work in convincing the proconsul (provincial governor) of Cyprus. He was not convinced by the miracle alone, however. The miracle only bore witness to the Spirit-anointed teaching and preaching that preceded it (13:7,12).

After Peter's first witness to the Sanhedrin, he and John went "to their own people" (4:23), which probably means to the Upper Room where they had been staying and where a large group of believers were gathered. Then "After they prayed, the place where they were meeting was shaken. And they were all filled with the Holy Spirit and spoke the word of God boldly" (v. 31). Again, the form of the verb indicates a new, special filling. The Sanhedrin had warned them "not to speak or teach at all in the name of Jesus" (v. 18). A new filling gave them the boldness, courage, and joyous confidence to speak the Word plainly and openly. Again, the terminology is not the important thing. Fresh fillings, fresh anointings, fresh moves of the Spirit, new manifestations of the hand or power of God are always available in time of need.

Attacks from Within

In addition to attacks from outside, the Church had to face enemy attacks from within. Ananias and Sapphira attempted to gain prestige in the Church without love or faith. This was the first step to the sort of political maneuvering that sometimes puts churches into the hands of unspiritual people. Actually, it was Satan who filled their hearts to lie to the Holy Spirit, which was the same as lying to God (Acts 5:3,4). Peter's discernment or knowledge of what they had done was a manifestation of the Spirit.

God's judgment on them not only saved the Church from danger, but put the fear of God on the believers and on the outsiders as well. Christians were stirred to a new unity in the Spirit. The rest of the Jerusalemites did not dare join them just for the sake of joining. But only the insincere were scared off. The high standards of truth and honesty caused the mass of the people around to hold apostles in high esteem. They showed this by bringing their sick to be healed. "Nevertheless, more and more men and women believed in the Lord and were added to their number" (v. 14; see vv. 13–16).

Full of the Holy Spirit and Wisdom

Another attack from within came when complaints and jealousy threatened to split the Church (Acts 6:1). As the number of believers continued to multiply, most of the men undoubtedly gained employment. The kind of sharing that called for the selling of property became less necessary. However, the same fund to which Barnabas contributed was still maintained to help the needy. Paul twice brought offerings to replenish it in times of special need (Acts 11:29,30; 1 Corinthians 16:1–3). But during much of the time only one group needed help. Widows in those days could not go out and get employment. In fact, widows without sons or brothers were known to have starved to death. So the Church used this fund to care for them.

Among the widows were those who had returned to Jerusalem from other lands and spoke only Greek. Like most minority groups, they were sensitive to slights and, as widows in that society, may have been timid about claiming their share. But by drawing attention to a language barrier they were in danger of splitting the Church.

The apostles, guided by the Spirit, directed the Church to select (elect) seven men for this ministry. Only one qualification was laid down. They must be men of good reputation, full of the Holy Spirit, and of (practical) wisdom. The Holy Spirit brought such love into the hearts of the majority group that the men chosen were apparently all from the Greek-speaking minority. All, at least, had Greek names, and any possibility of further neglect of Greek-speaking widows was thus avoided. This evidence of the Spirit's wisdom was followed by another increase of the Word of God (that is, of its effects), and the further multiplication of the Church (Acts 6:7).

Further Ministry

Stephen and Philip are examples of the fact that this fullness of the Holy Spirit, wisdom, and faith led to further ministry (Acts 6:5,8,10). The wonders and signs they did among the people were of the same dimension as those done by the apostles (6:8; 8:5–8). Though Stephen's witness brought death, to the end he remained full of the Spirit and bore witness to the glory of Jesus as His exalted Lord (7:55,56).[19]

Philip, on the other hand, was led by the Spirit, not only to witness in Samaria, but to win an Ethiopian eunuch to the Lord (8:26–38). One ancient Greek manuscript says the Spirit then fell on the eunuch, which certainly gave him another reason to go on his way rejoicing.[20] At the same time, the Spirit caught Philip up for what seems to be a supersonic ride to the seacoast. Going on to Caesarea, he made it his headquarters for continued ministry. Years later, he was still known as Philip the evangelist. Nor had he neglected to evangelize his own family. His four daughters were filled with the Spirit and prophesied (21:8,9).

Barnabas was also called a "good [noble, worthy] man, full of the Holy Spirit and faith" (11:24). He, too, continued in further ministry. Thus, there were not only specific fillings available for special needs; there was a continuous richness, a constant, powerful endowment of the Spirit that marked some as full of the Spirit.[21] Yet even these, who were so filled, could keep going deeper and higher in Him.

Breaking Down Barriers

Initially, the gospel spread only among Jews or those who were converts to Judaism. Even though the Old Testament does prophesy blessing and restoration for many from all nations, this was generally ignored by the Jews. Long-standing prejudices set up barriers that separated the Jews from the Samaritans on one hand and from the Gentiles on the other. One of the most important works of the Spirit for the spreading of the gospel was the breaking down of these barriers.

The first step came as a direct result of the death of Stephen. Instead of stopping the witness for Christ, the resulting persecution only spread the flame in all directions (Acts 8:1). The Book of Acts gives one direction as an example. Philip went to Samaria. There, his preaching and miracles convinced the people. Many were baptized in water to testify to their faith (v. 12). However, none received the gift of the Holy Spirit. There was no experience of the Spirit "come upon" them as He did on the Day of Pentecost (vv. 16,17).

Just why this is so presents a difficulty to those who hold that everything is received with water baptism. Some suppose the Holy Spirit should have been received and the deficiency was corrected as soon as possible. But it is impossible to explain why there should be such a deficiency on that basis. Others suppose the faith of the Samaritans was not real or was not saving faith until Peter and John came and prayed. However, Philip was a man full of the Spirit and wisdom. He most certainly would have had enough discernment and wisdom not to baptize people before they truly believed in Jesus.

Others suggest that perhaps Philip did not preach the full gospel to them. Since the Samaritans were on the other side of the fence, perhaps his prejudice kept him from telling the Samaritans of all the benefits that Christ as Savior and Baptizer offers to the believer. However, this idea is not borne out by what we find in Acts. The disciples were not able to withhold part of the message. They said, "We cannot help speaking about what we have seen and heard" (Acts 4:20). Philip preached the Word, preached Christ (8:4,5). The Samaritans believed what Philip preached concerning the kingdom (rule) of God and the name (authority) of Jesus. These things are often associated with the promise of the Holy Spirit. Philip must have included the exaltation of Jesus to the throne and the promise of the Father.

The problem seems to be on the side of the Samaritans. Now, they realized they had been wrong, not only about the deceptions of Simon the sorcerer, but also about their Samaritan doctrines. Perhaps, humbled, they found it difficult to express the next step of faith. When Jesus found faith expressed simply on the basis of His Word, He called it great faith, and things happened (Matthew 8:10). When faith rose above hindrances and testing, Jesus called it great faith, and things happened (15:28). But when faith was weak, He did not destroy what there was: He helped it, sometimes by laying on His hands.

When the apostles came, they prayed for the Samaritans to receive the Spirit. Then they laid hands on them, and as they did so the people received (were receiving, kept receiving) the Spirit (8:15–17). Simon the sorcerer, seeing this, fell back into his old greed and offered money for the authority to lay his hands on people that they might receive the Spirit.

Peter's rebuke to Simon for thinking the gift of God might be purchased with money is often interpreted to mean that Simon wanted to offer the gift for sale. But this does not seem to fit, since the apostles were going out and giving this gift freely, recognizing it came from God. It seems rather, that Simon simply wanted to restore his prestige among the people by becoming an authoritative giver of the gift of the Spirit. He misunderstood what had happened and jumped to the conclusion that authoritative laying on of hands was necessary to receive the Spirit. Many other passages show that this is not so. At Pentecost and at the house of Cornelius there was no laying on of hands. When Ananias laid hands on Saul (the apostle Paul), this may have been as much for healing as for receiving the Spirit.[22]

What Peter suggests is that all that is necessary to be able to pray for others to be filled with the Spirit is to receive the Gift yourself. Simon, instead of coming, acknowledging his need, and seeking help, came offering money to receive the gift. He had no understanding, no part or lot in this matter.

Something, however, must have happened when Peter and John laid hands on the believers, or Simon would not have wanted to buy what seemed to be their authority. Simon had already seen Philip's miracles. Prophecy would have been in his own language and not noticeably supernatural. There remains the same thing that attracted the attention of the crowd at Pentecost. They spoke with other tongues as the Spirit enabled them (Acts 2:4,33). Tongues, here, was not the point at issue. Nor did it have the same effect exactly, since there were not people of various languages present. Thus Luke says nothing about them in order to focus attention on Simon's wrong attitude.

Similarly, Ananias said Jesus sent him so that Paul might receive his sight and be filled with the Holy Spirit (9:17). Yet what follows does not give details about how Paul was filled, nor does it mention his speaking in other tongues. However, in the preceding verses that record the Lord's directions to Ananias, Luke does not record the promise that Paul would be filled with the Spirit either (vv. 11–16). As is so often the case, Luke does not mention everything every time, especially when what happened is clear elsewhere. (For example, he does not mention water baptism every time he tells of conversion.) Thus, what Acts 2:4 says surely applies here, especially since the apostle Paul himself said later, "I thank God that I speak in tongues more than all of you" (1 Corinthians 14:18).

A Convincing Evidence

On one occasion the evidence of the filling with or baptizing in the Spirit did become an important point in the issue. No other prejudice, no other barrier to fellowship was ever so great as that between Jews and Gentiles. Even though Jesus tried to prepare His disciples and actually commanded them to spread the gospel among all nations, they apparently took it to mean preaching only to the Jews scattered among the nations. Peter's prejudice was so great, the Lord had to give him a vision three times in order to make him willing to listen to the voice of the Spirit and go to the house of the Roman centurion, Cornelius (Acts 10:16,19). Peter knew this would not be acceptable to his Christian friends back in Jerusalem. Becoming a Christian never automatically removes prejudices. So Peter took along six good Jewish Christian brothers as witnesses (10:23; 11:12).

While Peter was preaching, the Holy Spirit fell on the whole household of the friends and relatives of Cornelius. The six Jewish Christians who were with Peter were astonished because "the gift of the Holy Spirit had been poured out even on the Gentiles" (10:45). The evidence that convinced them was "they heard them speaking in tongues and praising God" (v. 46).

Peter was not wrong about his reception in Jerusalem. As soon as he returned, the opposition became very vocal. But it was not directed so much at the fact that he had preached to the Gentiles as that he shared table fellowship with them and ate nonkosher food (11:3). Peter told the whole story, emphasizing that the Holy Spirit fell on the Gentiles "as he had come on us at the beginning" (v. 15). He also stressed that this was a fulfillment of Jesus' promise to baptize in the Holy Spirit. It was, in fact, the identical gift they all had received (vv. 16,17).[23] With this the Jewish Christians ceased their objections and recognized that God had "granted even the Gentiles repentance unto life" (v. 18).

From this it is clear that a convincing evidence was needed before Peter was willing to say, "Can anyone keep these people from being baptized with water? They have received the Holy Spirit just as we have" (10:47). Something had to show this was the identical gift with that given in Acts 2:4 before the Jerusalem Christians could be satisfied. Peter did not say, "I hope they received the outpouring, the overflowing experience of Pentecost." He did not say, "The Gentiles took it by faith, so I think they have it, I believe they have it." He knew they were filled, not by their testimony, but by the Holy Spirit's testimony through them. The Spirit gave the evidence, and He gave only one. "They heard them speaking in tongues and praising God" (10:46; exactly as in Acts 2:4,11).

Obviously, speaking in tongues was the convincing evidence. And in a day when so many think, hope, believe, and then wonder whether they have the baptism in the Spirit, a convincing evidence is still needed.

There are, however, other problems in the interpretation of this passage. Some suppose the fact that the Spirit came upon the Gentiles while Peter was still preaching means that their conversion experience and the outpouring of the Spirit were one and the same thing. We have seen, however, that at Pentecost and at Samaria, the recipients of the gift were already believers before the Spirit was outpoured on them. Since Peter identifies what happened here as the identical gift, there must be some distinction between their conversion and the gift of the Spirit here also.

The clue is in Acts 10:36,37. The word concerning Jesus that Cornelius and his friends knew was published throughout all Judea. "You" (v. 37) is emphatic. This seems to indicate that these Gentiles themselves knew the facts about Jesus, which would include the promise of the Holy Spirit. The word which God promised Cornelius that Peter would bring was not simply the gospel, but the good news "that everyone who believes in him [Jesus] receives forgiveness of sins through his name" (10:43).

Some believe Cornelius not only knew the gospel, but wanted to accept Jesus. Because it was being preached only to Jews, he may have been praying about taking the step of becoming a Jewish proselyte so that he could become a Christian. But whether this is true or not, it is clear he knew the gospel. It is also clear that God, through an angel, prepared him to accept whatever message Peter would bring (10:22,30–33). This meant also that their hearts were open to receive whatever God had for them. It took only a split second for them to believe and be saved. It took only another moment to receive the outpouring, which Peter saw as a baptism in the Spirit. Thus, though their conversion and baptism in the Spirit were not separated by a long period of time, there is no reason why they could not have been distinct events.

Peter at the Jerusalem Council (Acts 15:8) also indicates that the gift of the Spirit was God's way of bearing witness to them. This surely implies they were already converted. Their baptism in the Spirit thus witnessed to the fact that they were already believers. Verse 9 does mention the fact that God purified their hearts by faith. But the purpose of Peter in mentioning it last is not to indicate the time it happened, but to give it emphasis. The point at issue was primarily the question of whether Gentiles had to keep the Law and be circumcised, so Peter is not simply rehearsing what happened.

Others suppose Acts 10:47 means water was needed to complete the experience. Again, their hearts were purified by faith, not water (Acts 15:9).[24] Water baptism here was both a recognition by the Church that God had accepted these Gentiles, as well as a testimony to the world that they had indeed become members of the Church.[25] Thus, by the Spirit, the barrier was broken down. Gentiles were now members of the Church on equal terms with the Jews.[26]

Some problems, especially when they are connected with prejudices, have a way of coming up again, however. The Jerusalem conference became necessary when Jewish Christians again began to place restrictions on Gentiles and their salvation. But Peter's reminder of the Spirit's work at Caesarea, the testimony of Paul and Barnabas concerning what God was doing among the Gentiles, and the Spirit's message of wisdom through James again brought the believers into one accord (Acts 15:8,9,12–29). The Spirit's presence in their midst was sufficient for any problem, and they were willing to give Him the credit for it (v. 28).[27]

Have You Received?

At Ephesus speaking in tongues is again mentioned in connection with certain disciples whom Paul found there (Acts 19:1–7). Though the Book of Acts almost always uses the word disciple to mean a disciple of Jesus, a Christian, Paul sensed something missing here. Undoubtedly, these twelve men professed to be followers of Jesus. But, Paul asked them if they had received the Holy Spirit "since they believed" (v. 2, KJV)

Contemporary versions generally take this to mean "when they believed." But the Greek is literally, "having believed, did you receive?" The "believing" is a Greek aorist (past) participle, while "receive" is the main verb (also in the aorist). Since the tense of the participle often shows its time relation to the main verb, the fact that "believing" is in a past tense was taken by the King James Version translators to mean that it preceded the receiving.

Many modern Greek scholars point out, however, that the aorist participle often does indicate an action occurring at the same time as that of the main verb, especially if it also is in the aorist, as in verse 2. One writer, Dunn, goes so far as to say that anyone who suggests that the aorist participle here indicates action prior to the receiving is only showing that he (along with the King James Version translators) has an inadequate grasp of Greek grammar.[28]

Dunn draws attention to the many instances of "answered and said," which are really idiomatic and do not give much light on how to interpret other passages. Some of his other examples do show that the action of the participle and that of the main verb occur at the same time. But others are not so conclusive. Hebrews 7:27 does seem to be: "He sacrificed for their sins once for all, when he offered himself." Matthew 27:4, " 'I have sinned,' he said, for I have betrayed innocent blood,' " seems to be coincident, but the usage is not the same as in Acts 19:2. The sin is defined as betrayal. It hardly seems that "receiving the Spirit" is being defined as "believing" in Acts 19:2, especially since other passages indicate the receiving to involve a definite outpouring of the Spirit.

Another passage used by Dunn is 1 Corinthians 15:18: "Then those also who have fallen asleep in Christ are lost." However, Paul is not looking at the perishing as being the same as the falling asleep. Rather, the falling asleep was followed by perishing if Jesus did not rise. Dunn also takes Acts 1:8 to be coincident: "You will receive power, the Holy Spirit having come upon you" (literal). In a sense, the power may have come with the Spirit and the Spirit might be considered the power. But the power in the Book of Acts seems to come when it is needed. Thus it is the result of the Spirit's having come, rather than being the same thing.

Another example is Acts 10:33: "It was good of you to come." "Come" defines what Cornelius means by "It was good." But does "having believed" define what Paul meant by receiving the Spirit? It certainly does not seem to be all he meant. Then, Acts 27:3 is not nearly so obviously coincident as Dunn would have us believe. It is best translated, "Julius, having treated Paul with hospitality, gave him permission to go to his friends." It seems more than possible that there was hospitality preceding the permission to go to his friends.

Dunn overlooks other examples that are even less surely coincident. Speaking of seven brothers (Matthew 22:25), the Sadducees said of the first, "The first one married and died." Obviously, it does not mean the marrying and the dying were the same thing or even that they happened at the same time. They were distinct events, and the marrying clearly preceded the dying, probably by some time.

Similarly, Acts 5:10 is: "The young men . . . carried her [Sapphira] out and buried her." Again, the carrying out and the burying were not the same thing. The burying followed the carrying out in a simple historical sequence. Though there was not a long time between them, at least they were distinct events.

Other examples can be found in Acts 13:51 ("So they shook the dust from their feet . . . and went to Iconium"); 16:6 ("Paul and his companions traveled throughout the region of Phrygia and Galatia, having been kept by the Holy Spirit from preaching the word in the province of Asia"); 16:24 ("Upon receiving such orders, he put them in the inner cell"). In these cases and many more the action of the participle precedes the action of the main verb.

Thus, though there are some cases in which the action of an aorist participle is coincident with that of an aorist verb, this is not a strict rule. The whole impression of Acts 19:2 is that since these disciples claimed to be believers, the baptism in the Holy Spirit should have been the next step, a distinct step after the believing, though not necessarily separated from it by a long time.

The reply of these disciples, "We have not even heard that there is a Holy Spirit," may be translated "But we have not even heard if the Holy Spirit is" (v. 2). The meaning, however, does not seem to be that they had never heard of the existence of the Holy Spirit. What godly Jew or interested Gentile would or could have been so ignorant? It is more likely that the phrase compares with John 7:39. There, the condensed phrase, "It was not yet Spirit" (literal) means the age of the Spirit with its promised outpouring had not yet come. Thus, these disciples were really saying they had not heard that the baptism in the Holy Spirit was available.[29] In fact, several ancient manuscripts and versions of the New Testament do read, "We have not even heard if any are receiving the Holy Spirit."

Further inquiry by Paul showed that these disciples had only been baptized with John's baptism, which Paul explained was only preparatory. At this, they were baptized in the name (into the service and worship) of the Lord Jesus. Then, "When Paul placed his hands on them, the Holy Spirit came on them, and they spoke in tongues and prophesied" (Acts 19:6). It is better here also to take the laying on of hands as a means of encouraging their faith and as preceding or at least distinct from the coming of the Spirit. Then, probably to emphasize that these disciples had now received the full experience of the baptism in the Spirit, Luke definitely states that they spoke in tongues and prophesied. (The Greek also seems to imply that they continued to do so.)

Led by the Spirit

One of the most important evidences of the work of the Spirit, both in the Church and in the lives of individuals, was the way the Spirit led them. Several incidents in the lives of Peter and Philip have already been mentioned. But the guidance of the Spirit is even more prominent in the experiences of the apostle Paul.

The guidance to the spiritual leaders at Antioch was very specific (Acts 13:1–3). These men were prophets and teachers, men used and gifted by the Spirit, men who built up the church both spiritually and in numbers. Because they were sensitive to their spiritual needs as well as the needs of the church, they customarily spent time together in fasting and in prayer. They knew they must minister to the Lord (wait before Him in intercession and in seeking His presence and power) if they were to minister to the people.

On one of these occasions, the Holy Spirit spoke (probably through a prophecy). His command was to separate for Him Barnabas and Saul for the work to which He had (already) called them. After fasting and prayer, the others sent them away (let them go). Verse 4 emphasizes they were sent out by the direct agency of the Holy Spirit. The reason for the prophecy to the group was that Paul and Barnabas had accepted responsibilities with respect to the church at Antioch. It was not only necessary for the Spirit to deal with them about going; the church had to be willing to let them go. By laying hands on them they encouraged the faith of the apostles and indicated they would continue to stand with them in prayer. But they did not tell them where to go. The Spirit himself directed them to go to Seleucia and then to Cyprus.

Later, Paul recognized that elders of local churches were in the same class with these missionary apostles. The Holy Spirit made them "overseers [bishops, superintendents, pastors of local churches]. Be shepherds of the church [assembly] of God" (Acts 20:28). They, too, had their ministry and their call through the direct guidance of the Spirit. He was the source of the gifts of administration they needed to direct the work of the church as well (1 Corinthians 12:28).

Bound by the Spirit

Being led by the Spirit means more than enjoying the freedom, boldness, and victories He brings. There is, above all, no liberty for selfish or arbitrary expressions of one's own will.[30] On the contrary, those who are called and led by the Spirit may find they are not only set free by the Spirit, they become His (willing) prisoners. They accept the boundaries He sets for them and the constraints. They heed when He checks them. They recognize that He knows what He is doing and that constraints are necessary for His purposes.

A striking example is found during Paul's second missionary journey. Paul, with Silas and Timothy, was forbidden by the Spirit to speak the Word in the Roman province of Asia (Acts 16:1). This, too, was probably by a prophecy, since the Greek indicates a direct command by the Spirit. Think what this must have meant to a man who said, "Woe to me if I do not preach the gospel!" (1 Corinthians 9:16).

Actually, God did give Paul a great ministry in the province of Asia on his third missionary journey. But God had another direction for Paul to go at this time. However, the Spirit did not give positive guidance. So Paul just kept going on the way that was open to him. As they came opposite Mysia it became necessary to make a decision. The road to the north would soon end. Since there was still no positive guidance from the Spirit, Paul turned eastward and made an attempt, took definite steps, toward going into Bithynia. Not until then did the Spirit (called the Spirit of Jesus here in some ancient manuscripts) give direction. Again, it was by a definite refusal to permit them to go in that direction (Acts 16:6–8).

Paul then turned westward toward Europe only because the Spirit prevented him from going in any other direction. But at Troas he was in the place where the Lord could give him another sort of direction through the vision of the Macedonian call (v. 9). The previous checks of the Spirit prepared him to accept this as the Lord's will. In Macedonia he did not doubt that the Lord had sent him, even when he was thrown into a Philippian jail (v. 25).

As Paul made his last journey to Jerusalem, he went "compelled by the Spirit" (Acts 20:22). It was not his personal desire to go to Jerusalem. He wanted to go to Rome and then on to Spain (Romans 1:10–13; 15:23,24). But he was bound by the Spirit to go to Jerusalem. The same verb is used of prisoners. Paul later went to Rome in chains as a prisoner of the Roman government (though he always looked on himself as being a prisoner of Christ). But he was just as much a prisoner of the Spirit. The Spirit was taking him to Jerusalem to minister there by bringing an offering from the churches in Macedonia and Greece (Romans 15:25–27).

This did not mean Paul was unwilling to go, even though the Spirit kept bearing witness from city to city that real bonds and persecution awaited Paul. Paul was not moved in his purpose to obey God. He looked forward to finishing his course with joy (Acts 20:23,24).

More details of how the Spirit bore witness are given in the next chapter of Acts. At Tyre, while the ship was unloading, Paul and his friends spent seven days with the Christians there. They, "through the Spirit," told Paul to stop going up to Jerusalem (21:4). However, the word *through* is not the word used in previous passages for the direct agency of the Holy Spirit. It can mean "in consequence of the Spirit," or "because of what the Spirit said." The Spirit himself definitely did not forbid Paul to go on.[31] The Spirit was constraining Paul to go. The Spirit does not contradict himself.

The details of what happened at Paul's next stop, Caesarea, make the picture clearer (Acts 21:10–14). A prophet, Agabus, came down from Jerusalem, took Paul's belt and used it as an object lesson to illustrate the Spirit's message that Paul would be bound by the Jews of Jerusalem and turned over to the Gentiles. Because of this prophecy, everyone begged Paul not to go up to Jerusalem. This, undoubtedly was the case at Tyre. The people, when they heard the Spirit's message, expressed their own feelings that Paul should not go.

Paul, however, stated he was ready not only to be bound but to die in Jerusalem for the sake of the name of the Lord Jesus.

He knew it was God's will for him to go. Then the others finally said, "The Lord's will be done." That is, they recognized that it really was the Lord's will for Paul to go.

Actually, it was very important for the Christians to know it was God's will for Paul to be bound. There were still Judaizers around who opposed the gospel Paul preached and wanted to force the Gentiles to become Jews before becoming Christians. In effect, they were saying that the Gentile Christians were not really saved.

Had Paul gone to Jerusalem without all these warnings to let the churches know what was going to happen, the Judaizers might have taken his arrest as the judgment of God. This could have brought great confusion to the churches. But the Spirit bore witness to Paul and the gospel he preached through this. At the same time the Church itself was protected from the forces which cause division. The Spirit is truly the Guide and Protector the Church needs.

The Book of Acts thus emphasizes that the Holy Spirit in the very nature of things is closely bound up with every aspect of the life of the Church and the Christians. Jesus is the Savior. Jesus is the Baptizer. Jesus is the Healer. Jesus is the Coming King. But the Holy Spirit reveals Jesus and does for us all Jesus promised He would do. We are baptized in the Spirit, empowered by the Spirit, taught to be disciples by the Spirit, guided and checked by the Spirit. Nor is this limited to apostles or other leaders. In the Book of Acts, every believer is a witness. Every believer is filled. Every believer has the joy of the Lord. What a picture of what the Church should be!

The Spirit
in Everyday Living

The Book of Acts shows that Paul and his fellow evangelists were filled (kept on being filled) with joy and the Holy Spirit (Acts 13:52). Persecution and trouble only made them press on with even more joy. Paul's converts also were filled with the same joy (16:34). It was a joy that came as the Holy Spirit gave honor and glory to Jesus.

Paul also gave all the glory to Jesus. His message, ministry, and personal life centered in Jesus. He never forgot that heavenly vision (26:19). Constantly, he spoke of being in Christ. He refused to try to satisfy the Jews with signs or the Greeks with (philosophic) wisdom. He simply preached Christ crucified (1 Corinthians 1:22,23; 2:2). Then the signs followed in the demonstration of the Spirit and of power (v. 4). That is, signs followed, not to convince skeptics, but in response to the faith of those who believed. A good example is the response of the cripple at Lystra to Paul's preaching and to his command (Acts 14:7–10).

Paul's writings also show that the Holy Spirit was just as real and personal to him as Jesus was. He recognized the important place the Spirit had in his ministry, in the Church, and in the lives of individual believers. He also gave definite teaching concerning the Holy Spirit and His gifts, especially in Romans, 1 Corinthians, and Ephesians.

Romans and Galatians emphasize the contrast between the new life in the Spirit and the old life of self-effort under the Law as well as the old life of sin. Corinthians and Ephesians emphasize the work of the Spirit both in the hearts of believers and in

167

the Church. But in all Paul's epistles the work of the Spirit is evident and important, even in Philemon, which does not specifically mention the Spirit. This is true also of the remaining books of the New Testament including Revelation.

Don't Put Out (Quench) the Spirit's Fire

Paul's letters to the Thessalonians speak only briefly of the Holy Spirit. He expresses deep concern over the new converts. God had established the Church through a mighty move of the Spirit. But, because of violent opposition, Paul was forced to leave. He wrote to encourage them. They must not forget that the gospel came to them "not simply with words, but also with power, with the Holy Spirit and with deep conviction" (1 Thessalonians 1:5). As a result, the believers became "imitators" of the evangelists and "of the Lord; in spite of severe suffering," having "welcomed the message with the joy given by the Holy Spirit" (v. 6).

From this we see that Acts, even with as much attention as it gives to the Holy Spirit, does not always mention things made clear elsewhere. Acts tells of the opposition at Thessalonica, but does not mention the Holy Spirit's work there. The nearest it comes is to quote the Jewish opposition: "These men who have caused trouble all over the world have now come here" (Acts 17:6). But from what Paul says it is clear that the signs that followed the other apostles (2:43) were present. Joy as well as the Holy Spirit filled the believers here also, just as in every other church.

Paul, however, had to go on and urge these Gentile converts to abstain from sexual sins (1 Thessalonians 4:3). They had come from a Greek culture which had no idea of moral purity or of what the Bible teaches about marriage (Matthew 19:4–6). Paul reminded them that "God did not call us to be impure, but to live a holy life. Therefore, he who rejects [does not recognize] this instruction does not reject man but God, who gives you his Holy Spirit" (1 Thessalonians 4:7,8). The call to a holy life dedicated to God's will and way is in line with the nature of God as well as the holy nature of the Spirit. He is the Holy Spirit.

Probably with this in view, Paul goes on to say, "Do not put out the Spirit's fire" (5:19). The joy they had in the Spirit as they served God and waited for Jesus (1:9,10) could be lost if the Spirit was stifled or suppressed by sin.

The Holy Spirit's fire may be put out, too, by a wrong attitude, as Paul's next appeal indicates. "Do not treat prophecies with contempt. Test everything. Hold on to the good" (5:20,21). They were rejecting prophecies and treating them as if they were worthless. An arrogant, disdainful attitude is implied. Possibly some of those who claimed this gift did not measure up to biblical standards of holiness. Or, perhaps some spoke out of their own desires or enthusiasm rather than from the Spirit. Such prophecies would indeed be without meaning and might predict things that were not fulfilled.

Contempt and arrogance, however, are not the work of the Spirit either.[1] The answer is not to reject all prophecies for fear some might be false. Instead, they should be put to the test, the bad rejected, and what is good held fast. (See Deuteronomy 13:1–4; 18:21,22; 1 Corinthians 14:29.)

That there were prophecies in the church which needed to be put to the test is shown in 2 Thessalonians. Some had come in upsetting the believers by teaching them they could not make the meeting with the Lord in the air their hope (1 Thessalonians 4:16,17). Their claim was that Paul had changed his mind and was now teaching that they were already in the Day of the Lord. This would imply they could expect nothing but to remain on earth during the judgments that were coming. To reinforce their ideas they not only brought reports and forged letters supposedly from Paul, but claimed support "by some prophecy" (2 Thessalonians 2:2).

Paul definitely had not changed his mind. He was proclaiming the truth given him by Christ himself (Galatians 1:8,11). They could test these reported prophecies, testimonies, and letters by the Word of God that he had already given them (2 Thessalonians 2:5).

Actually, they could still look ahead to salvation, not to the wrath that was coming on the earth (1 Thessalonians 5:9; 2 Thessalonians 2:13; compare Revelation 16:1). God's purpose for believers has always been salvation (including our full inheritance in Christ and in the new heavens and new earth). Two things are necessary for us to continue on the way toward the fulfillment of this salvation, however. They are "sanctifying work [dedication, consecration to God and His work and will] of the Spirit and through belief in the truth [the gospel]" (2 Thessalonians 2:13). Actually, both are made effective in our lives by the work of the Spirit. Both also call for our response.[2]

Received through Faith

Romans and Galatians deal with many of the same subjects. But Galatians was written in the heat of Paul's battle with the Judaizers. Romans was written later as a more general treatment of the meaning of the gospel to prepare Roman believers for Paul's expected visit.

Paul was surprised at the Galatians. How could these new converts listen to people who wanted them to make their salvation depend on their own efforts? What value did they see in keeping the Law and following current Jewish customs? Jesus had been publicly portrayed among them as the crucified One. That had been sufficient for their salvation.

Paul then asked one question that would give them a conclusive answer: "Did you receive the Spirit by observing the law, or by believing what you heard [the preaching that called only for]?" (Galatians 3:2; compare believing/having faith in Hebrews 4:2, "the message they heard . . . combine it with faith," and 1 Thessalonians 2:13, "the word of God, which you heard from us . . . which is at work in you who believe").

There was obviously nothing vague or indefinite about the experience of the Galatian believers. They received the Spirit in a definite act. They knew it. Paul knew it. Paul could never have used their experience in this kind of argument if it had not been as definite as the experiences in Acts 2:4; 10:46; and 19:6.[3] It may very well be that their response of faith came during Paul's preaching, a response not only for accepting Christ but also for receiving the baptism in the Holy Spirit.

Paul then asked, "Are you so foolish [unintelligent]? After beginning with the Spirit, are you now trying to attain your goal by human effort?" (Galatians 3:3). Some take this to mean that "beginning with the Spirit" refers back to the moment of becoming a Christian (as "began" seems to do in Philippians 1:6, which promises that God who began a good work in us will complete it).[4] It seems rather that Paul means the whole period of the beginning of their Christian life while he was with them. He compares this with their present sinful, human efforts to perfect themselves by attempts at keeping the Law.

The thing that stands out in Paul's argument is the fact that faith is the key to our participation in all the work of the Spirit. Does God minister the Spirit (keep giving you the Spirit in abundant supply, that is, in Pentecostal overflow)? Does He keep working miracles (deeds of mighty power) among you? On what grounds does He do so, the works of the Law or believing what you heard (that is, on the ground of faith in and obedience to the message heard)? (Galatians 3:5).

The Law, rather than bringing a blessing, brings a curse. From this curse Christ has "redeemed us in order that the blessing given to Abraham might come to the Gentiles through Christ Jesus, so that by faith we might receive the promise of the Spirit" (v. 14). Thus, two gracious purposes of Christ's redemption are linked together for all who share the faith of Abraham. The blessing he enjoyed is now ours, as is the promised Holy Spirit.[5]

Since the blessing of Abraham and the promise of the Spirit are coordinate here, some take this to mean Paul identified the two. The blessing given Abraham (justification by faith, Genesis 15:6) and the blessing promised for all nations (Genesis 12:3) are thus made ours through the promised Holy Spirit. This is a possible interpretation.[6] But it seems better to take the promised Holy

Spirit not only as coordinate with the blessing of Abraham but as climactic and as specifically related to Galatians 3:2. The blessing of Abraham thus comes on all nations through Christ. Then, both Jews and Gentiles who have faith may receive the Spirit.[7]

What an assurance this is of God's favorable attitude toward all nations, including the Jews. The baptism in the Holy Spirit thus gives clear, positive, identifiable evidence that God has accepted the Gentiles by their faith and that He does not require them to keep the Law. This is exactly the conclusion the Church came to as the result of Peter's experience at the house of Cornelius (Acts 10:44–47; 11:15–18). Moreover, God was continuing to pour out His Spirit on and do miracles for Gentile believers who acted in faith but did not keep the Law (Galatians 3:5). Truly, the experiences recorded in Acts and the doctrine in Paul's epistles are very closely correlated.

Abba, Father

To bring out the same truth in another way, Paul says God sent Jesus (as a Man) to live under the Law in order "to redeem those under law, that we [Jews and Gentiles] might receive the full rights [adoption] of sons" (Galatians 4:5). By "full rights" or "adoption" he means entering into the privileges and responsibilities of sonship. He uses it also of the sonship of Israel (Romans 9:4). Galatians 4:1,2 indicate that the son and heir of a wealthy family in Paul's day would be treated as a slave until he became of age. Then he would receive the *adoption,* that is, all the rights, privileges, and responsibilities that belonged to an adult member of that family. *Adoption* was also used in the modern sense, so that Gentiles who were not sons of Abraham became true heirs, true sons of God, by faith. Jesus died, not just to save us from the fires of hell, but to make it possible for us to receive all the blessings that go with being a member of the household (family) of God (Ephesians 2:19).

Then, because you are sons, and because all the promised blessings of sonship now belong to you, "God sent the Spirit of

his Son into our hearts, the Spirit who calls out, 'Abba, Father' "
(Galatians 4:6; Romans 8:15). The Holy Spirit is probably called
"the Spirit of his Son" to remind us of the words of Jesus in
Luke 24:49. There, Jesus used the same verb, "send," to say, "I
am going to send you what my Father has promised."

This sending of the Spirit is clearly the baptism in the Holy
Spirit, as explained in Acts 1:4,5; 2:4. That Paul refers to it as
the Spirit coming into their hearts is not strange. He still has the
same definite coming of the Spirit in mind as in Galatians 3:2.
Moreover, we have already seen in Acts the variety of terms the
Bible uses for the Spirit's coming in the Pentecostal experience.

It is of great importance here, however, that Paul distinctly
makes the fact that they are sons the ground for sending the
Spirit. Some have tried to reinterpret Galatians 4:6 to avoid a
difference between the experience of the new birth and the sending of the Spirit. But the verse is a plain, simple sentence that can
bear no other meaning.[8] Some try to make the sons only poten-
tial sons, not yet born again, but this is only another clever argument to try to avoid the plain meaning. Sonship, clearly, must
precede the sending of the Spirit in Pentecostal fulfillment.

That Paul still had a distinct experience in mind that people
can know whether they have it or not is seen in the next verse
(v. 7): "So you are no longer a slave, but a son." By saying this
Paul brings it home to each individual that the fact he experienced the baptism in the Spirit is positive confirmation that he is
indeed a son and heir, not a slave to the Law.

This is confirmed by the Spirit himself who comes into our
hearts and continually "calls out, 'Abba, Father' " (v. 6). "Calls
out" usually means loud cries, shouts, such as might be needed
to get attention in a marketplace or public square. It expresses a
depth of intensity, fervency, and urgency by which the Holy
Spirit within us cries out to God as Father.

The repetition of the cry gives added solemnity.[9] It is often
said today that Abba was the Aramaic equivalent of "Daddy!"
as a familiar form of address. It does sound good to think of

how we have the privilege of the most intimate fellowship with the Father through the Spirit. Indeed, we do. Yet, *Abba* is actually Aramaic for "The Father," or "O Father!" It was used in the family circle. But in that society children did not say, "Daddy." Very respectfully, they said "Father." There is no thought of a loose or careless familiarity in the intense cries of the Spirit.

A better explanation might be that the early believers had heard Jesus address God in Aramaic as *Abba*. This became the common address in prayer and was taken over by the Greek-speaking Gentiles. But it could easily become a meaningless form, especially to those who did not speak Aramaic. So the Holy Spirit directed their hearts to God, calling Him by the precious term *Abba*, but immediately adding "Father" in their own language. He wanted them to feel that God was truly their Father.

"*Abba*, Father," of course, was not something said in tongues, but was the Spirit's own continued inner cry. It is implied, however, that this stirs a response in the heart of believers so that they too call out to God as Father. Because these cries are real and meaningful, they give believers further assurance that they are children and heirs of God.

Righteousness by Faith

Not only does God's bountiful supply of the Spirit show we are sons; it should make us realize we do not need to add anything to God's provision. Those who taught that Gentiles must keep the Law apparently said that only by keeping the Law can anyone be righteous before God. Paul pointed out that our hope is in a better righteousness (Galatians 5:5). The Law cannot hope to achieve true righteousness or even help to achieve it.

The Gentiles who listened to the Judaizers were putting their trust in circumcision (as a sign of the Old Covenant) for their standing before God. By this, they were actually rejecting Christ and were fallen from grace. We do not need the Law, "By faith we eagerly await through the Spirit the righteousness for which we hope. For in Christ Jesus neither circumcision nor uncircumcision has any value. The only thing that counts is faith expressing itself through love" (vv. 5,6). Faith is the key. Faith does what the Law cannot do when faith is operative, effective through love (or in an atmosphere of love). We can only expect a righteousness that pleases God, then, by the Spirit through (out of) faith (or, through the Spirit which is received by faith energized by love).[10]

Live by the Spirit

Paul was always careful lest by overemphasizing a truth he would have caused people to go in the wrong direction. The Gentiles were indeed free from the Law. But this must be balanced by the fact that they were free, not for self-indulgence, but for life in the Spirit. They were not to "use [their] freedom to indulge the sinful nature [to allow the desires and impulses of the sinful nature to take over]." Rather, they were to "serve one another in love" (Galatians 5:13). This means having the same self-discipline that Jesus showed when He, the Lord of glory, humbled himself and was among us "as one who serves" (Luke 22:27—see vv. 25–27; Philippians 2:5–8).

In some passages Paul used the Greek word *sarx* to mean the physical body (2 Corinthians 4:10,11), but in Galatians 5 he meant the evil tendencies within us that lead to selfish indulgence and strife: the sinful nature. Thus, the desires that come from the sinful nature in this sense are directly opposed to the desires that come from the Spirit (v. 17). Nor was it enough for these believers simply to be baptized in the Holy Spirit. It takes living by the Spirit to have victory over the desires and impulses of the sinful nature (v. 16).

The problem with these Galatian believers was that they were biting and devouring one another (v. 15; compare James 4:1). This strife showed that they were not living by the Spirit, for if you live by the Spirit you will definitely not fulfill the cravings (desires, sinful desires) of the sinful nature and the mind (Galatians 5:16; the Greek is emphatic). This showed also that putting themselves under the Law was not giving them victory over the sinful nature either. In fact, the Law was encouraging the impulses of the sinful nature, so they could not do even the good things they wanted to do, nor could they bring the peace they wanted to see. The only way to win the victory in this conflict between the sinful nature and the Spirit was to come over completely to the side of the Spirit and let Him lead. This, again, would mean they were not under the Law (the Mosaic Law).

To live by the Spirit and be led by the Spirit then means something more than miracles. It means victory over the desires and impulses of the sinful nature. It means crucifying those desires. It means cultivating the fruit of the Spirit, for the fruit of the Spirit is the best antidote to the cravings of the sinful nature.

The guiding principle, then, is in verses 16 and 18. But Paul never left people with general principles. He stated exactly what he meant by the works of the sinful nature that arise from its impulses and cravings (desires, or lusts). He identified clearly the fruit that would arise in the lives of those led by the Spirit. He did not mean these lists (vv. 19–23) to be all inclusive. (Notice the word "like" in v. 21 and "such" in v. 23.) But they are full enough to make clear what he is talking about.

Actually, we need to see the fruit of the Spirit against the background of the cravings of the sinful nature in order to see whether we are living by the Spirit or not. There is no middle ground here for Paul. The works of the sinful nature are not possible if we are being led by the Spirit. If they appear, it means we have stopped living by the Spirit; we have turned away from His leading. This does not mean the Spirit has left us, but that we are giving the sinful nature opportunity instead of giving Him opportunity. However, those who do (keep on doing, make a practice of) these things "will not inherit the kingdom of God" (v. 21).

The Works of the Sinful Nature

The works of the sinful nature may be classified into four groups (vv. 19–21). First, "sexual immorality, impurity and debauchery [unrestrained willfulness, wanton acts against decency]" (v. 19) have to do with sexual immorality. Much of this was not even considered sin by society in general. Second, "idolatry [including both images and the worship of the gods they represented] and witchcraft [including sorcery, enchantment, and possibly the use of drugs in religious rites]" (v. 20) have to do with religions of human origin. Third are "hatred [hostility], discord [strife, quarrels, wrangling], jealousy [over what others have], fits of rage [outbursts of anger, losing one's temper], self-ish ambition [selfish intrigues with mercenary motives, selfish devotion to one's own interests as in office-seeking], dissensions [as between political parties], factions [differences of opinion, especially when pressed to the point of causing division] and envy [expressed in ill will and malice]" (vv. 20,21). These all have to do with conflicts that arise from our own selfish impulses and desires. And fourth are "drunkenness, orgies [the carousing that usually results from drunkenness]" (v. 21).

These are our natural impulses that do battle against the desires of the Spirit for us. Civilization, education, culture, and good family upbringing may put a thin veneer over these things so that an unbeliever may have a good appearance. But it usually does not take much for some of these works of the sinful nature to break through the veneer.

The Christian, in identifying himself with the crucified Savior, did crucify the sinful nature with its cravings. But that victory which is ours potentially must be made active and actual. We as Christians live by the Spirit in the sense that we have our life by the Spirit. But we must also live by the Spirit if tendencies, impulses, and desires of the sinful nature are to be truly crucified in our daily experience (Romans 8:4,5).

The Fruit of the Spirit

Nothing shows this more than our relationship with one another. If we "become conceited [if we become boasters with excessive ambition]" we provoke and envy one another (Galatians 5:26). If we are spiritual (living by the Spirit, walking by the Spirit, living in active fellowship with Him) we will take the humble place. Instead of putting other people down, instead of seeking our own pleasure, we will bear one another's burdens and be concerned about restoring the fallen brother (6:1,2).

Actually, this is an illustration of the fruit of the Spirit (5:22,23), fruit that begins with love and is all summed up in love. It is called the fruit of the *Spirit* because the Spirit is its source. It does not grow naturally out of the soil of our human nature.[11] "Love" is the kind of love God showed at Calvary when He sent His Son to die for us while we were yet sinners (Romans 5:8). It is described in 1 Corinthians 13:4–7 as patient (toward those who provoke and injure us), kind (returning good for evil), free from envy (including malice, ill will), humble ("does not boast"), free from self-importance ("not proud"), never rude or discourteous, never selfish or greedy ("self-seeking"), never provoked or irritable ("not easily angered"), never mindful of evil done to it, never delights in the iniquity or downfall of others. It bears up with faith and hope in every circumstance of life. No wonder it will never fail, never cease!

"Joy" is something the world knows nothing about. Many are in a mad pursuit of pleasure. Some have found a measure of happiness or satisfaction. But they cannot even imagine what it is like to have the deep, continuing joy that is the fruit of the Spirit. It comes as the Spirit makes Jesus and His work of salvation more and more real to our hearts. It is expressed in an active rejoicing in the Lord (Philippians 3:1). Yet it is there, nurtured by the Spirit, whether there is opportunity for expression or not, and whether the outward circumstances are joyful or not. (See also Romans 14:17; 15:13; 1 Thessalonians 1:6; Philippians 1:25).

Real "peace" also comes only from the Holy Spirit. It includes a quiet spirit, but it is more than that. It is the consciousness that we are in right relationship with God, a sense of spiritual well-being. It includes the assurance that we can trust God to supply all our need "according to his glorious riches in Christ Jesus" (Philippians 4:19). Along with love and joy it becomes the help of the Spirit for the development of the rest of the fruit.

"Patience" is having patience with people who deliberately try to upset us or harm us. Unbelievers may do everything they can to injure us or make us angry. But the Spirit helps us to take it all in love with the joy of the Lord. Thus there is no temptation for revenge (Ephesians 4:2; James 1:19; Romans 12:19).

"Kindness" is a kindness and generosity that tries to put people in the best light. It is sympathetic and gives the soft answer that Solomon said turns away wrath or avoids causing angry outbursts of temper (Proverbs 15:1).

"Goodness" has the idea of the development of character that is truly good, upright, dependable, and yet still generous and good to others. This is what makes us God's noblemen. The best way to describe it is being like Jesus. (He embodied all the fruit of the Spirit in His life and ministry.)

The words *faithfulness* and *faith* are both translated from the same Greek word *(pistis)*. As a fruit of the Spirit, it is often distinguished from the faith that brings salvation and the faith that works miracles.[12] Faith in both the Old and New Testaments does include faithfulness and obedience. Here, since it is a complement and constituent of love and since it is being contrasted to the works of the sinful nature, the emphasis is on "faithfulness." It is a faithfulness shown not merely toward God, but toward others as well. Yet this does not make it essentially different from saving faith, since saving faith involves both trust and obedience. The fruit of the Spirit must grow. Faith should grow and develop within us.

"Gentleness" is not a self-debasing or a belittling of oneself. Rather it is a true humility that does not consider itself too good to do the humble tasks. It is not too big or self-important to be courteous, considerate, and gentle with everyone. It is modest, yet willing to try when a job needs to be done.

"Self-control" is not mere moderation. The corresponding verb is used of athletes who must exercise self-control in everything if they are going to win (1 Corinthians 9:25). The Spirit does not always take away all the desires and certainly not all the impulses and tendencies of the sinful nature. But part of His fruit is that He helps us develop self-control that masters those desires, impulses, passions, and appetites.

Self-control does not come automatically, however. What the Spirit does is help us to discipline ourselves. Cowardly fear is another thing that can arise out of the sinful nature. But, as Paul told Timothy, "God did not give us a spirit of timidity [cowardly fear], but a spirit of [mighty] power, of love and of self-discipline" (2 Timothy 1:7). We do not get rid of timidity or cowardly fears that keep us from witnessing for the Lord or doing His will by simply sitting in the sun and drinking in the rain. We have to make up our minds and then do the thing we know we should do. In other words, we have to cooperate with the Spirit in disciplining ourselves if the fruit of self-control is to grow.

This cooperation with the Spirit is necessary for the growth and development of all the fruit of the Spirit. Some suppose that just because we have life in the Spirit or are baptized in the Spirit, the fruit is sure to come. But all that grows automatically in most gardens are the weeds. If fruit is desired it must be cultivated. God does some of that (John 15:1). But we have our part.[13]

Peter, dealing with some of the same fruit, calls us to "make every effort to add to [our] faith goodness" (2 Peter 1:5). This can mean we supply through our faith goodness (moral power). Or, better, it means we must exercise our faith in such a way as to produce goodness and the other fruit in turn: "knowledge; self-control; . . . perseverance [steadfast endurance in the face of difficulty]; . . . godliness [in worship and in practical religion]; brotherly kindness; and . . . love [the same love that is the fruit of the Spirit]" (vv. 5–7). This is what it means to walk by the Spirit, actively responding to His leading in obedience and faith.

Peter adds that if these things be in us and abound we shall not be barren or unfruitful in the (personal) knowledge of our Lord Jesus Christ. But if we lack them we are in terrible danger (2 Peter 1:8–10). Paul adds that if we keep on sowing to our sinful nature, we shall of the sinful nature "reap [eternal] destruction," while if we keep sowing to the Spirit we shall of the Spirit "reap eternal life" (Galatians 6:8). Then he gives a word of encouragement: "At the proper time we will reap a harvest if we do not give up" (v. 9). With the help of the Spirit the fruit will grow and bring a bountiful harvest. Nor do we have to wait to the end to enjoy the fruit. While it is growing and developing we can experience love and joy welling up within us by the Spirit. We can sense the reality of that inner peace even when death threatens us. We can lean hard on the Holy Spirit and receive His help when things go wrong and others take advantage of us. We can take the way of peace when others are trying to stir up strife and division. Thus, the fruit will not be something secret and hidden that gives no evidence of its presence. We can know whether it is developing in us. So can those around us (Matthew 12:33).[14]

The Spirit of Holiness

Paul's letter to the Romans had in view further evangelization of the Gentiles (Romans 1:13; 15:28). Thus it stressed the Christian's freedom from the Law, as does Galatians. Many of its teachings concerning the Holy Spirit are also parallel to those in Galatians.

As always, Paul keeps Jesus Christ central. The first reference to the Holy Spirit in Romans is in relation to Him (1:4). The phrase is actually "through the Spirit of holiness." Because of a parallel phrase "as to his human nature" in verse 3, many take this to mean Christ's human spirit which was without sin (Hebrew 4:15).[15] Or, they take it as His human spirit being "the seat of His divine nature."[16] Thus, they do not see the Holy Spirit as the active Agent of His resurrection here. Instead, His lack of sin made it impossible for death to hold Him (as some interpret 1 Timothy 3:16, also). There is truth in this, of course. But the Spirit of holiness is similar to such expressions as the Spirit of Truth. Nor is there anything against considering the Holy Spirit as the active Agent by whom God raised Jesus from the dead.[17]

Actually, the contrast can hardly be between Jesus in a human body and the human spirit of Jesus. It is rather between His former humble state during His earthly ministry and His present power and glory in heaven.[18] The sequence in Romans 1:3–5 begins with Christ's first coming as the Son of David, the branch growing from the roots of a cut-down tree, a root out of a dry ground (Isaiah 11:1; 53:2). But that humble existence on earth is over now. We can no longer look at Christ (from a human standpoint) as a Man on earth with physical, earthly relationships (2 Corinthians 5:16). He has been declared to be the powerful Son of God by the Resurrection from the dead. (See Philippians 2:9.) The Pentecostal outpouring and the ministries of the Spirit also bear witness to this.[19]

Paul had his personal evidence that Jesus rose and is now exalted, not only by the appearance on the Damascus Road that made him a firsthand witness of the Resurrection, but also through the grace and apostleship he received. The same sort of evidence comes to every believer who is baptized in the Spirit according to Acts 2:4. Jesus promised He would ask the Father and the Father would send the Spirit. When we receive the Spirit with the same definite evidence of speaking in tongues, we become firsthand witnesses that Jesus is indeed enthroned in heaven doing what He said He would do.

"Through the Spirit" (Romans 1:4) may mean also "as foretold by the Spirit"[20] or "in the realm of the Spirit."[21] Now Jesus is manifest to us, not in physical existence, but in the power of the Spirit. It is a new age, with the triumphant Resurrection power of the glorified Christ available through the Spirit to every believer.[22]

True Jews

As Paul goes on to deal with the gospel that is the power of God unto salvation (Romans 1:16), he recognizes that the Gentiles turned away from God and desperately need the gospel. But so do the Jews. Their circumcision, the sign of the old Covenant of the Law is robbed of meaning by their sin. God wanted righteousness, not religious forms (2:26). Thus the real Jew is not the one who appears to be one outwardly (by circumcision). The real Jew is the one who "is one inwardly; and circumcision is circumcision of the heart [an inner separation to God performed], by the Spirit" (v. 29; see Galatians 6:15, where a new creature or creation is what counts; see also Philippians 3:3, where this is demonstrated by worshipping God in the Spirit.) Jew (from Judah) means "man of praise" in the sense of one praised by his brothers (Genesis 49:8). But the praise of the real Jew comes not from men but from God (Romans 2:28,29).

This inner work of the Holy Spirit is done by grace through faith (Ephesians 2:8). The same faith brings a positive hope and assurance of sharing the glory of God (Romans 5:2). This hope will never make us ashamed for having held it. That is, it will never disappoint us, because "God has poured out his love [abundantly] into our hearts by the Holy Spirit, whom he has given us" (5:5).

The gift of the Spirit refers to the baptism in the Holy Spirit. God's love is the love He poured out supremely on Calvary. But the outpouring of that love did not end at the Cross. Paul goes on to say that the God who loved us enough to send His Son to die for us, surely loves us enough to make available everything we need to take us all the way to heaven (Romans 5:8–10; 8:37–39).[23]

The Law of the Spirit

Paul contrasts the law of Moses with grace in Romans chapters 5 through 7, rather than with the Spirit. The real conflict, however, is not between the Law and grace but between the Law and sin. The Law was not evil or wrong. It was "holy, righteous and good" (7:12). Sin, not the Law, brings death (vv. 10,11). In fact, sin showed how bad, how very sinful it is by taking a good thing like the Law and using it to stir up more sin (vv. 7,8).

The problem was not the Law, but man's weakness (8:2). The Law was like a mirror that could show men their faults, but could not help them do better. By delivering men from the Law, Christ made it possible to serve God in a new way. Serving Him by the Holy Spirit is a far better way than the old way of trying to follow what was literally written in the Law (7:6).

This anticipates Romans 8, which speaks of a new law, "the law of the Spirit of life" (v. 2). This law makes the believer free from the old law of sin and death. The person under the law of Moses could not possibly provide the righteousness God required. The Law only condemned his sin and brought death. Thus, his actions were guided by a law (a principle) of sin and death. But the Holy Spirit brings life in Christ.

By speaking of the law of the Spirit, Paul is not putting the Spirit in a class with the law of Moses. The Bible does not substitute one list of rules for another when the Spirit sets us free from the Law. Lists of rules that say, "Do not handle! Do not taste! Do not touch!" (Colossians 2:21) are nothing but the teachings of men. They are the sort of thing the world calls religion. But they are of no value in keeping us from indulging the sinful nature (vv. 20–23). That is, if all you have is a list of rules, you can still do something that is not on your list and be just as much in the sinful nature as any drunkard or adulterer. But it will not bother you because it is not on your list. We must put to death the gross sins of the sinful nature, of course (3:5–9). But we must also seek the "things above," clothe ourselves with the fruit of the Spirit, and "let the word of Christ dwell in [us] richly" in worship and praise (vv. 1,2,12–17).

When the Spirit sets us free from the Law, He does not enslave us. He just gives us opportunity to serve the Lord by our own free choice.[24] By the law of the Spirit, Paul means a principle, something that guides and governs our actions.[25] With the Spirit in control as we yield to Him, we have victory instead of defeat. There is still a battle (Ephesians 6:12,16). But we have help: the Holy Spirit (Romans 8:13)!

Sharing Christ's Victory

The Law's failure to produce righteousness was not due to the Law, but to our human weakness. God knows this and has compassion on us (Psalm 103:13,14), but our weakness does not excuse us. God, therefore, sent Jesus "in the likeness of sinful man [as a real man, but without any sin] to be a sin offering" (Romans 8:3). As a man, without using any of His divine powers, Jesus defeated temptation in the same areas where Eve failed and where we all fail ("the cravings of sinful man, the lust of his eyes and the boasting of what he has and does," the same desires and tendencies that characterize the world; 1 John 2:16). By this He condemned sin in sinful man, that is, He showed we sin, not because we have to sin, but because we choose to sin and because we ignore the help available through the Word and the Spirit. We are indeed guilty. But He has removed our guilt by His sacrifice on Calvary (Romans 8:3). By walking by the Spirit we share the results of His victory and do the good things the Law really wanted (v. 4).

Galatians also stressed living in and by the Spirit. Romans adds that this involves a mind-set, a directing of our thoughts, intents, aims, and aspirations. The person "according to the sinful nature" (v. 5) lives in the realm of the sinful nature and looks at everything from the point of view of the desires and impulses of the sinful nature. (See Matthew 5:28; 6:19–21,31,32.) But those who live by the Spirit and in the Spirit look at everything from the point of view of the Spirit. He loves to glorify Christ and He directs our aims and our strivings toward heavenly things, the things of Christ (Matthew 6:33; Colossians 3:1,2).

The sinful mind-set only leads to death (Romans 8:6). In fact, it is already death in the sense of separation from God.[26] By its very nature, it is "hostile to God" and cannot bring itself under the law of God, under the principles of life that please Him (v. 7). But the mind-set given us by the Spirit brings "life and peace" (v. 6) including fellowship with God in contrast to the separation brought by yielding to sinful desires, or as Galatians says, "the acts of the sinful nature" (Galatians 5:19).

Beginning with Romans 8:9, Paul speaks directly to the believer. We "are controlled not by the sinful nature [or in the realm of the sinful nature and its desires] but by the Spirit [in the realm of the Spirit and the guidance and help He gives]." But there is a condition: "if the Spirit of God [continually] lives in you." Paul obviously is not talking about the baptism in the Holy Spirit here, but of the Spirit's presence that comes in regeneration. The condition that brings about this mind-set that is according to the Spirit is a matter of belonging to Christ. If we are His, we have the Spirit. If we do not continue to have the Spirit, we are not His.

If we have the Spirit, then, Christ is in us, and the body is dead because of sin, but "your spirit is alive because of righteousness" (v. 10). The word *spirit* here means the human spirit on the basis that the conflict between the sinful nature and the spirit is only in born-again believers. Thus, the body (of sinful desires) in now dead because of sin, but our human spirits are alive because of the righteousness of Christ ministered by the Spirit.[27] But the conflict in the preceding verses is between the sinful nature and the Holy Spirit, not between the sinful nature and the human spirit.[28] Thus, physical death is in this body (we are already dying) because of sin, but the Spirit at the same time ministers spiritual life within us because of righteousness.

The whole point of verses 10 through 13 is related to the Resurrection life of Christ which is ours by the Spirit. Our physical bodies are mortal, subject to death because of sin. No matter what we do for these bodies, there is only one thing our bodies can do for us. They can only bring us down to death. While we have them, we can use them for God's glory. We recognize also that they are temples of the Holy Spirit and must take care of them and keep them morally clean for that reason. But there is no reason why we should cater to sinful desires and impulses (such as jealousy, hatred, strife, anger) that arise from the body. In fact, to do so brings more than physical death.

According to 1 Corinthians 9:27, Paul beat his body (that is, treated it with severe discipline) and made it his slave (brought it into subjection), "so that after I have preached to others, I myself will not be disqualified" and fail to receive his eternal inheritance, become reprobate like the false teachers who were on the way to hell and dragging others with them). Eternal death, the complete loss of our eternal inheritance, is the result of living in the realm of the sinful nature, as we saw in Galatians 5:21.

On the other hand, "if the Spirit of him [God] who raised Jesus from the dead is [continually] living in you [as evidenced by the fact that we keep putting "to death the misdeeds of the body," Romans 8:13]," then the God who resurrected Jesus "will also give life to your mortal bodies through his [indwelling] Spirit (v. 11).

Sharing Christ's Inheritance

As Galatians indicated, living by the Spirit means being led by the Spirit. This is also evidence that we are sons and heirs of God. Those who put themselves under the Law are in bondage, becoming slaves to sin and death. But the Spirit we have received is not "a spirit that makes you a slave again to fear, but you received the Spirit of sonship. And by him we cry, "Abba, Father" (v. 15). In Galatians, the "Abba, Father" is the inner voice of the Spirit. Here it is also our cry. By it, or in this cry, "the Spirit himself testifies with [or, to] our spirit that we are God's children" (v. 16). In other words, we can repeat the words, "Abba, Father," and they will mean nothing unless the Spirit is actually present in us witnessing to our spirits that we really are the children of God.

Paul is speaking of actual experience here. The witness of the Spirit is not something vague. When we cry out to God as Father we know we are not just saying words. The Holy Spirit makes us conscious that God really is our Father. From this we know also that our sonship is meaningful. We are not only heirs of God, we are fellow heirs with Christ. That is, we must not think of our inheritance as insignificant. A man might be an heir of a millionaire and only get $10. But Christ is the Son of God in a special sense. As the heir, He now reigns triumphantly in glory. But we are fellow heirs with Him, sharing the whole of that glory which is His inheritance, sharing even in His throne (vv. 17,18; Revelation 3:21).

Paul has the same thing in mind when he wrote: "Though outwardly we are wasting away, yet inwardly we are being renewed day by day. For our light and momentary troubles are achieving for us an eternal glory that far outweighs them all" (2 Corinthians 4:16,17). He was willing to suffer with and for Christ in view of the glory to be revealed. (Romans 8:17,18; 2 Corinthians 1:5–7; Philippians 3:10; Colossians 1:24).

The gift of the Holy Spirit is really part of this glory to come.[28] What we have received in our present experience is actually the firstfruits of what we are yet to receive (Romans 8:23). In its literal meaning, the firstfruits were not only the first part of the harvest; they were the assurance and pledge that the remainder of the harvest would come. Thus, the outpouring of the Spirit we have received so far is only a small token of the overwhelming experience in the Spirit that is part of our adoption, part of the privileges of our sonship that we shall receive in the future.

The Redemption of the Body

The problem is in our present mortal bodies. Our sonship promises us something more than even the healing of our bodies, wonderful as that is. For even the part that is healed keeps on aging and decaying and goes down to death. Healing is indeed a wonderful way the Spirit breaks down the power of the enemy in sickness and drug addiction, but there is also a redemption of our bodies for us in that sonship. At the time of the resurrection and the Rapture (1 Thessalonians 4:16), we shall be changed (1 Corinthians 15:51,52). Our present bodies will be swallowed up by a new body that is as much different from what we have now as the entire wheat plant is from a bare grain. It will be a spiritual body, not in the sense of being ghostly or unreal, but in the sense of being perfectly suited to be the temple of the Holy Spirit. The Holy Spirit works in us now in spite of our weakness and inability. But our new bodies will be the perfect instruments for the expression of the life in the Spirit (1 Corinthians 15:43,44).

Some have supposed it is possible to have the redemption of the body now through the Spirit. But though it is assured to us, it remains a hope and will not be part of our experience until Jesus comes again (Romans 8:24,25). We are indeed the sons of God now, but "what we will be has not yet been made known" (1 John 3:2). Not until Jesus comes shall we be like Him in His glorified state. In the meantime, we groan in our weakness with the rest of creation, waiting for that day when we shall receive that adoption, that redemption of our bodies (Romans 8:23).

We remain in the weakness of our present bodies, therefore. But the Holy Spirit is with us. Though our experience with Him in the age to come will be beyond anything we know now, He is still with us in person, ready to help us in a real and personal way. Though Paul does not call the Spirit the Counselor, the Paraclete, he certainly sees the Spirit as our Helper here. He is right here to help us in our weakness. In our weakness we often do not understand ourselves or our needs. We want to do God's will, but we do not even know how to pray as we should. Then the Spirit comes to our aid and makes intercession for us (instead of us) with groanings too deep for words (vv. 26,27).

These groanings are not expressed in words, not even in tongues (though the Spirit might well be interceding in these inexpressible groans while we are speaking in tongues or while we are praying or praising God). But they do not need to be expressed in words. The same God, the same Heavenly Father who knows what is in our hearts also knows what is in the mind of the Spirit. So there is perfect communication between the Father and the Holy Spirit without the necessity of words. Moreover, the Holy Spirit knows what the will of God is, so we can be sure that His intercession is according to the will of God. In other words, we can be sure His prayers will be answered. No wonder Paul says that nothing can separate us from the love of God which is in Christ Jesus our Lord.

An Enlightened Conscience

Chapters 9 through 11 of Romans deal with Paul's concern for the Jews who were rejecting Jesus, Jews who had a spirit of slumber instead of the Holy Spirit (11:8). Because Paul turned to the Gentiles in his ministry some supposed he did not care about the Jews any more. But he always went to the Jew first (even in Rome; Acts 28:17). Moreover, he had a deep and continuous concern, as his conscience bore witness in the Holy Spirit (Romans 9:1–3).

This seems to mean his conscience was guided and enlightened by the Holy Spirit, who knows the will of God.[29] Our consciences are never a sufficient guide in themselves. They need the Word. They need the enlightenment of the Spirit if they are to help us. Paul knew by the Word and by the Spirit that God is still concerned over the Jews; so Paul was. Thus, the Holy Spirit also let him know that his conscience was correct and his concern was correct. His concern was more than a fellow feeling for his own people. It came from the love of God.

Spiritual Worship

After showing that God still has mercy for both Jews and Gentiles who will believe, Paul goes on to give practical guidance for believers. The sacrifices in the temple are no longer needed. Christ has fulfilled them once for all (Hebrews 9:11,12,25–28). But this does not mean we can take it easy or go our own way. God still calls us to present, not slain sacrifices of animals, but living sacrifices, our own bodies (Romans 12:1). Bodies that are holy (separated, dedicated to God and His service) are the only sacrifices now acceptable to Him and are our reasonable service (or spiritual worship). As Peter puts it, we who have come to Christ are living stones built up into a spiritual temple. We are also a holy priesthood offering up spiritual sacrifices to God by Jesus Christ (1 Peter 2:5).[30] This too is the work of the Holy Spirit, for the word *spiritual* here really means caused by, filled with, or corresponding to the Holy Spirit.

The Use of Spiritual Gifts

The following passage (Romans 12:3–8) gives us one of the five lists of spiritual gifts found in the Bible. (See also 1 Corinthians 12:8–10,28,29,30; Ephesians 4:11.) Paul's purpose here, however, is not to give an inclusive list, nor is it to describe the gifts. This was not needed. The Christians in Rome were experiencing these gifts, just as were the other churches. But they needed guidance concerning their use.

The great danger in being used by the Spirit in the ministry of any of His gifts is to begin to imagine there is something special about us because we are being used by the Spirit. It is imperative, therefore, that all believers think "with sober [sensible] judgment" about themselves and their gifts, recognizing that the measure of faith each one has is distributed or assigned by God (Romans 12:3).

When it comes to ministry, we do not have a right to choose what we would like to do or what function we want to fulfill in the Body. "You did not choose me, but I chose you" (John 15:16) refers, not to salvation, but to the choice of the twelve apostles to special training and ministry. No one has a right to decide simply by his own will to be a pastor or missionary. The same is true of the various functions in the Body that are accomplished through spiritual gifts. No one in himself has the faith to prophesy, nor can he develop it or work it up. It has to be given by God. All the glory goes to God, then. We are just members of the body of Christ, all working together, all needing each other, but we "do not all have the same function" (Romans 12:4).

The word "function" has nothing to do with the functions of formal offices today, nor is it limited to officers in the church. The comparison is simply of a human body where different parts of the body have different functions. The representative gifts in this passage are not limited to offices or officers. They are simply illustrative of some of the variety of ministries or services which the Spirit gives through various individuals in the church. Every believer has a measure of faith from God for at least one of these or other similar gifts.

Instead of exalting ourselves we must recognize that the various spiritual gifts *(charismata)* are expressions of God's free grace (unmerited favor) given to us (v. 6). This rules out the slightest thought of any credit being due us for them or for their use, since the faith to exercise them is also from God.[31]

Not only does the gift come through the measure of faith: it must be exercised according to the proportion of faith. This is sometimes understood as "in agreement with the faith" taking "the faith" to be the teachings of the gospel (as in Galatians 1:23). But this is an exception to the normal use of the word *faith*. It is better to give it the same meaning as in Romans 12:3. The most common meaning of *faith* (even when the Greek says "the faith") is an active belief and trust in God, a faith that is the opposite of the unbelief that kept Israel and will keep us from entering God's promises (Hebrews 3:19; 4:1,2). In this case, it is a faith given by God with the power to minister the gift the Spirit gives.[32] Faithfulness is also implied. The prophet has a responsibility to carry out the ministry God gives him. And since the faith comes from God one needs to keep that faith "living, strong, and enlightened by hours of communion with God."[33]

What is said about the prophet's exercising his gift, prophesying (speaking for God) according to the proportion of faith could just as well apply to all the other gifts mentioned. If we step beyond the faith we have into self-effort, we fall. If, like Peter walking on the water, we take our eyes off the Lord and consider the difficult circumstances around us, we will sink. (Prophecy is dealt with more fully in 1 Corinthians chapters 12 through 14.)

"Serving" (Romans 12:7) seems to mean the work of deacons who served in the routine matters of keeping the work going, keeping accounts, ministering aid to the poor, and otherwise helping in the church. They need the Spirit's gift for this work so that it does not become mere perfunctory service, but a real ministry.

The teacher needs to give himself to the gift of teaching. This also means preparation, study, prayer. But the teacher needs the Spirit's gift if he or she is to bring true understanding. Exhortation which includes prophetic encouragement needs the Spirit's gift if it is to challenge the heart, the conscience, and the will. (See 1 Corinthians 14:3, where exhortation is included in the gift of prophecy, but is here considered separately.)

The remaining gifts may not seem so supernatural, but actually, they are. Giving needs to be done with simplicity (with a single-minded motive), in the manner of Barnabas, not that of Ananias and Sapphira (Acts 4:36,37; 5:1–3). Barnabas, you remember, was full of the Holy Spirit, while Ananias lied to the Holy Spirit. Some give because others give. Some give hoping for something in return. But the giving that pleases God and blesses the Church is the giving that comes because God has put it in your heart to give and the Spirit's gift of giving keeps your motives pure. As you follow the Spirit's leadings in this gift, He will use you to meet specific needs and will enable you to do more and more.

"Leadership" has to do with any kind of administration or oversight, any presiding or superintendency. This needs to be done with diligence, earnest devotion, good will, and spiritual zeal or enthusiasm. Natural ability, human skill, and specific education and training may be useful in any such position. But they are never enough for the work of God. The Spirit's gift makes the difference.

"Showing mercy" or doing acts of mercy such as personally taking care of the sick or scrubbing their floors, taking help to the needy, visiting those in prison may seem to be the natural realm. But not everyone can do them and be a blessing. They need to be done with cheerfulness, that is, not out of compulsion, not out of a sense of duty, but because the Spirit's gift in your heart makes you feel glad to do them.

It is not enough to have gifts, then. The motive, the love, the zeal, the state of the heart and mind of the person who exercises the gift is Paul's chief concern. He goes on, without making any sharp distinction, to exhort us that our love be without hypocrisy, that we abhor the evil and cling to the good, that we have strong affection toward one another with brotherly love, that we give higher honor to others than to ourselves. When earnestness or zeal is needed we should never be reluctant or lazy. Rather, we should be fervent (boiling, burning, aglow) with the Spirit,[34] serving the Lord, obeying Him as our Master (Romans 12:9–13).

The Spirit and the Kingdom

There are only a few more brief references to the Holy Spirit in the Book of Romans. The next one is very significant with regard to the nature of the Kingdom. Paul has very little to say about the kingdom of God in his epistles, probably because the kingdom (rule, reign) of God is active in this age primarily through the Holy Spirit. But the work of the Spirit in preparing for the coming age and in bringing in the coming age is very much in view.

Many take this verse (14:17) to mean that God's kingdom has to do basically with spiritual realities and is not much concerned about material things.[35] The point of the verse, however, is related to Paul's concern that we show love toward the weaker brother who might be caused to stumble by our freedom to eat or drink things he feels he cannot. We must be careful not to let these things become an issue. The things that show we are under the rule or kingdom of God, the things that show God is really King of our lives are not what we eat or drink. They are "righteousness, peace and joy in the Holy Spirit" (v. 17). Eating meat offered to idols was the problem then. Now it may be other things. But we do not show that Christ reigns within by insisting on our rights and freedoms.

Actually, the righteousness, peace, and joy are all ours in and through the Holy Spirit. He helps us to stand by faith in Christ's righteousness. He helps us win victories over sin, giving us power to yield ourselves to God in obedience and faithful service. He gives us power to live out our salvation in a fullness of peace and spiritual well-being. He gives us joy that breaks out in positive rejoicing and praise to God even in the midst of persecution or suffering (Matthew 5:10–13). His strength, His joy made Paul and Silas sing praises to God from the inner dungeon of the Philippian jail (Acts 16:25). Paul at the time of writing to the Romans was expecting to come to them in peace (Romans 1:10). He did not know he had an arrest, trials, two years of imprisonment in Caesarea, and a shipwreck ahead before he would reach Rome. He had been through such things before (2 Corinthians 11:23–28). But he did not break under them. The Spirit continued to reveal Christ in and through all these experiences and he could still rejoice.[36]

Paul, then, in Romans 14:17 is not saying that "righteousness, peace, and joy in the Holy Spirit" are all there is to the Kingdom. He looked ahead to the future age. In fact, these blessings are blessings of the future Kingdom. But, through the Spirit, they are our present possession as well. By the gifts and fruit of the Spirit the Kingdom has its present manifestation in the Church.

Paul goes on to show that this present manifestation of the Kingdom only increased his anticipation of his future hope. His prayer is that in view of God's promises concerning Christ, the God of hope will fill all the Christians "with all joy and peace as you trust in him, so that you may overflow with hope by the [mighty, supernatural] power of the Holy Spirit" (15:13). Again, this joy and peace is not negative or hidden but is a powerful accompaniment and expression of our believing.

Paul found this power and joy expressed especially in connection with the ministry God gave him to the Gentiles. He compares this ministry to a priesthood where he offers the Gentile converts as an acceptable offering to the Lord. His enemies among the Jews and Judaizers said the Gentiles who did not keep the Law were unclean (Acts 10:14,15,28,34; 11:3). But

Paul presented them as "an offering acceptable to God, sanctified [made holy] by the Holy Spirit" (Romans 15:16).

The success of his mission to the Gentiles was not the result of his own efforts. He did work hard, not only in preaching, but also in the tentmaking by which he supported the whole evangelistic party. But it was the work of Christ through mighty miracles and signs and the power of the Holy Spirit that brought in the Gentiles and made them obedient to the gospel (vv. 18,19).

Finally, Paul asked the Romans to strive along with him in prayer through the Lord Jesus Christ and through the love inspired by the Spirit. They did not know Paul, but they did know Jesus. They had no opportunity to learn to love Paul, but love for him could be created by the Spirit so they could pray with real concern (v. 30).

Each of Paul's requests was fulfilled, but not in the way he expected or hoped for. He was delivered from unbelieving Jews who were trying to kill him and from more than forty Jews who took an oath not to eat or drink until they had killed him (Acts 21:31,32; 23:12–24). The journey to Rome brought more victories and deliverances. In Rome, even with Paul a prisoner, the gospel spread. Thus, though the prayers of the Romans were inspired by love through the Spirit, the Holy Spirit knew better than they, better than Paul, what the will of God was. Yet Paul was not disappointed. He just kept on living in the Spirit and by the Spirit. Then the Spirit just kept making Jesus real in his life and ministry.

The Spirit
in the Ministry of
Believers

From the beginning of 1 Corinthians, Paul drew attention to the gifts of the Spirit. He thanked God for the grace given to the believers by Christ Jesus, that in everything they were enriched by Him, especially in the two gifts highly prized by the Greeks, speaking and knowledge (1:5). In fact, the testimony of Christ was confirmed in them so that they were lacking in no spiritual gift *(charismata)* (v. 7).

But Paul was just as concerned about the fruit of the Spirit. He reminded them that Christ would "keep [them] strong to the end, so that [they] will be blameless on the day of our Lord Jesus Christ [when it comes and when we stand before His judgment seat]" (v. 8; Romans 14:10; 2 Corinthians 5:10). Paul came back to the matter of spiritual gifts in chapters 12 through 14. But he found it necessary in the first eleven chapters to give most of his attention to problems arising from a deficiency of the fruit of the Spirit.

The chief problem had to do with divisions and contentions in the Body that came from the sinful nature, not the Spirit. Christians were using personal preferences for Paul, Apollos, or Cephas (Peter) as a basis for setting up what almost amounted to political parties. Some were even considering themselves superior to the others and calling themselves the Christ party. By these divisions they were breaking up the spiritual fellowship of the church and stirring up strife.

Paul's concern over the fellowship and unity of the body of Christ runs through the entire epistle. He dealt with the divisions first by showing that they had come from a failure to take in the full meaning of the Cross. Second, he showed that he and Apollos are fellow laborers with the Lord. They are servants who belong to the people. But the people belong to Christ (1 Corinthians 3:22,23).

The failure to take in the meaning of the Cross came because they were still looking at spiritual things from the standpoint of human reason. The Corinthians, as Greeks, had a background of seeking for and exalting wisdom, but it was a human wisdom, the result of human deductions, the application of human philosophies. Because of their love for this wisdom, they had looked at the Cross as foolishness (before they found the reality of Christ through Paul's preaching; 1:18).

But even though they had accepted the Christ of the Cross, they still did not see the Cross in the fullness of its meaning as an expression of divine wisdom and as an example of love and humility. Nor had they left behind their tendencies to interpret everything in the light of what man calls wisdom. To each of the groups that were forming in the church, their loyalty to a particular teacher seemed logical. Those who claimed they were holding to Paul probably felt it was right and wise to be loyal to the founder of the church. Those who held to Apollos probably argued that his knowledge of the Bible had done much to teach the Church and that his eloquence had caused it to move forward (Acts 18:25,27).[1] Those who took Peter's name as their banner probably said they were honoring him as one of the original apostles.

It was all reasonable, logical. But it was in the spirit of Peter when he wanted to build three shelters on the Mount of Transfiguration. Suddenly a bright cloud cut off the revelation and a voice said, "This is my Son, whom I love; with him I am well pleased. Listen to him!" (Matthew 17:3–5). The Corinthians needed to get a new vision of Christ crucified, Christ the power of God, Christ the wisdom of God (1 Corinthians 1:24).

The Wisdom of God

To help correct the Corinthians' dependence on human wisdom Paul contrasts the wisdom of God with the wisdom of men. He reminds them that his own speech and preaching "were not with wise and persuasive words [of man's natural wisdom], but with a demonstration [convincing proof] of the Spirit's [mighty] power" (2:4). What Paul brought them was not just another teaching, not just another philosophy, not just some human ideas to argue about. They had already had enough of those in their heathen condition. He took them into the laboratory of the Holy Spirit and showed them the power of God. He encouraged them to step out in the same mighty power that their faith might stand in that power (including the gifts of the Spirit).[2]

The work of God was a mystery, in the sense that it was not revealed in its fullness before the Cross, and also in the sense that men were not able to figure it out by their human wisdom or powers of reasoning. If they had been able to do so, "they would not have crucified the Lord of glory" (v. 8).

Paul explained this by a free paraphrase which gives the sense of Isaiah 64:4 (in the light of Isaiah 52:15). "No eye has seen, no ear has heard, no mind [including the imagination] has conceived what God has prepared for those who love him" (1 Corinthians 2:9). The things God has prepared here are not primarily the glories of heaven but the glories of the Cross and all it means in the plan of God. They include what we are already enjoying through the Spirit.

The meaning of the Cross in relationship to the Christian life in the present and the life to come cannot be understood by the natural mind. But we as Christians are not left in the dark. God has revealed His whole plan to us by His Spirit. This, of course, we now have recorded in the New Testament, but Paul indicates we share in the same revelation in the sense that the Spirit illuminates and explains these truths to our hearts.

We can have confidence in what the Spirit makes real to us because the Spirit really knows what is in the heart of God for us.

He "searches [penetrates] all things, even the deep things of God" (v. 10). Think of all the contradictory things human philosophies say about the nature of God. The human mind simply cannot penetrate the depths. But the Spirit can.

Paul illustrated what the Spirit does by comparing Him with a man's human spirit. No one knows what a man is really thinking, but his own spirit knows what is going on inside him (v. 11). So no one by human wisdom trying to look at God can figure out what is going on in the mind of God. But the Spirit of God knows. We cannot, of course, press this analogy too far. The Holy Spirit's relationship with God the Father is not exactly like our spirit's relationship with us, for the Holy Spirit is a distinct Person from the Father. But He knows God from the inside. He is thus able to reveal correctly what God's thoughts and purposes are.[3]

What we receive through the Spirit is not like the spirit of the world. Its great thinkers may be geniuses. But they can only guess about the things that really count. We do not need to guess or imagine what is in the mind of God, for the Holy Spirit which we have received is of God "that we may understand what God has freely given us" (v. 12). Paul included his readers here. The same certainty of truth that Paul received from the Holy Spirit is available to every believer.[4]

To show further the difference between earthly and heavenly wisdom Paul said he did not use "words taught us by human wisdom but in words taught by the Spirit, expressing spiritual truths in spiritual words" (v. 13). That is, Paul did not use the kind of rhetoric, logic, or deductive thinking that characterized human wisdom. He did not start from the standpoint of human wisdom and try to move toward the spiritual, going from the known to the unknown. He simply presented what the Holy Spirit teaches, including what the Holy Spirit brings from the Old Testament and the teaching of Jesus. (An examination of Paul's sermons in the Book of Acts shows how much the Spirit used the Old Testament. See Acts 13:17–42.)[5]

The phrase "expressing spiritual truths in spiritual words" (1 Corinthians 2:13) is a difficult one to interpret. Some take it, "explaining spiritual truths to spiritual people." Others, "comparing spiritual gifts and revelations we already have with those we receive and judging the new by the old." Still others read, "bringing together spiritual truths in a spiritual form." The Greek is not conclusive. In verse 6, Paul did say he spoke the wisdom of God among them that are perfect (mature), which seems to mean those who are spiritual, filled with and guided by the Spirit. Verses 14 and 15 go on to compare the natural man and the spiritual man. This would fit in with the first explanation given above. But in verse 13 itself Paul compared the words of man's wisdom with the words the Holy Spirit teaches. This points to the third interpretation concerning spiritual truths. Perhaps this is one of those cases where two meanings are possible because Paul meant both.

What the Holy Spirit teaches does not satisfy the natural (or unspiritual) man who is oriented only to the things of this world. He does not receive the things of the Spirit of God, for "they are foolishness [silly] to him" (v. 14). He just has no way to grasp their true meaning because they must be "discerned" (examined and judged) in the light given by the Holy Spirit. (Discerned is the same verb translated "makes judgments" in verse 15 and "examined" in Acts 17:11 where the Bereans searched the Scriptures.)

In contrast to the natural, worldly-minded man, "the spiritual man makes judgments about [and examines] all things, but he himself is not subject to any man's judgment [and examination]" (1 Corinthians 2:15). We do not need to submit what we learn from the Spirit to the inspection and judgment of the wise men of this world. In all their wisdom, they do not know the mind of the Lord. They might want to instruct us. But they are surely presumptuous if they think they are going to instruct God. That is really what they are trying to do when they try to evaluate the Bible as if it were a merely human document like Shakespeare's plays. But the Christian has the mind of Christ. That is, he has the fullness of the revelation of God given in Christ. The Holy

Spirit reveals Christ and enables us to see spiritual things from the divine point of view.

We probably should not limit verse 15 to spiritual or even religious things, however. The "all things" may mean that the person who is filled and led by the Spirit can judge and evaluate everything. The Bible does not draw a line between the sacred and the secular in this respect. God is as much concerned about the wonders of nature and the glories of the stars as He is about heaven itself. He is in control of kingdoms and nations and is working out His purposes in the world of men (without destroying their free will) just as much as in the Church. The person led and illuminated by the Spirit sees everything from a completely different perspective than does the unspiritual person of the world.[6]

Living Like Ordinary People

The real problem of the Corinthians was not primarily intellectual, however. It was moral. Paul said that even when he was present with them, he could not speak to them "as spiritual [truly Spirit-led] but as worldly [dominated by the weaknesses of the sinful nature]—mere infants in Christ" (3:1). They had gifts, but had not developed the fruit or the maturity available through the Spirit.

Their carnality was shown by works of the flesh, chiefly in envying, strife, and divisions, so that they walked "like mere men [i.e., people]" (v. 3). That is, they were living, acting, and arguing like ordinary men, instead of like spiritual men. They were following the desires of the flesh and the mind just as much as the heathen around them. They expressed their ideas in a different realm, perhaps, since they talked about teachers and apostles. But their attitudes and motivations were the same. They needed to recognize there was a judgment day coming (v. 13). The fires of that judgment would reveal the character of their works and leave them without reward.

The seriousness of these works of the sinful nature is seen in the light of the fact that God wants a unity in His holy temple (in this case, looked at as the local church). Paul implies in verses 16 and 17) that they did indeed know they were (as a local body) the temple (sanctuary, Holy of Holies) of God, and that the Spirit was dwelling in them (in and among the Body, not just in the individuals here). In the light of the holiness of God's Spirit-filled temple, then, God must destroy anyone who destroys this temple. The Church as a body is holy, set apart for His use, sanctified by the presence of the Holy Spirit. (See 2 Peter 2:9,10,12, where eternal judgment is reserved for such destroyers.)

Let us not forget, then, that the destroying of the temple was being done by their human wisdom which was not giving the Lord the right place, but was glorifying humanity. Such thoughts were wise in this world's way of thinking. All great people of this world do everything they can to gain a following. It may be that those who were promoting these divisions were really trying to find a way to exalt themselves and their own leadership. But we do not need to exalt ourselves. We belong to Christ. We are already seated together in heavenly places in Christ "far above all rule and authority, power and dominion, and every title that can be given, not only in the present age but also in the one to come" (Ephesians 1:21; 2:6). Nothing we can do can give us a better position than that. Therefore, we can afford to take the humble place and serve one another in love wherever the Lord puts us.

More Works of the Sinful Nature

The carnality in the Corinthian church was not limited to strife and division. Paul dealt with that first because it was doing the most damage. There was also sexual immorality among them (1 Corinthians 5:1). They were tolerating among them a man involved in a sin that even the heathen around them considered shameful. The Christians were saying nothing to this man, partly because of their background and possibly partly because of false doctrine. Corinth was noted as a lewd and immoral city. But it is possible that false teachers were claiming liberty in Christ to do anything they felt like doing. Paul gave them his judgment that the man be disfellowshipped and turned over to the realm of Satan (for discipline, v. 5). The idea is probably that sickness might come and cause the man to repent and seek both healing and forgiveness (James 5:15).

Paul went on to warn the whole church against the works of the sinful nature. As in Galatians, he emphasized that those who practice these things will not inherit the kingdom of God. But with the Corinthians, he was a little more specific about naming things common in Corinth, such as homosexuality and extortion (1 Corinthians 6:9,10).

He does not say that the situation of those who commit these sins is hopeless, however. Instead, he says, "That is what some of you were. But you were washed [from your sins, through the cleansing of the blood of Jesus], you were sanctified [dedicated to God and His service], you were justified [acquitted from your sin and guilt and freed from the fear of judgment] in the name of the Lord Jesus Christ and by the Spirit of our God" (v. 11). What the Lord had done for them, He could do for the worst of sinners.

The Lord for the Body

Two more things Paul emphasized in this connection. One is that sin enslaves. Even things that are not sinful in themselves can enslave us. Paul did not intend to make Christian liberty an excuse for letting oneself be enslaved by anything. The other point is that sexual immorality is not natural for the human body. The heathen considered immorality such as adultery, prostitution, and homosexuality simply "doing what comes naturally." But Paul denied that these things are really in line with the nature of our bodies (including the human personalities that go with our bodies). Our bodies are not evil in themselves. The body is not meant for immorality but for the Lord, "and the Lord for the body" (v. 13).

Some take the statement in the Bible that precedes this ("Food for the stomach, and the stomach for food") to be a parallel in the temporary realm of the present. Just as the stomach needs food to carry out what it was created to do, so the body needs the Lord if it is to carry out the service it was created for. (See Philippians 1:20, where Paul is concerned that Christ be magnified or glorified in his body, whether by life or by death.)[7]

The fact that God is truly concerned about our body and is "for" our body is further shown by His raising up Jesus from the dead, which means He will also raise us up by His own power (1 Corinthians 6:14). Thus, the body will still have a place in God's purposes—or He would not bother to resurrect it. (See 15:35.)

In view of the Lord's concern for the body, we must therefore not suppose it is just our spirits that are members of Christ. Our bodies also are members of His body. How then can a Christian take a body that is Christ's and join it to the body of a prostitute, making the body of Christ one flesh with a sexually immoral person (6:15)?[8] The argument against immorality is made even stronger by recognizing that we who are joined to the Lord are one spirit with Him. Our bodies and our personalities, controlled by the Holy Spirit, are united with Him in the Spirit. In fact, our union in the Spirit is closer than the union of a husband and wife in the natural.

Immorality is also not only a sin against the Lord; it is a sin against our own bodies. We must flee from every sort of sexual sin for the body of each Christian is individually a temple of the Holy Spirit. Thus, these sins are totally contrary to the nature of Christ's body as well as to the nature of the Holy Spirit who dwells in the temple. We have the Holy Spirit from God. This makes the temple of the body belong to God, so that we are not our own. We are doubly not our own because we are bought with a price (1 Peter 1:18,19, "the precious blood of Christ"). We have no right to use our bodies or our lives for the gratification of the flesh or the exaltation of self.

Both our bodies and our spirits belong to the Lord. Therefore, our object should be to use them both to glorify God (1 Corinthians 6:20). This again means we must take care of the body. But we are not to use this as an excuse for catering to the impulses and desires that come from the lower nature. Even legitimate pleasure must not become our reason for living. We have something more wonderful to do as we glorify God in service and sacrifice.[9]

I Also Have the Spirit

Chapters 7 through 11 of 1 Corinthians deal with a variety of other questions and problems, with only a few brief allusions to the Spirit and His work. After giving his judgment on certain questions concerning marriage, Paul said, "I think that I too have the Spirit of God" (7:40). He had already stated he had the Spirit. Some take it that he did not have an actual saying of Jesus about this matter, but that he indeed had the Spirit of God. Others take it as irony, with Paul saying that he too could say he had the Spirit just as much as (and more than) any of his enemies who opposed his teaching.[10]

While dealing with Christian liberty Paul reminded us that knowledge only puffs up, but love edifies (builds up). Knowledge, probably meaning knowledge as it is developed by our human reason, even though we may begin with or be dealing with spiritual truths may cause a person to put on airs. Without love it breeds pride, arrogance, conceit, and the kind of clever answers that humiliate others. But love honors God and man and promotes the good of all (8:1). This love is first of all a love for God that comes because He loves us. By it we are known (acknowledged) by God (v. 3). The love that builds up and edifies is, of course, the fruit of the Spirit.

One other note (11:4,5) will be considered further later. While talking about customs in the churches, Paul made it clear that men and women were equally free to pray and prophesy (publicly, that is, in the congregation).[11]

Understanding Needed

Paul begins the great passage on spiritual gifts (1 Corinthians 12 through 14) by saying, "Now about spiritual gifts, brothers, I do not want you to be ignorant" (12:1). By this, he did not mean they were totally ignorant of the gifts. He had already said they were not lacking or deficient in any gift (1:7). He meant he wanted them to know the gifts in the sense of having some real understanding of both the gifts and their use.

In a sense, Paul was not really changing the subject. Even in this discussion of the gifts of the Spirit, he was still primarily concerned with the fruit of the Spirit. First Corinthians 12 does little more than list the gifts. There is no systematic classification, no detailed description of the individual gifts, no discussion of their nature, no examples given by which we might better identify them. The problem at Corinth was not the gifts themselves but the way they were being used. The gifts are supernatural and from God. Paul never questioned their gifts. There was nothing wrong with the gifts as such. But they were being used wrongly.[12] This is the reason for the emphasis on love in chapter 13 and for the detailed discussion on how to use tongues and prophecy in love found in chapter 14.

Paul recognized that the Holy Spirit was active in the church through the gifts. But his chief purpose was still to deal with the division and strife caused by their carnality and immaturity. As "mere infants in Christ" (3:1) the same lack of the fruit of the Spirit that made them fail to "recogniz[e] the body of the Lord" in their fellow believers (11:29; 10:17; 11:21,33,34), made them exercise the gifts of the Spirit without recognizing the unity of the body of Christ.

Many of them apparently felt that the gift was theirs to use as they pleased. Others may have been exalting one gift as more important than others. Still others may have failed to recognize the necessity and interdependence of all the gifts. Some may have gone in the other direction and felt that certain gifts were completely unnecessary.

This may seem strange today to some who persist "in imagining that those who enjoyed these supernatural gifts of the Spirit were models of perfect holiness and spiritual maturity."[13] It must be remembered that fruit is something that grows, that must be encouraged, that takes time to develop. It must be kept in mind also that these Corinthians did not have the good background in morals and in the Scripture that men like the apostle Paul had. God always begins where people are, gives them as much as their faith is able to receive, and leads them on.

What God gives is always truly a gift. We shall one day have our reward. At the judgment seat of Christ, we shall be judged on the basis of our works (2 Corinthians 5:10). But now a gift is a free gift. It would not be a gift if there were any good works necessary as a prior requirement for receiving it. People have a tendency to forget that the gifts of the Spirit must be received on the same basis as the gift of the Spirit and the gift of salvation. "It is by grace you have been saved, through faith—and this not from yourselves, it is the gift of God—not by works, so that no one can boast" (Ephesians 2:8,9). When the lame man at the Gate Beautiful was healed, the people began to give their attention to Peter and John in awestruck amazement. Peter had to rebuke them, "Why do you stare at us as if by our own power or godliness we had made this man walk?" (Acts 3:12).[14]

That the gifts of the Spirit are by grace through faith is implied also by the most common Greek word used to describe these gifts. They are *charismata*, "freely and graciously given gifts," a word derived from *charis*, "grace, the unmerited favor of God." *Charismata* are gifts given us in spite of the fact that we do not deserve them. They bear witness to the goodness of God, not the goodness of those who receive them.

A common fallacy that often leads people astray is the idea that because God blesses or uses a person, this means He is putting His approval on everything else the person does or teaches. Even when there seems to be "anointing," this is not guaranteed. When Apollos first came to Ephesus, he was not only eloquent and biblical in his preaching; he "spoke with great fervor [boiling]" (Acts 18:25). He had the fire. But Priscilla and Aquila saw something was missing. So they took him aside (probably home to dinner), and explained the way of God more accurately (v. 26).

It is the way of God with respect to the gifts, then, that Paul, as a spiritual father, wanted to explain more accurately to the Corinthian believers. He called these gifts in 1 Corinthians 12:1 just "spirituals" (the word "gifts" is not in the Greek). The word by itself might include other things directed by the Holy Spirit and expressed through Spirit-filled believers. But in this passage Paul is clearly limiting the word to mean the free gracious gifts or *charismata* which are mentioned again and again (vv. 4,9,28, 30,31; 14:1). All the early Christian writers took the word *spirituals* as "spiritual gifts," therefore, recognizing them to be supernatural gifts with the Holy Spirit as their immediate source.[15]

A Variety of Gifts

In chapter 12, Paul gives three lists of gifts. The first (vv. 8–10) lists nine gifts, which are probably classes of gifts, each with a variety of ways in which it can be manifested. The second list (v. 28) gives eight gifts including people used in ministry. Three of these gifts are not mentioned in the first list. The third list (vv. 29,30) lists seven gifts with elements taken from both of the previous lists.

Many consider the first list of nine gifts as complete and comprehensive. This means that the other gifts listed elsewhere must be taken as expressions or interweavings of these gifts ("the message of wisdom," "the message of knowledge," "faith," "gifts of healing," "miraculous powers," "prophecy," "distinguishing between spirits," "speaking in different kinds of tongues," "the interpretation of tongues," vv. 8–10). One writer states that "every supernatural happening in the Bible or out of it, except of course counterfeit miracles of satanic origin, must be included in the sweep of the Nine Supernatural Gifts."[16] But Paul did not say even of these nine gifts, "These are the gifts of the Spirit." He simply goes down the list saying, here is a gift given by the Spirit, then another by the same Spirit, and another by the same Spirit. The emphasis is on the fact that all come from the one Holy Spirit, not that all the gifts are being named.

It seems better to take all of these lists as merely giving samplings of the gifts and callings of the Spirit, samplings taken from an infinite supply. How can there be any limit to the abundance of His gifts that are available for the fellowship, life, and work of the Church? Paul seemed to be more concerned with their variety than with any kind of classifying or categorizing. He did not give them all in the same order in the various lists. Frequently, he mentioned what we might consider entirely different sorts or classes of gifts, putting them together without any distinction. Whatever the need of the Church, the Spirit has some gift to meet it.

By combining these lists with the lists in Romans 12:6–8 and Ephesians 4:11 in various ways, it is possible to come up with a total of eighteen to twenty gifts.[17] But some of these gifts overlap. Romans 12 lists exhortation as a distinct gift. In 1 Corinthians 14:3 it is included as a function of prophecy. Ephesians 4:11 seems to include the pastor and teacher together as one. There are probably many other interrelations.

Honoring Jesus

Before listing the gifts, Paul drew attention to the fact that the Holy Spirit will always glorify Jesus (1 Corinthian12:3). We have seen that Paul always kept Christ central in his ministry. He was led of the Spirit to do this, for the Holy Spirit wants to honor Jesus. Jesus is the living Word. He came to unfold God and His ways to us (John 1:14,18). Now Jesus has gone back to heaven, but the Holy Spirit still makes Him God's living Word to us. What a contrast this is to the former state of these Corinthian believers who were once led astray by dumb idols, mere nothings that had no meaning, no word for them (1 Corinthian12:2). This ultimate lack of meaning is true of everything outside of Christ.

The word the Holy Spirit gives can thus be tested by the fact that He always recognizes Jesus as the divine Lord exalted above every other power and authority, real or imaginary, that men recognize. He is King of kings and Lord of lords (8:5,6; 15:24,

25; Philippians 2:9–11; Romans 14:9). On the other hand, no one speaking by the Spirit will ever say, "Jesus be cursed!" (1 Corinthian 12:3). Some take this curse to be the utterance of a demon spirit. Others think it was said by false teachers who in the spirit of Antichrist were making a difference between the man Jesus and the spiritual Christ. (See 1 John 4:2,3.)[18] Still others believe it was from ignorant or unlearned listeners who misunderstood Paul's teaching about Christ being made a curse for us (Galatians 3:13).[19]

Not only does the Holy Spirit exalt Jesus: no one can truly say "Jesus is Lord!" (1 Corinthian 12:3) except by the Holy Spirit. Anyone can say the words, of course. But they will be empty, meaningless, unless the Holy Spirit personally makes Jesus the divine Lord in our lives as we respond to Him. ("Lord" is the common title applied by the Jews to God.) Thus, in all our witnessing we need the illumination, anointing, and gifts of the Spirit. It is the Spirit who gives wisdom and who applies the truth to hearts (Ephesians 1:17).

There is encouragement here for us also. We need never be afraid to seek the Holy Spirit and His gifts. Yielding to Him will never lead us astray, for He will always exalt Jesus and honor His Lordship. The exercise of the gifts of the Spirit becomes an opportunity to bring honor to Jesus.

Keeping Jesus central, then, will help us see the wonderful unity that runs through all the variety of spiritual gifts. This unity is seen also in the way the entire Trinity cooperates to bring all the diversity of the gifts into a beautiful harmony of expression (1 Corinthian 12:4–6).

The variety is always needed, and the Corinthians had it. But because of their strife and division they were running off in all directions, so that the gifts did not bring the profit and use to the church that God intended. They needed to see the harmony and cooperation of the Trinity at the very source of the gifts.

Paul speaks first of the Spirit as the One who directs the operation of the gifts in our lives (see v. 11). Then, he speaks of the

Lord (Jesus), by whose authority the Holy Spirit works in the world today; then of God the Father, who is the ultimate Giver of every good and perfect gift (James 1:17).

Three different terms are used of these gifts as Paul refers to them in their variety of expression and distribution (1 Corinthians 12:4,5). There are varieties of gifts *(charismata)*, but the same Spirit; varieties of administrations (ministries, ways of service), but the same Lord; and varieties of operations (activities), but the same God who works effectively in everything and in everyone. (See Ephesians 3:20; Colossians 1:29.)

It is evident from this also that God does not give out His grace and gifts in one big deposit. There is no reservoir of these gifts in the Church or in the individual. For each gracious gift we must look to the Source anew. It is also evident that the various gifts involve willing ministry and service on our part. God does not force us to respond in these activities. The gifts of the Spirit are necessary if the Church is to continue the work of Jesus as He intended in this age. But He does not cause us to enter into these ministries against our will. Nor does the Holy Spirit knock us down and make us exercise these gracious gifts or *charismata*. He does not give His gifts to those who do not want them or even to those who are not eager for them. They are too valuable to be wasted.

In fact, the gifts are given with the divine intention that everyone will profit by them (1 Corinthians 12:7). This does not mean that everyone has a specific gift, but there are gifts— manifestations, disclosures, means by which the Spirit makes himself known openly—being given continuously for everyone for the "common good." The word translated "common good" has the idea of something useful, helpful, especially in building the Church, both spiritually and in numbers. (The Book of Acts has a theme of numerical and geographical growth. God wants the gospel spread in all the world.) It might be illustrated by the Parable of the Ten Minas (Luke 19:12–27). The king commanded his servants to put what he gave them to work "until I come back" (v. 13). As we step out in the ministry of His gifts, He helps us to grow in efficiency and effectiveness, just as those did who used what the Master gave them (vv. 15–19).[20]

Given as the Spirit Wills

The first list of gifts with its repetition of the fact that each is given by the same Spirit (1 Corinthians 12:8–10) leads to a climax in verse 11 which says: "All these are the work of one and the same Spirit, and he gives [distributes] them to each one [individually], just as he determines."

There is a parallel here to Hebrews 2:4, which speaks of the apostles who first heard the Lord and passed on the message: "God also testified to it by [supernatural] signs, wonders and various miracles [various kinds of deeds of mighty power], and gifts of the Holy Spirit distributed according to his will."

From these passages it is evident that the Holy Spirit is sovereign in bestowing gifts. They are apportioned according to His will, which is the will of God. We can seek the best gifts, but He is the only One who knows what is really the best in any particular situation. It is evident also that the gifts remain under His power. They really remain His gifts. They never become ours in the sense that we do not need to depend on Him in faith for every expression of them. Nor do they ever become a part of our nature so that we cannot lose them or have them taken from us.[21] The Bible does say the "God's gifts and his call are irrevocable" (i.e., God does not change His mind about them), but this is speaking about Israel (Romans 11:28,29). The principle seems to be, however, that "God's gifts and his call," once given, remain available. Israel did lose much through unbelief, and so can we. But we can also always come back in faith and find the gifts are still there to claim once again.

The sovereign Holy Spirit is himself the same, whether He is called the Holy Spirit, the Spirit of Christ, the Spirit of Jesus, the Spirit of Truth, or the Spirit of God. Thus, the Source is the same no matter what the gift is or who is being used. It is clear, also, that the gifts may be apportioned by Him to a person for more or less regular ministry in some gift or combination of gifts. For example, the lists of gifts include prophets. Or He may apportion the gifts for a brief ministry or a single manifestation of the gift in a particular gathering of the assembly. Thus, the lists include prophecy.

We see also that unity does not mean uniformity. When the Church fails to achieve unity through the operation of the Spirit's gifts in love, an appearance of unity is sometimes obtained by an insistence on uniformity. But the unity the Spirit brings is the unity of a living organism. It retains its variety. It is able to adjust to new situations and meet new opportunities and challenges. It continues to live and grow. Uniformity can sometimes be obtained by human means and human organization. But it is mechanical and superficial. Worse than that, it can be dead.[22] This does not mean, of course, that organization as such is to be shunned. Nothing in nature is more highly organized than a living organism. The Bible teaches organization, not for organization's sake, but to get the job done. On the other hand, if all we have is organization we cannot live or grow in God any more than an automobile can, no matter how fine a piece of machinery it might be.

One Body with Many Members

To illustrate the unity of the working of the Spirit and to show that the gifts of the Spirit are not intended to be used out of relation to the body of Christ, Paul next makes comparisons with the physical body. "The body is a unit, though it is made up of many parts; and though its parts are many, they form one body. So it is with Christ" (1 Corinthians 12:12).

This means that the purpose of the variety is to make it possible for the whole body to function as a unit. The variety is thus not for the advantage of the individual in giving us more things to enjoy. It is rather for the advantage of the Church. In the case of the body of Christ, the comparison is really to the gifts that are manifested through the different members of the Body. So, the various gifts and ministries of the Spirit are as important and necessary to the body of Christ as the parts of the natural body are to us as individuals. God has given no other means to carry out His purposes in this present age. How terrible to let them atrophy through disuse![23]

Unity, the Spirit's Work

The unity of the body of Christ is actually part of the first work of the Holy Spirit. He does not just give us spiritual life and let us go off by ourselves. He baptizes us into the body of Christ (1 Corinthians 12:13). He plunges us in, no matter who we are, right along with Jews and Gentiles, slaves and free. Then he makes us all drink (be watered, saturated) with the same Spirit. But not for self-exaltation or rivalry. God's continuing purpose is that we serve and build up the Body.

Verse 13 is interpreted in a variety of ways. One group insists that this is the same as Christ's baptism of the believer into the Holy Spirit. They usually identify this with regeneration through the Spirit and often with water baptism. Or they may say that Pentecost brought a massive deposit of the Spirit into the Church and we get our share automatically when we are baptized into the Church. Others allow for fillings of the Spirit but not baptisms after regeneration. These claim it should be translated, "For in one Spirit also we all were baptized so as to form one body," that is, they make the Spirit the element into which we are baptized at conversion.[24] The argument for this translation is that "by" one Spirit should be "in" one Spirit. They argue that the Greek word *en* always means "in" when it is used with the word baptize.[25]

This is true of the six cases that compare John's baptism in water with Jesus' baptism in the Holy Spirit. But, in spite of the fact that most traditional scholars identify verse 13 with water baptism, we must recognize that a believer should already be part of the spiritual body of Christ if water baptism is to be a meaningful testimony. Thus, the baptism into the Body cannot be identified with water baptism.

Moreover, the word *en* often does mean "by." In some cases it is used with the Holy Spirit to mean "by the Holy Spirit." Luke 4:1 uses it of Jesus led by the Spirit into the wilderness. Mark 1:12 confirms emphatically that the Spirit was indeed the agent. Luke 2:27 is a similar case: "moved by the Spirit." Ephesians 3:5 is also: "revealed by the Spirit."

Though many feel that the evidence is not conclusive or that the translation is just a matter of choice, the context really is clear. An examination of the whole passage in 1 Corinthians 12 gives a firm backing for the translation "by one Spirit."

The entire preceding passage emphasizes the unity of the Body by the fact that the various gifts are given by the one and the same Spirit. The Spirit is the one who is the agent giving the gifts. In verses 8 and 9, the word *en* is used interchangeably with the word *dia,* meaning "through." Whether by the Spirit or through the Spirit, the Spirit is clearly the agent.[26] The baptism in verse 13 is thus very definitely by the Spirit into the body of Christ and is therefore distinct from the baptism by Christ into the Holy Spirit on the Day of Pentecost. This fits in well with the distinction between conversion and the baptism in the Holy Spirit found in the Book of Acts.

Holdcroft suggests that there are actually at least four choices held by Bible-believing scholars. One is that "the believer's total experience with the Holy Spirit is His role to baptize him into the body of Christ." This is sometimes taught by default and sometimes by design. A second group believes that "being placed in the body of Christ is the only experience of Spirit baptism, and although there is a subsequent filling with the Spirit it is not called baptism. This is the position of Merrill Unger, Samuel Ridout, Kenneth Wuest, and many others." A third group distinguishes between the baptism by the Spirit into the body and the baptism by Christ into the Spirit for service. "This is the position of Jasper Huffman, John R. Rice, R. A. Torrey, René Pache, and many others." A fourth group includes Pentecostals who distinguish between the two baptisms and the evidence for the second baptism is speaking in other tongues. "It has been expounded by R. M. Riggs, E. S. Williams, Donald Gee, P. C. Nelson, Myer Pearlman," and many others.

Holdcroft goes on to suggest that the rejection of the Pentecostal position often leads to a downward trend that ends in the neglect of the work of the Spirit in the believer's life. Thus, "quite apart from the issue of tongues, it is clearly of manifest spiritual importance to enjoy a meaningful, personal baptism with the Spirit."[27]

Only One Body

Coming back to the chief emphasis of 1 Corinthians 12:13, we see that with all the variety in the Body there is still only one Spirit and one Body. If a person is in Christ at all, he is part of the Body even if he thinks he is now a member of some Apollos party, Cephas party, or even Christ party. Obviously, any church or denomination that begins to say it is the only one is sidetracked in its thinking. But even these are still part of the Body, if they have been born again by the Spirit.

Paul compared this, further, with the human body (vv. 14–20). The foot cannot say it is not of the body because it is not the hand. Nor can the ear say it is not of the body because it is not the eye. If every part of the body had the same function, if it were all a big eye or a big ear, it would not be a body and would not be able to function. Thus, a church where everyone had the same gift or ministry would be a monstrosity, not a functioning body of Christ.

Carrying the analogy further, Paul emphasized the interdependence of the human body. There are indeed many members, but still one body, each part in need of the other. The eye cannot say it does not need the hand, nor the head the feet. Even the parts of the body that seem to be weaker or less important are necessary. God has so formed and unified the members of our bodies that they work together in perfect harmony and interdependence. When one part of the body hurts, our whole body (and person) is concerned about it. When one part is honored, the whole body rejoices. The same thing should be true of the body of Christ and its individual members (v. 27).

Just as God formed the human body in such a way as to bring unity and harmony, so "in the church God has appointed first of all apostles, second prophets, third teachers, then workers of miracles [deeds of mighty power], also those having gifts of healing, those able to help others, those with gifts of administration, and those speaking in different kinds of tongues" (v. 28).

Some take the enumeration here to be in order of value, so that prophets and teachers are more important than miracles, and apostles most important of all.[28] If this is so, we should still remember that every member of the Body is both necessary and important. Even the last named, the gift of tongues, if it is less important it is still necessary just as is the ministry of apostles, prophets, and teachers. In fact, since it is easy to see the importance of the apostles, more attention should be given to honoring the last four of the list, which are really grouped together.

Others take it that the order is chronological. Jesus appointed the apostles as primary witnesses of His resurrection and His teachings. Next, prophets and teachers were given to build up the Body so they could all share in the ministries and gifts of the Spirit. Then the rest of the gifts and ministries were distributed among them. But this cannot be pressed too far. Many take this as a listing without any thought of precedence, since Paul's concern is still about the unity and variety necessary in the Body.

Paul, in fact, went on to ask, "Are all apostles? Are all prophets? Are all teachers? Do all work miracles? Do all have gifts of healing? Do all speak in tongues ? Do all interpret?" (vv. 29,30). These questions are stated in such a way as to call for the answer, "No!" God has purposely given different gifts and ministries to different people. He wants us to realize we need each other. The Church as a body should not be satisfied with merely the first gifts. The Holy Spirit wants to use every member and bring in all the variety that will build up the Church in unity.

There is no intention here of setting up sharp distinctions between clergy and laity, either, nor between full-time and part-time ministries. All are working together under the direction of the Holy Spirit as He wills. It is clear that some will be regularly used in particular ministries. Some are prophets, some are teachers. The tense of the verbs used in verse 30 are continuous present. Some do keep on ministering gifts of healings. Some do regularly minister to the Body in various kinds of tongues. Some do regularly interpret these tongues for the congregation. It should be noted here also that since these are talking about regular ministries to the Body, the fact that the questions call for negative answers should not be pressed too far. The fact that all do not have a ministry along the lines of gifts of healing does not mean that God cannot use them occasionally to minister healing to the sick. The fact that all do not have a ministry of tongues does not mean that all could not speak in tongues on occasion or in their private devotions. Nor does it rule out tongues as the initial physical evidence of the baptism in the Spirit according to Acts 2:4.

Paul went go on to challenge the Corinthians to "eagerly desire the greater gifts" (1 Corinthians 12:31), that is, strive for the more valuable spiritual gifts (*charismata)*. This can hardly mean the enumeration given in verse 28. It may refer rather to whatever gifts are most needed and most edifying at the time. The command also reemphasizes the fact that we do not have the gifts automatically just because we have the Spirit. Further steps of faith are needed. In addition, it is clear from this that though we may have a gift or ministry, we need not be limited to the same one forever. The Holy Spirit does apportion the gifts "as He wills," but He does not disregard changing needs. Nor does He violate the integrity of our personalities by forcing a gift on us for which we do not have this earnest desire (v. 31).

The Most Excellent Way

First Corinthians 12, as we have seen, takes people who were coming behind in no spiritual gift and shows them a better way to exercise them. The better way is to appreciate the variety of gifts and use them to promote the unity of the Body. Then Paul wrote; "I will show you the most excellent way" (v. 31). What he means is, "I am about to point out and explain to you an even better way to exercise the gifts." This is the way of love, for love will do everything called for in chapter 12 and more.

This does not mean, however, that love may be substituted for the spiritual gifts. Many say love is a gift of the Spirit.[29] Some even say other spiritual gifts are not needed if we have the supreme gift of love. Love, however, is never called a spiritual gift. God's love is indeed a gift to us. The love of Christ has been given to us. The consciousness of Christ's love is also the work of the Spirit in our hearts (Romans 5:5). But love as a motivating factor in our lives is always a fruit of the Spirit, not a gift of the Spirit. Nor is there ever a contrast between the fruit of the Spirit and the gifts in the sense of saying that if you have the fruit you do not need the gifts.[30] The whole of 1 Corinthians 12 shows that the gifts, by the very nature of the Body, are both important and necessary for its life and ministry.

The contrast here is rather between spiritual gifts without love and spiritual gifts with love. There is no thought of degrading the value of spiritual gifts or of saying that love is better than spiritual gifts. The whole point is simply that without love the highest gifts lose their proper effectiveness, value, and reward.[31]

Gifts without Love

To bring this out Paul pointed to seven examples of spiritual ministry, seven things highly valued by Corinthian believers no matter which division of the church they were supporting.

Speaking in tongues without love has no more effect than a noisy brass gong or "clanging cymbal" (13:1). It gets attention, but does not contribute to the harmony of the music. Prophecy, understanding of mysteries (with supernatural insight), knowledge (supernaturally received), and faith so great that it removes not just one mountain, but "mountain after mountain," will accomplish more than tongues. But without love, the person who is used in these gifts is nothing (v. 2). Personally, as far as his place in the body of Christ is concerned, he is nothing, no matter how much people may acclaim him for his gifts.

Others may sacrifice their money and personal possessions for the work of the Lord. They may even give their bodies to be burned as martyrs because of their faith (v. 3). Many may be helped by such gifts. Multitudes may be challenged to serve the Lord through the death of a martyr. But if those who give their goods and their lives do not have self-giving, Calvary love, love that gives itself to the undeserving, love that seeks nothing in return, it will profit them nothing. That is, when they stand at the judgment seat of Christ, their works will turn out to be mere wood, hay, and stubble, as far as reward is concerned (3:12).

Love must go to work in our hearts until it becomes the controlling motive of all we do. Such love brings with it all the fruit of the Spirit as well (as the description in 13:4–7 shows). Such love will never fail (in the sense of coming to an end because not needed or because no longer valid).

In contrast to love, prophecies will "cease" (v. 8, a different word than "fail"). Tongues will "be stilled" (come to an end, a still different word). Knowledge (probably the spiritual gift of the message of knowledge here) will "pass away." Now "we know in part [imperfectly] and we prophesy in part, but when perfection [what is complete, in full measure] comes, the imperfect disappears [ceases]" (vv. 9,10).

Some say that Paul by "perfection" meant the Bible, so that we do not need these gifts now that we have the Bible. On the surface, this may appear logical, since prophecy and knowledge were of special help to the first generation of believers who did not have the New Testament. However, this interpretation does not fit the illustration Paul used. During the entire present age our understanding and knowledge are partial, mediated to us indirectly like the dim image in an imperfect mirror. (Ancient mirrors were really metal imperfectly polished and leaving much to be desired.) This did not suddenly change when the Bible was completed. In fact, with all our knowledge of the Bible, we still see imperfectly. Otherwise, we would not find so many differences of opinion even among Spirit-filled Christians.

Everything the Bible says about the spiritual gifts shows that they are all still needed today. They are part of what God has appointed (placed, fixed, established) as an integral part of the Church just as He has set the various members or parts of the human body in their place to fulfill their proper function (12:18, 28). This clearly means that they are intended for the entire Church Age. But they are temporary in the sense that they are limited to the present age.[32] Today they are still needed, but when Christ comes again, the perfect state will be unveiled. We shall be changed into His likeness. No longer shall we be limited by these present decaying bodies. With new bodies, new maturity, and the visible presence of Christ with us, we shall not need the partial gifts. The things that perplex us now will perplex us no more. It will be easy to surrender our present partial and incomplete understanding when we shall see Him as He is (1 John 3:2).

The thought, then, is not that these gifts will cease at the end of the Apostolic Age. Paul is simply saying that we must not expect to find the kind of permanence in spiritual gifts that we find in faith, hope, and love.[33] They will always continue. Even when faith becomes sight, faith in the sense of trustful obedience will always be the right attitude toward God. Even when hope is realized and we receive the fullness of our promised inheritance, hope in the sense of expectation of future good will abide. Love, of course, cannot end, for God is love. The more we have of Him, the more we shall have of love. And since He is infinite, there will always be more throughout eternity. These things that are permanent must therefore be the guide for the exercise of spiritual gifts. Above all, they must be exercised in love.

The Spirit in the Ministry of the Church

With love in mind, 1 Corinthians 14 goes on to give practical directions for the exercise of two spiritual gifts—tongues and prophecy—in the Church. As we go though the chapter, we see again and again that love is the guiding principle from which these directions flow. Nor would we limit what is said to tongues and prophecy alone. Most of the basic instructions can be applied to other gifts was well.

Greater Is He Who Prophesies

One of the problems in the Corinthian church was the overuse of the gift of tongues in their worship when they came together as a body. Since speaking in tongues is the initial physical evidence of the baptism in the Holy Spirit (as the examples in the Book of Acts indicate), it is easy to reach out in faith and claim the gift of tongues. Because the individual's heart goes out to God as he speaks in tongues and he is blessed and edified, it then becomes easy to respond in tongues every time one feels the Spirit move. In Corinth this meant tongues were exercised so often in their meetings that other gifts were neglected. Sometimes also, the spontaneity of their response and the fact that numbers spoke in tongues at the same time, gave the impression of confusion.

Correction and instruction were needed, but Paul was careful to give correction in a way that makes it clear he still appreciated the gifts of the Spirit. He was glad for all of them, including tongues. He had no intention of bearing down so hard in his instructions that he would discourage the use of any gift.

This is why he made it clear again and again that he was not trying to stop the use of tongues. Specifically, he stated, "I would like every one of you to speak [to keep on speaking] in tongues" (1 Corinthians 14:5; the Greek is a continuous present tense). He did not tell those who were speaking in tongues to quit. He directed them rather to pray that they may interpret (v. 13), which implies there will still be tongues to interpret. People who give thanks in tongues have done nothing wrong. In fact, they give "thanks well enough [rightly, commendably]" (v. 17).

Paul himself was thankful to God that he continued to speak in tongues more than all the Corinthians. Yet in the church (the assembly of believers coming together for instruction and worship), he said he would rather speak five intelligible words to teach others than ten thousand words in tongues (vv. 18,19). Yet he did not mean to rule out tongues even by this. They are still a legitimate part of their worship (v. 26).

Before leaving the subject, Paul warned them to stop forbidding speaking in tongues (v. 39). Apparently, some disliked the confusion caused by overuse of tongues. They were trying to solve the problem by forbidding speaking in tongues altogether. But the experience was too precious and the blessing too great for the majority of the Corinthians to accept this. Some today say, "There are problems with speaking in tongues, so let us stay away from them." But this was not Paul's answer either for himself or for the Church. Even the limits he did put on tongues were not intended to hinder tongues. They were only meant to give more opportunity for greater edification through other gifts.

Edification is the key. Paul wanted to see the gifts manifest in such a way as to build the Church both spiritually and numerically. In fact, it is quite clear as we go along that Paul always had a deep concern for the salvation of souls (vv. 23–25).

Paul, however, did not begin by castigating the Corinthians for their wrong use of tongues. In fact, he began on a very positive note. It took him five verses to lead into the subject. Even then he gave the primary emphasis in what follows to the fact that tongues need interpretation (vv. 6–13).

First (v. 1), Paul called on them to pursue love, strive for love. But this does not mean neglecting spiritual gifts. We must also desire (be deeply concerned about and strive earnestly for) spiritual gifts. Every member needs to have the gift or gifts that will enable him to function in the Body as the Spirit wills.

Prophecy, however, brings such edification to the Body, that all should desire it. Its value is easily seen when it is contrasted with tongues. When a person "speaks in a tongue [that person] does not speak to men but to God" (v. 2). No one can understand him (no one learns anything), for in the Spirit he is speaking "mysteries" (secret truths, known only to God). Thus he edifies only himself (v. 4).

Paul did not say this was wrong. Each of us does need to be edified, built up spiritually, and God wants us to be. Nor is it selfish for us to want to be built up, for this will help us to build up others. But Paul is talking here about what is best for the assembly when they come together (v. 26). It is selfish to take the assembly's time to build up yourself which you might better receive in the privacy of your own devotions. Since Paul spoke in tongues more than all of them, yet not in the assembly, it is evident that he spent time alone with the Lord where he let the tongues roll out while his heart was lifted up in faith and in praise to God.

Prophecy, however, does more than build up the individual. When a person prophesies (speaks for God by the Spirit in a language everyone understands), he or she speaks to men and women, not just to God. His or her words strengthen the Church spiritually (and develop or confirm faith), exhort (encourage and awaken, challenging all to move ahead in faithfulness and love), and comfort (that cheers, revives, and encourages hope and expectation).

Actually, the principles of 1 Corinthians 12 show the importance of the gift of prophecy. There it was emphasized that the Holy Spirit wants to use the individual to bless and build up the whole Body. He wants us to grow up into Christ, for only as the whole Body is fitted together and united, with every part receiving a supply from the Head, does the Body grow to the upbuilding of itself in love (Ephesians 4:15,16). The love of 1 Corinthians 13 will also lead us to strive for prophecy above other spiritual gifts because it does more to edify the Church. For this reason, he who speaks in prophecy to the Church is more important than he who speaks in tongues. The only exception is when he interprets the tongues so that they will speak to the people.

Tongues Need Interpretation

Some take the latter part of 1 Corinthians 14:5 to mean that tongues with interpretation is the equivalent of prophecy. What Paul was actually saying is that tongues with interpretation bring edification to the Church just as prophecy does. Tongues with interpretation may bring various kinds of edification, including revelation (insight into the meaning of spiritual truths), knowledge (spiritual understanding), prophesying (a message to encourage or exhort), word of instruction (not in the sense of establishing new doctrine, but giving practical instruction or clarifying spiritual truth; v. 6).

On the other hand, tongues without interpretation may be compared to a flute or harp played without clear notes or a definite melody (v. 7). It will be just noise to the listener. Similarly, a trumpet is of no value to an army if its notes are uncertain (indistinct and unrecognizable; v. 8). Any speech that is unintelligible is just speaking into the air. It does not communicate. Paul compared it to the speech of barbarians. (In those days anyone who could not speak Greek was called a barbarian. Greeks seldom bothered to learn other languages. They just made everyone learn Greek, which was a great help in the spreading of the gospel.) The point is that there is no communication in either direction. Thus tongues without interpretation gives no communication to others. But the speaker himself also misses the message the Spirit may want to give.

Again, Paul quickly added that he was not trying to quench their zeal for spiritual gifts. His purpose rather was that they continue to excel (seek to keep on overflowing and abounding) to the edification of the Church (v. 12). In other words, the gifts of the Spirit should be exercised with such maturity, order, love, and fullness that they will be a beautiful evidence of the Holy Spirit's desire and power to build the Church.[1]

Interpretation should therefore be sought by all who speak in tongues, but not only for the edification of the Church. Paul went on (vv. 14,15) to show that though the individual is edified when that person speaks to God (v. 4), he or she receives greater personal benefit even if there is interpretation. As a person speaks in tongues, he or she speaks by the Holy Spirit, and that person's own spirit goes out to God in praise and is edified and enriched. But the mind or understanding cannot enter in, so remains unfruitful (unproductive). Thus, a person should exercise tongues in the church with a desire and expectation that he or she will interpret. The Corinthian church did not measure up to this, for there were times when no interpreter was present (as implied by v. 28). Yet this was the ideal toward which they should strive.

Again (v. 15), Paul stated that he was not trying to stop speaking in tongues. He would keep on praying with the Spirit (by the Holy Spirit; that is, in tongues). In addition, he would pray using his mind and understanding. When the Spirit moves, he would break out in spontaneous singing in tongues. (The Greek usually means singing with musical accompaniment, so this probably means the musicians will also be led by the Spirit.) He would also sing praise with the mind and understanding.

From this, we see that in addition to what is mentioned in verse 6, tongues can include giving thanks, blessing, praise, or worship. But if it is not interpreted, the one who does not understand cannot join in or put an amen to it. Verse 16, in fact, can mean that the one who worships in tongues without interpretation puts the whole church in the place of those who are ignorant, unlearned, untrained.

This suggests also that worship in the church should be in one accord with everyone joining in, united in heart, mind, and soul. Yet this does not imply that worship in tongues even without interpretation has no value at all. The person who speaks in tongues worships or gives thanks well, but a person who loves would want the others edified. Nor does verse 19 indicate Paul is trying to suppress tongues in the Spirit-filled life, as some would say.[2]

As we have noted, Paul must have exercised the gift of tongues primarily in his personal devotions, but he did consider it an important part of his spiritual life. It may be that some Corinthians were neglecting the blessing this gift could bring when used in this way.

Nor was Paul arbitrary in this limiting of his own expression of tongues in the assembly. He had the heart of a true shepherd. He wanted to feed the flock. Divine truth from the Word is the food our souls need (1 Peter 2:2). Teaching puts it in a form that may be received and assimilated with profit and blessing. For Paul to take up all the time of the congregation with a gift that brought edification primarily to himself would hardly show a shepherd's heart, nor would it show the love of 1 Corinthians 13.

In Understanding, Be Mature

Because Paul wanted the Corinthians to share the same concern for building up each other, he takes time out to try to get them to accept what he is teaching (14:20). He was about to give specific limitations for the use of the gift of tongues in the assembly. But he knew how they loved the free expression of the Spirit. He knew also that already some of them were probably closing their minds. Some were perhaps even becoming angry, finding fault, or beginning to feel malice or ill will. It is so easy to feel insulted when someone tries to direct our actions, especially when we have been perfectly happy and often blessed with things as they are.

Paul therefore called on them to be men; that is, to be mature, grown up. One does not expect a small child to understand spiritual things. But an adult who is mature in this thinking is willing to seek understanding. On the other hand, children do not develop deep-seated malice or habitual faultfinding. They are quick to forgive and forget. So far as malice is concerned, then, we should remain as children, even as babes. But in our thinking and understanding we need to be mature adults. It takes mature thinking to receive teaching on spiritual gifts. But Paul expected it of the Corinthians, and God expects it of us all.

Tongues as a Sign

Again, Paul made it clear he was not saying that tongues are not needed in public worship. Speaking in tongues is a sign to the unbeliever that is indeed still needed. First, it is a judgment sign, parallel to the tongues or languages of Isaiah 28:11. As we have seen, Isaiah was warning those who were turning a deaf ear to God's clear revelation. God would send them foreign conquerors (the Assyrians) whose language would seem like nonsense syllables to them, but whose actions would make it clear that the Israelites were separated from God, cut off from His blessing, and under His judgment. So tongues today are a sign to the unbeliever, making that person realize he or she is separated from God and cannot understand God's message. Tongues are a sign to unbelievers also in that they draw attention and let them know something supernatural is present. This was true on the Day of Pentecost when the sound of the tongues brought the crowd together.

But tongues bring only a sign to the unbeliever, not a message. If the whole church keeps on speaking in tongues, the initial effect will pass. Unbelievers or those who are do not understand will say the people are mad (out of their minds, overcome by uncontrolled enthusiasm).

As at Pentecost

Many try to make a distinction between the tongues in Corinth and the tongues given by the Spirit on the Day of Pentecost. Some versions of the Bible even translate "speaking in tongues" in the Book of Acts different from the epistles to the

Corinthians. In Acts, they translate it "speaking in foreign languages." In Corinthians, they make it "speaking ecstatically" or "speaking with strange sounds." But there is no evidence that the Corinthians were speaking in ecstasy in the sense of being in a trance. "The spirits of prophets are subject to the control of prophets" (1 Corinthians 14:32). Paul's directions concerning courtesy and love and the limitations on tongues would have no meaning if believers were not fully in control of their senses and aware of what was going on around them.[3]

Actually, what was happening in Corinth is exactly parallel to what happened on the Day of Pentecost. At Pentecost, the crowd initially was amazed, but no one was saved by the tongues. Eventually, as the one hundred twenty kept on speaking in tongues, many could not see a reason for what the believers were doing and said, "They have had too much [sweet, very intoxicating] wine" (Acts 2:13). This was just another way of saying they seemed out of their minds, mad. There have been occasions today where unbelievers have heard tongues given in their own languages and have marveled at the wonderful works of God as at Pentecost (v. 11).[4] But Paul made it clear that in the ordinary gathering where people of various languages are not present, the purpose and use of tongues is somewhat restricted.

On the other hand, the gift of prophecy is not a (supernatural) sign to the unbeliever (1 Corinthians 14:22). The word "sign" is one of the biblical words for miracle. Because prophecy is in his or her own language, the unbeliever does not see it as obviously supernatural. Yet prophecy is indeed a miracle sign to the believer. He or she is in tune with the Spirit. The believer does not need tongues to let him know that the supernatural is present. But when the gift of prophecy is manifest, he or she recognizes it as a supernatural work of the Spirit, full of His power.

Since the Holy Spirit works through the truth, applying it to the hearts of unbelievers in His convicting, convincing work (John 16:8), the unbeliever must be able to understand what the Spirit is bringing. It must go through his mind in order to reach his heart.

Thus, prophecy, given in the language that is understood by all, brings the unbelievers or spiritually ignorant to where they see themselves in the light of the gospel and recognize that the message is from God. This makes them fall down to worship and honor God. Instead of saying that the speaker is out of his mind, they recognize that "God is really among you" (1 Corinthians 14:25).

This, too, was exactly the situation on the Day of Pentecost. When Peter stood up to speak, he did not give his own reasoning or thoughts. He spoke (uttered forth) as the Spirit enabled him, but this time in prophecy and not in tongues. The word of prophecy spoke to their hearts, as Acts 2:37,41 shows.

Continuing the comparison with the Day of Pentecost, we see that the new Church did not spend all their time speaking in tongues, but "devoted themselves to the apostles' teaching and to the fellowship, to the breaking of bread and to prayer" (v. 42). The word of God increased, and the number of disciples multiplied (6:7). Stephen, "full of God's grace and power, did great wonders and miraculous signs . . . but they could not stand up against his wisdom or the Spirit by whom he spoke" (Acts 6:8,10). From the beginning, a variety of spiritual gifts were manifest in the Church.

Paul recognized that this variety of expression is normal. The words "What shall we say then?" (1 Corinthians 14:26) show that Paul wanted the Corinthians to see this. The first rule for the expression of spiritual gifts, as chapter 12 indicates, is that no gift is unimportant and no gift should be set aside. "Everyone has" means everyone should have something to contribute to building up the Body. No one is to sit back and just enjoy what he receives. Nor is there any implied distinction between the natural and the supernatural in the ministry of the believers. It is all from the supply of Christ (Ephesians 4:16), and is ministered by and through the Holy Spirit.[5]

As the believers came together then (usually in a home), one may have a psalm (probably a psalm from the Book of Psalms) sung under the anointing of the Spirit (usually with musical accompaniment). Another may bring a doctrine (a teaching), that is, Spirit-illuminated instruction from God's Word. Another may bring a revelation; that is, one of the gifts of revelation such as a message of wisdom or a message of knowledge. Still another may bring a tongue and another an interpretation. There is no fixed "order of service" in this picture of a New Testament gathering.[6]

Regulations for the Expression of Tongues

To make room for this variety of expression, Paul gave four specific directions to guide the expression of the gift of tongues in public worship. First, the number should be limited to two or at most three (1 Corinthians 14:27). Some interpret this to mean two or three in succession, then allowing two or three more later on in the meeting. Others say it means two or three by the same person, thus allowing two or three more by the next person. But neither of these ideas is in line with the purpose to allow a greater variety in the manifestation of the gifts. In each meeting or each time believers gather, two expressions should be considered quite sufficient, but three is allowable. Again, the purpose is not to quench the Spirit, but to encourage believers to seek and exercise other gifts of the Spirit.

Second, tongues should be by course, given by one person at a time. Love and courtesy do not allow two to speak in tongues at once as if they were in competition.

Third, one should interpret. That is, opportunity should be given for an interpretation after a "message" in tongues. If one person stands up to give it, another should not get up, too; the first should be allowed to interpret. Some take this to mean that one person in the congregation should do all the interpreting. But this idea does not fit well with the command that each person pray that he may interpret the tongues he himself has given (v. 13).[7]

Fourth, if no interpreter (no one who has been used in the gift) is present, then no tongues should be given aloud, for to do so would not edify the Church. The person can still express the gift, however, in a right way by speaking quietly directly to God

(v. 28). This will still fulfill the chief purpose of the gift (v. 2). The exhortation to pray that we may interpret (v. 13) should also be kept in mind.

Prophecy Must Be Judged

The gift of tongues is not the only gift needing direction and instruction, however. Principles that will help toward edification of the Body should be sought for all the gifts.[8] Paul indicated that prophecy is greater than tongues because it brings greater edification. But this does not mean the prophets have free reign to exercise the gift as they please. Prophecy, too, needs direction and guidance for its expression.

First, of the prophets, two or three may speak and then they should let others "weigh carefully what is said" (v. 29). The sense seems to be that two or three people in succession may prophesy. Then before others minister, these messages must be evaluated.

Second, to "weigh carefully what is said" implies a deliberate consideration of what the Spirit is saying, how it lines up with the Word, and what the Lord wants to do about it. Prophecy is not merely spiritual exercise. It brings a message from the Lord. If prophecy after prophecy continues on and on, the effect will be lost and there will be little edification. Thus, even the gift of prophecy must not be allowed to become a means of being blessed, and then doing nothing about it.

After two or three messages in prophecy, then, others need to examine, differentiate, evaluate what was said. It is implied that the judging will be done with the help of the same Spirit who gives the prophecy.[9] But it is also clear that the Bible does not intend for us to sit with our mouths open taking in everything that is said without thinking about it. The Bereans were more noble because they searched the Scripture to see whether the things Paul said were so (Acts 17:11). We must do the same to the gifts of the Spirit.

Sometimes, also, our conclusions need to be evaluated. It is possible to see a prophecy in the light of our own feelings, as in

Acts 21:4,12. (One's own feelings may be injected unintentionally, I believe.)

Third, if a person is giving a message in prophecy and another person stands indicating God has given him revelation (by some gift of the Spirit), then the first person should give the second an opportunity to speak. Thus, love will not permit any one person to monopolize the time. Then, as prophecies continue, one at a time, various individuals may be used, and all may learn, all may be comforted (encouraged and challenged; 1 Corinthians 14:31).

Peace, Not Confusion

Love, the governing principle for the exercise of the gifts, brings peace, not confusion. It can do so, however, only as those who minister in the gifts recognize that the "spirits of prophets are subject to the control of prophets" (v. 32). If the prophet does not show love, courtesy, and consideration for others, it is his own fault, not the Holy Spirit's. From this we see also that Spirit-filled believers do not need to be afraid that they will do something unedifying in spite of themselves. Those who exercise spiritual gifts are not hypnotized, nor are they in a state like that of sleepwalkers. Heathen prophets and mediums are used by evil spirits and are not always able to control what they do. But the New Testament never considers tongues or prophecy or any other manifestation of the Spirit uncontrollable.[10] The Holy Spirit respects us as children of God. God makes us fellow laborers so that we cooperate with Him, exercising the gifts in obedient faith as we willingly yield to Him.

From this also we see that any confusion the Corinthians were experiencing was their fault, not God's. We note also that Paul does not put the responsibility for order or for the regulation of the gifts on the elders or pastors. As someone has said, the call is for moderation (self-discipline) not for a moderator. The responsibility for order is to be shared by each individual member of the congregation. Even the Holy Spirit respects our integrity and will not force us to obey the instructions given here. For example, if there are more than three messages in tongues this does not mean the fourth was not of the Spirit. He puts the responsibility on us. If all we will respond to is tongues, He will keep giving us nothing but tongues—and let us stay spiritual babies if we want to.

Again, Paul is not trying to put the Corinthians in bondage. Nor is he giving them special directions that only they needed. The same problems, the same need for variety of gifts, the same need for courtesy and love is seen in all the churches of the saints (the believers who are dedicated to God). What he is saying in verses 33 and 26 is just meant to bring the Corinthians in line with the directions Paul has expressed for all the churches.[11]

This seems to mean that a person should not interrupt other ministry the moment he feels the Holy Spirit moving or prompting him to exercise a gift. Nothing is lost by waiting until the Spirit provides the opportunity to exercise the gift in love without causing confusion or disorder. Holding steady will, in fact, only deepen the Spirit's impression and make the expression of the gift even more effective.

While Paul was speaking about interruptions and disorder, he suggested that another type of interruption should be avoided. Women (who were usually uneducated in that day) were asking questions in an improper manner and thus contributing to the confusion. They were instructed to hold their questions and ask their husbands at home. This should be applied to both men and women in matters that custom considers unbecoming. But Paul is in no sense trying to hinder women from prophesying, speaking in tongues, singing, or otherwise contributing to the worship. He expected women to pray and prophesy if the Spirit gave them a ministry (11:5). The Bible makes no difference in spiritual manifestations between men and women.

Paul then stated that those who consider themselves prophets or spiritual (filled with and guided by the Holy Spirit) will accept these directions concerning the use of the gifts (14:37). They will not consider themselves superior to God's Word. They will appreciate variety and harmony. They will submit themselves to the judgment of others. Only the spiritually ignorant will reject these instructions. But they are not to be embarrassed in public. Just let them be ignorant, but recognize that they remain so at their own peril. God still wants all things to be done decently and in order. But, as Donald Gee said, "Not the order of a graveyard, but the order of a corporate life performing all its functions with ease and effectiveness to all concerned."[12]

The expression of the gifts, however, and Paul's concern over them, must not make us forget that his major concern was the preaching of the glorious gospel which declared Christ's resurrection and ours (1 Corinthians 15). Through Christ we shall receive a spiritual body, a real body that is the perfect temple, the perfect instrument for the expression of the Spirit. What we have now is only partial and can be only partial because of our present limitations. But that which is perfect is indeed coming. We look for something even better than what God gave Adam in the beginning. Our restoration is not merely to what Adam lost, but to what Christ has prepared. He will see to our resurrection and to our inheritance, for He is a life-giving Spirit (v. 45). (This may mean He gives life from the spiritual realm where He is now reigning in glory.)

The Deposit of the Spirit

Second Corinthians also has that forward look. Along with Ephesians it speaks of the deposit (earnest, first installment) of the Spirit and connects it with a sealing by the Spirit. After emphasizing that God has established us in Christ and anointed us, Paul said that God "set his seal of ownership on us, and put his Spirit in our hearts as a deposit, guaranteeing what is to come" (2 Corinthians 1:22). Then, after speaking of the time when we shall receive our new bodies, he said: "Now it is God who has made us for this very purpose and has given us the Spirit as a deposit, guaranteeing what is to come" (5:5).

Ephesians 1:13,14, after talking about God's purpose and our inheritance, speaks of how the believers trusted "in Christ when

[they] heard the word of truth, the gospel of [their] salvation. . . . [They] were marked in him with a seal, the promised Holy Spirit, who is a deposit guaranteeing [their] inheritance until the redemption of those who are God's possession—to the praise of his glory." Then, Ephesians 4:30 goes on to say we are not to grieve the Holy Spirit of God whereby we are sealed "for the day of redemption."

The ideas of the seal and the deposit are closely related. Both emphasize the fact that what we have through the Spirit now is a guarantee of a greater fullness to come. Both are closely related to the idea of the firstfruits (Romans 8:23) as well.

Some translate "deposit" as "down payment," but "first installment" is preferable. Just as the firstfruits are an actual part of the harvest, so the deposit is an actual part of the inheritance, and is the guarantee of what we shall receive in larger measure later.[13] Our inheritance is more than a hope. Now, in the midst of the corruption, decay, and death of the present age, we enjoy in and through the Holy Spirit the actual beginning of our inheritance.[14] In fact, the Holy Spirit himself is the deposit, though all His gifts and blessings are undoubtedly included.

The seal is related to the thought of 1 John 3:2. Though we are already sons of God, there is no outward glory yet. We still have these dying bodies with all their limitations. We still have many of the difficulties, problems, and sorrows common to humanity. But we have a present possession of the Spirit which is the seal giving us assurance we are God's children and that our hope will not disappoint us (Romans 5:5). When Jesus comes we shall be changed into His likeness and share His glory and throne. In the meantime, we enjoy a real part of our inheritance in the Holy Spirit.

Assurance, Not Protection

Some have taken the seal to mean protection, safety, or security. But the seal is a present acknowledgment that we are the Lord's. Of itself, it does not mean we cannot lose our salvation.

Nor does the Greek imply here the kind of sealing that is done when food is sealed in a jar or tin can to protect it from contamination. We are indeed kept by the power of God through faith unto salvation (1 Peter 1:5), but this is not automatic. Faith must be maintained.

Jesus, in John 6:27, said the Father put His seal on Him, but not for protection. Rather, the Father sealed or designated Him as the Son of God and the Giver of eternal life. Then, when we receive the testimony concerning Christ we "set to [our] seal that God is true" (John 3:33, KJV) or have "certified that God is truthful" (NIV).

The seal in Old Testament times was a recognition that a transaction was completed. A seal was placed on a deed to property indicating that the price had been paid and the transferal had taken place (Jeremiah 32:9,10). The sealing of the Spirit thus indicates we are delivered from the power of darkness and transferred "into the kingdom of the Son he loves" (Colossians 1:13).

The seal in the New Testament also has the idea of a designation of ownership, a trademark indicating we are His workmanship (Ephesians 2:10).[15] Since an ancient seal often impressed a picture, the seal may be related to the fact that the Spirit brings the impress of Christ "until Christ is formed in [us]" (Galatians 4:19).[16] The seal is also a mark of recognition that we are indeed sons, and an evidence that God has indeed accepted our faith.

The Time of the Sealing

In view of Ephesians 1:13, "Having believed, you were marked in him [Christ] with a seal, the promised Holy Spirit," some draw attention to the fact that Christ is the One doing the sealing after the believing. Therefore, they identify it with the baptism in the Holy Spirit. At this point even Dunn admits that the aorist (past) participle (used here of the believing as in Acts 19:2), would usually mean that the believing comes before the sealing.[17] But like the majority of the commentaries, he says that the context demands that the believing and the sealing take place at the same time. That is, the majority take the sealing to refer to the Spirit's coming in regeneration.[18]

The argument is that the context shows attention to spiritual life, not power for service. However, anointing is listed in 2 Corinthians 1:21,22, which usually indicates service or ministry. Others say we belong to the Lord the moment we are saved and we cannot make God's ownership dependent on a later experience.[19] But this argument is not well taken either. The seal did not cause ownership. It only recognized ownership. Thus, the blood of Jesus is the purchase price. By faith we believe and are made His. Then, the baptism in the Holy Spirit comes as the seal, the assurance by Jesus that God has accepted our faith.

Some take the seal as an invisible designation.[20] But this does not seem to fit the normal meaning of a seal that was intended to give visible identification for others to see. The seal is certainly something more than the believing.[21] Most commentators forget also that the baptism in the Holy Spirit was the normal experience of all believers in New Testament times. Therefore, in Paul's mind he is not drawing a line between sealed believers and those who do not have that privilege. He sees all believers as having had the experience and as therefore included.

Even the sealing of the 144,000 in Revelation 7:3 may involve the sealing of the Spirit. It is true they are sealed with a mark in their foreheads. But even in the Old Testament, God did not command an outward sign without the inward reality to go with it. David was anointed with oil, but the Holy Spirit came upon him from that day forward (1 Samuel 16:13).

The deposit, however, speaks of a first installment of our future inheritance. Thus, it must include the continuing moving and power of the Spirit in our lives. This is the most important thing to keep in mind. It fits also with the third chapter of 2 Corinthians where Paul considers the whole lives of his converts to be his living letters "written not with ink but with the Spirit of the living God, not on tablets of stone [as was Moses' Law] but on tablets of human hearts" (3:3).

The Glory We Share

Paul saw the glory of his inheritance also, not only in the age to come, but realized also in his present life and ministry. His ministry of the New Covenant was not by the letter that kills (and leaves in condemnation)[22] but by the Spirit that gives life (v. 6). This ministry was much more glorious than that which caused Moses' face to shine (vv. 7,8).

Moses put a veil over his face to hide that glory. Unfortunately a veil over the minds of many of the Jews was keeping them from seeing a greater glory, the glory in Christ. Actually, the prophecies concerning Christ were hidden even to the apostles until Jesus himself opened their minds and made their hearts burn within them. (See Luke 24:27,32,45–49.) The Spirit wants to do the same for us as He makes the Word live. (See 2 Timothy 3:16,17.)

The Jews also when they turn to the Lord will have that veil taken away from their minds. But the Lord they see will not be the Lord whom Moses saw, yet it will. For the Lord they see will be Christ revealed by the Spirit. "Where the Spirit of the Lord is," then, the veil is gone and "there is freedom" from the bondage of the Law that put the veil over their minds (2 Corinthians 3:17; see also John 8:31,32.) Then we all, both Jews and Gentiles, with open, unveiled faces now do behold by the Spirit, the glory of the Lord. (Second Corinthians 3:17 does not mean Christ and the Spirit are the same person or even that the Lord (*Yahweh*, Jehovah) of the Old Testament and the Spirit are the same person. It is simply that the Holy Spirit brings the glory of the Lord and mediates Christ to us.)[23]

As we continue to behold the glory of the Lord, even though as in an imperfect mirror, therefore imperfectly seeing Him, we are "being transformed into his likeness with ever-increasing glory (from one degree of glory to another), which comes from the Lord, who is the Spirit (v. 18). That is, Moses was the only one who saw the glory at Sinai. Then, he only had the one experience and had to veil the glory. But, through the Spirit, the glorified Christ who is our Mediator at God's right hand is continually revealed to us all (5:16), and we keep on being changed.[24]

The context shows, however, that Paul expected that glory to be revealed, not on his face as in Moses' case, but in his ministry, especially in the proclamation of the glorious gospel of Christ (4:1,5).[25] This ministry of Paul's found its approval and its increasing glory through the faithfulness of his converts, through his sufferings, through the Holy Spirit, and through his love (6:4–6).

One Temple, One Body

In Ephesians, Paul goes on to pray for the believers that God may give them the "Spirit of wisdom and revelation, so that [they] may know him better" (1:17), not merely for the fulfillment of their own desires, but so that they can see Christ as He is, the risen and exalted Head of the Church (1:20–23).

Paul was just as concerned that churches in Asia see that the Spirit's work is to maintain the unity of the body of Christ. In Corinth, the problem was that different factions were arising in a largely Gentile church. In Ephesus and the churches of Asia, there seems to have been a large body of Jewish believers among the Gentile believers still. Thus the line of cleavage was primarily between Jews and Gentiles. They needed to be reminded that the Church has been made one through the death of Christ which broke down the wall (the Law) that separated Jew from Gentile. Now through Him (Hebrews 10:20), we both have access by one Spirit to the Father (Ephesians 2:18). Now we are joined together, growing into one holy temple "a dwelling in which God lives by his Spirit" (v. 22).

Paul also reminded them that the mystery of the Gentiles being fellow heirs with the Jews was not revealed in former times. The Old Testament makes it very clear that Gentiles would share the blessing. (Genesis 12:3, for example.) But it was not clear that God would count both Jews and Gentiles as sinners, put them all in the same boat, and then show His mercy by letting them both into the Church on the one basis, by grace through faith.

This mystery was not revealed just to Paul, but to all the holy apostles and prophets of the Early Church by the Spirit (Ephesians 3:5). Paul, however, was made the chief announcer of this good news to the Gentiles. Through him and through the conversion of the Gentiles is made known to the principalities and powers in heavenly places "the manifold wisdom of God" (v. 10). This was no afterthought. It was "according to his [God's] eternal purpose which he accomplished in Christ Jesus our Lord" (v. 11). Thus, through the Church, God is still revealing His eternal purpose.

With this in mind, Paul prayed that God would grant believers to be strengthened "with power through his Spirit in [their] inner being" (v. 16). The supernatural power is not for miracles, but for the greatest miracle, the continuing miracle of Christ dwelling in their hearts by faith. It is also to help them be "rooted and established in love" so that they can "grasp how wide and long and high and deep is the love of Christ," and "be filled to the measure of all the fullness of God." For He is able to do "immeasurably more than all we ask or imagine, according to his power that is at work within us" (vv. 17–20). What an overwhelming concept! Not only does God want us to have a panoramic view of His plan. He wants to fill us with himself, which must mean with His own nature, His own holiness, love, and grace.

We, however, have our part in endeavoring "to keep the unity of the Spirit through the bond of peace" (4:3), for we must cultivate the fruit of the Spirit, especially love. This unity is maintained also by recognizing there is one Body, and one Spirit, as we are called in one hope of our calling (that is the upward calling which causes us to press on toward the goal in Christ, Philippians 3:14). This means honoring "one Lord" (Jesus), confessing "one faith" (one body of belief, one gospel), "one baptism" (probably not water baptism, but the baptism into Christ by the Spirit that makes us all one), "one God and Father of all" (Ephesians 4:5,6). The emphasis is on one God, one Christ, one Holy Spirit, and therefore one Body. The emphasis is not on anything outward here, and certainly not on any outward forms or outward organization. There is still unity with variety. But the variety, the diversity, should bring blessing and strength to the local body, not split it into factions. For "to each one of us grace has been given as Christ apportioned it" (v. 7). The grace, of course, includes gifts of the Spirit without which "the church cannot subsist in the world."[26]

Gifts Given to People

To illustrate what he means by grace ministered by the gift of Christ, Paul quoted from Psalm 68:18, indicating that the gifts received were given to people (Ephesians 4:8). Verses 9 and 10 are a parenthesis. Then, in verse 11, Paul went on to say that these gifts are apostles, prophets, evangelists, pastors, and teachers (or pastor-teachers). That is, Christ in ascending on high as our exalted Lord has taken people captive to himself. Then He has given them as gifts to the Church to mature the saints (God's people, all believers) so that they can do the work of ministry and build up the body of Christ (v. 12). Through this, the whole Body will come to a maturity where they are no longer spiritual babies led astray by every deceiver who comes along (v. 13). Instead, they will keep growing up into Christ in all things and receive from Him a supply that will enable them to minister a variety of gifts for the upbuilding of the Body, both spiritually and in number (vv. 13–16).

Obviously, the gifts of Christ here are the same as are identified in Corinthians as gifts of the Spirit. But the emphasis is on people and ministries. The chief emphasis in this passage concerns what God did at the beginning to establish the Church. But the Bible also indicates a continuing need for ministries that will establish the Church and bring believers to maturity. The growth of the Church plus the needs of young people and new converts demand this.

Renewal by the Spirit

The key to the success of this ministry in the Spirit is still the fruit of the Spirit. Paul went on to urge believers to turn away from the ways of the Gentiles with all their uncleanness and greediness.

They must put off the old way of life that seemed natural to them when they were Gentiles. They need to be renewed in the spirit of their mind and "put on the new self, created to be like God [in the image of God] in true righteousness and holiness" (v. 24).

This means quitting specific sins common among the Gentiles, such as lying and stealing. It means not grieving the Holy Spirit by "bitterness, rage and anger, brawling [excited yelling or shouting at each other] and slander [abusive speech], along with every form of malice" (v. 31). The Holy Spirit works best when we are "kind and compassionate to one another, forgiving [and graciously giving to] each other, just as in Christ God forgave [and graciously gave to]" us (v. 32).

This means living as children of light, recognizing that all the fruit of the Spirit is "in all goodness, righteousness and truth" (5:9). It means also that we must not become drunk with wine (or any of the false stimulants of the world) leading to debauchery, dissipation, and incorrigible profligacy. Instead, we are to keep being "filled with the Spirit" (v. 18). This is, as the Greek indicates, not a one-time experience, but a continued filling or, better, repeated fillings, as the Book of Acts suggests.

If we are truly continuing to be filled with the Spirit, it will show up in our worship as we "speak to one another with psalms, hymns and spiritual songs" and as we "sing and make music [playing musical instruments]" in our hearts to the Lord (v. 19). Psalms and hymns are probably out of the Book of Psalms (in Hebrew called *Tehillim*, "Praises"). Spiritual songs are other songs given by the Spirit (not necessarily in tongues, but given in the same sense that wisdom and understanding are given by the Spirit).

Our obedience to the command to be being filled with the Spirit will also show up in our love for one another, especially in our families (5:21 to 6:9). This will not be easy. We are in a battle against the devil, and we need the whole armor of God to take our stand against him (v. 11). But we must do more than keep on the defensive against him. We need to take "the sword of the Spirit, which is the word of God" (v. 17). The Word is, in fact, the Spirit's only tool, only weapon, only instrument. We become the Spirit's agents, not His instruments. An instrument, like a sword or a hammer, is used without any sense of cooperation on its part. It is picked up and laid down arbitrarily. But we are agents of the Spirit, ambassadors for Christ, fellow workers with the Lord, friends to whom He reveals His will and plans. The Word through us, however, becomes the Spirit's tool.

We need to carry on the battle positively by the means of prayer also. The shield of faith will stop all the fiery arrows from the enemy (which always come from outside the believer, never from evil spirits within). But we need to balance by praying "in the Spirit on all occasions with all kinds of prayers and requests" (v. 18).

Stand Fast in One Spirit

To the Philippians, Paul gave the good news that in spite of his bonds and all the opposition, Christ was being preached. He rejoiced also because he knew this would turn out to his deliverance (probably from prison) through their "prayers and the help [unfailing support] given by the Spirit of Jesus Christ" (1:19).

Paul's concern for the Philippians themselves was again for the unity and effectiveness of the Body. He wanted to hear that they were standing "firm in one spirit, contending as one man [person] for the faith of the gospel (v. 27).

The fruit of the Spirit is still the key. If there is "any encouragement from being united with Christ, if any comfort from his love, if any fellowship (sharing) with the Spirit, if any tenderness and compassion" then let the Church be in one accord and let them show the fruit of the Spirit by their concern and love for one another (2:1–4), and by their moderation or self-control (4:5).

Judaizers were still a problem in Philippi also, for Paul had to warn them of the concision (mutilators of the flesh, those who circumcise for the hope of salvation). Jews called themselves the circumcision. The real circumcision, the true Israel of God, however, consists of those who worship God in the Spirit (3:2,3). (Or, as some ancient manuscripts read, "who worship by the

Spirit of God.") In our worship by or in the Spirit we rejoice in Jesus and have no confidence in the flesh, that is in anything we can do in ourselves.

Making the Word Central

Colossians does not specifically mention the Spirit as often as Ephesians, but the emphasis of Colossians is on Christ as the Head of the Body. Paul saw all things in Christ, but these things are also the work of the Spirit.

Paul was thankful for the good report of their love in the Spirit (a fruit of the Spirit. (See Romans 15:30.) The things he asks them to put off are the same works of the flesh he mentions in other epistles (Colossians 3:8,9). What he asks them to put on are the same virtues that he also calls fruit of the Spirit. Above them all he says put on love, which is the bond of perfectness; that is, it unites and holds together all the other virtues (v. 14).

Instead of the command to be filled with the Spirit, Paul gave another command that draws attention to another important basis for spiritual worship: "Let the word of Christ dwell in you richly as you teach and admonish one another with all wisdom" (3:16). This is, of course, the work of the Spirit. Because we are filled with the Word as well as the Spirit, our worship will involve teaching and admonishing, that is, instructing and warning one another in "psalms, hymns and spiritual songs with gratitude in your hearts to God." Clearly, the Word and teaching must have a central place. Our songs must have a biblical message.

Rekindle the Gift of God

In writing to Timothy, Paul gave special attention to encouraging Timothy's own ministry as a ministry in the Holy Spirit. He wanted the truth to be passed on to future generations, and he knew that the conflict he had had with false teachers was not going to end with his death. In fact, the Spirit kept speaking explicitly that in "later [future] times some will abandon the faith and follow deceiving spirits and things taught by demons [having demons as their source] (1 Timothy 4:1). It is very important, therefore, for Timothy to entrust what he had heard from Paul to faithful men who would teach others as well (2 Timothy 2:2).

This is the very thing Paul has in mind in 1 Timothy 1:18 where he entrusted a charge (a body of instruction) to Timothy to pass on to others in accordance with the prophecies "once made about" him, that by following them (inspired by them, or in fulfillment of them) he might continue to "fight the good fight" of faith.

This same ministry of teaching is in mind also when Paul (1 Timothy 4:12–16) said, "Don't let anyone look down on you because you are young, but set an example for the believers in speech, in life [conduct], in love, in faith and in purity. Until I come, devote yourself to the public reading of Scripture [the Old Testament], to preaching [by the Spirit's gift, but in relation to the Scriptures read] and to teaching [Christian truth to others]. Do not neglect your [spiritual] gift, which was given you through a prophetic message when the body of elders [or leaders of the local assemblies] laid their hands on you. Be diligent in these matters [put them into practice]; give yourself wholly to them [be in them, live in them], so that everyone may see your progress. Watch your life and doctrine [teachings] closely. Persevere in them, because if you do, you will save both yourself and your hearers."

Apparently Timothy needed this kind of encouragement in view of the increasing persecution. Thus in 2 Timothy 1:6–8 Paul went on, "For this reason [Timothy's unfeigned, sincere, genuine faith, verse 5] I remind you to fan into flame [keep rekindling, keep stirring to a blazing flame] the [spiritual] gift of God, which is in you [given in accompaniment] through the laying on of my hands. For God did not give us a spirit of timidity [cowardly fear], but a spirit of [mighty] power, of love and of self discipline [prudent, thoughtful self-control]. So do not be ashamed to testify about our Lord, or ashamed of me his prisoner. But join with me in suffering for the gospel, by the power of God."

Finally, in 2 Timothy 1:13,14, Paul said, "What you heard from me, keep as the pattern [the standard] of sound [healthy, correct] teaching, with faith and love [which come by being] in Christ Jesus. Guard the good deposit that was entrusted to you—guard it with the help of the Holy Spirit who lives in us."

Some have tried to use these passages to promote the idea that by prophesying over someone spiritual gifts may be given or transmitted to that person. Others have taken the laying on of hands to be a means of bestowing spiritual gifts. We must not forget, however, that the Spirit gives gifts as He wills. But even this is not the point here. These passages are better understood in the light of Acts 13:2,3 and Acts 16:2. In Acts 16:2, Timothy was brought to Paul and joined his company with the approval of the brethren who were at Lystra and Iconium. Acts does not give further details here. But from what Paul said to Timothy, it is evident that something similar to what happened at Antioch in Acts 13:2,3 took place. Why did the brethren want Timothy to join Paul's missionary party? It can only be that there was prophecy that directed the churches to set apart Timothy for the work to which the Lord had called him. Then Paul and the elders prayed and laid hands on him expressing their faith and their acceptance of Timothy's call. "Through a prophetic message when the body of elders laid their hands on you" or the putting on of Paul's hands (which undoubtedly occurred at the same time as that of the elders) only mean "accompanied by." Neither prophecy nor the laying on of hands is the cause of the gift.[27] Rather, they endorsed the gift God had already given.

The important thing is that God has a deposit (an investment) in Timothy which Timothy must guard through the Holy Spirit who indwells us. Throughout all these passages also is the repeated emphasis on teaching. Timothy must be taken up with teaching and live what he teaches if he is to save himself and his hearers. This suggests that the spiritual (charismatic) gift, which Paul repeatedly mentioned, had to do with teaching, especially the establishing of believers by a teaching ministry. It is true

Timothy was to preach the Word and do the work of an evangelist (2 Timothy 4:2,5), but he was to do it all "with great patience and careful instruction."

To fulfill this gift, Timothy needed to keep the full flame of it blazing. He could not neglect it. The fact that prophecies were given and hands laid on him was not enough. Constant attention to this ministry was needed. He could become too busy in other things, neglect it, and the fire would burn low. Or he could let the threat of suffering keep him from seeing what the power of God could really do. "Timidity" or cowardly fear does not come from the Holy Spirit. But power and love do. So does self-discipline. All this is necessary also to guard the deposit of the gospel God has given. Many have tried to do it with human reasoning, by setting up creeds, by excellent apologetics, but have failed. It cannot be done apart from the ministry and gifts of the Spirit.[28]

Paul also reminded Timothy of the work of the Spirit in relation to Christ (1 Timothy 3:16). "[God] appeared [was revealed] in a body [in the Man Jesus], was vindicated by the Spirit, was seen by angels, was preached among the nations, was believed on in the world, was taken up in glory." Some take "vindicated by the Spirit" to mean "proved to be right by entering into the realm of the Spirit." But it seems more likely to be speaking of the vindication brought when He was raised from the dead by the Spirit.[29] Some take this verse to be a fragment of a hymn concerning Christ that was actually given by the Spirit and sung in churches Paul established. In any case, it is a beautiful summary of what the Christian religion teaches about Him. (Some take "seen by angels" to refer to the welcome given by angels after His ascension. The "taken up in glory" refers to His taking the Church with Him to heaven when He comes again.)

Poured Out Abundantly

Much of the instruction Paul gave Titus is similar to that given Timothy. But in Titus 3:5–7 is a fine but tightly compressed statement of what Christ has done for us: "He saved us, not because of righteous things we had done, but because of his mercy. He saved us through the washing of rebirth and renewal by the Holy Spirit, whom he poured out on us generously through Jesus Christ our Savior, so that, having been justified by his grace, we might become heirs having the hope of eternal life."

Many take this of water baptism and suppose Paul has changed his mind about the means of salvation. But the emphasis is till the same, and salvation is not by works. The washing or bath is the new birth itself. The same word is used in Ephesians 5:26: "the washing with water through the word." It relates to Romans 10:8,9, " 'The word is near you; it is in your mouth and in your heart,' that is the word of faith we are proclaiming: That if you confess with your mouth 'Jesus is Lord,' and believe in your heart that God raised him from the dead, you will be saved." The bath, even the water bath, is the Word that the Holy Spirit uses, for He is the Spirit of Truth, not the Spirit of water. (Compare also John 13:10; 15:3.)

The *renewal* by the Holy Spirit probably has to do with new relationships, since the word *regeneration* has to do with new life. It may speak of the baptism into the body of Christ by the Spirit (1 Corinthians 12:13). Then, as a further thought, the Holy Spirit is the One whom God has poured out generously through Jesus Christ our Savior. The pouring out by Jesus refers to Acts 2:33 and Joel 2:28. But the chief reference is not to the Day of Pentecost, since Paul and Titus are both included. Each one had his own Pentecost mediated to him by Jesus Christ.[30] From this it is evident that every new believer since Pentecost can have his or her own personal Pentecost, his or her own experience of the baptism in the Holy Spirit, and that it can be the same rich outpouring given in Acts 2:4.

That Paul went on to say "having been justified by his grace, we might become heirs" (Titus 3:7) does not affect this assurance. He is simply concluding by recognizing that justification by grace (and of course, through faith; Ephesians 2:8) is what makes it possible for us to be heirs. In fact, Titus 3:7 is just an amplification of the phrase "he saved us . . . because of his mercy" in verse 5.[31]

Gifts According to God's Own Will

Hebrews also speaks of gifts of the Holy Spirit as part of God's miraculous supernatural witness to the message of salvation preached by the first generation of believers (2:4). But, where in 1 Corinthians 12:11 they are distributed by the Spirit according to His own will, in Hebrews 2:4 they are said to be according to God's own will. But this is only in line with what Paul says about the Spirit knowing the will of God (Romans 8:27).

Believers are also made tasting (partaking, possessing) of the Holy Spirit, an experience which is parallel to tasting (partaking) of the powers (mighty, supernatural powers) of the coming age (Hebrews 6:4,5).[32]

The Holy Spirit is also a witness to us that God has accepted Christ's sacrifice and "has made perfect forever those who are being made holy" (10:14,15). This is further confirmed by Jeremiah's prophecy (v. 16; Jeremiah 31:33), even though Jeremiah himself did not mention the Holy Spirit. In this context, being "made perfect" was accomplished in the sacrifice of Christ on Calvary. "Forever" means either continuously or for all time and refers to the fact that His sacrifice was "once for all" (Hebrews 9:26). "Being made holy" is in a continuous form of the Greek verb that means "those who are being sanctified or consecrated, dedicated to God and His service."

Though the Spirit bears witness to this, the dedication or separation to God is brought about by the death of Christ. (See also Hebrews 13:12.) This is in line with the general emphasis in Hebrews which gives prominence to Christ as the divine Son and on the whole has less to say about the Holy Spirit than Epistles such as Romans and Corinthians. The same sort of thing is true of the Spirit's convicting, convincing work, which Hebrews shows is a matter of making men see their relationship to a living God.[33] (See 3:12; 9:14; 10:31; 12:22.)

Hebrews also, instead of giving the human author of a quotation from the Old Testament, always refers it to the Holy Spirit, the divine Author (3:7; 9:8; 10:15). Hebrews 9:8 is interesting also in that it shows the Holy Spirit had the typology referring to Christ in mind while He was inspiring the writing of Old Testament passages. That is, in the very writing of the Old Testament, the Spirit was preparing for and pointing to the work of Christ.

Jealous Yearning

The Epistle of James mentions the Holy Spirit only once: "The spirit he caused to live in us envies intensely" (James 4:5). The context deals with the fact that friendship with the world makes one an enemy of God and with the need to submit to God and His grace. It is possible to take the verse to mean that God yearns jealously over the Holy Spirit that indwells us, wanting us to give Him opportunity to develop His fruit and give His gifts. It is also possible to take it that the Holy Spirit himself yearns over us and desires us to cooperate with Him in His fruit and gifts. The effect is the same, whichever way the verse is interpreted.

James also spoke of every good gift coming from the Father, who "chose to give us birth through the word of truth" (1:17, 18). This indicates that what Paul and John ascribed to the Holy Spirit is actually also of God the Father. But this is just another evidence of the perfect cooperation of the entire Trinity.

Obeying the Truth through the Spirit

Peter's Epistles also show the Holy Spirit inspiring the Word and the preaching of the gospel (1 Peter 1:11,12). He emphasizes that "no prophecy of Scripture came about by the prophet's own interpretation [is not a matter of someone giving his own explanation]. For prophecy [the Word of God] never had its origin in the will of man, but men spoke from God as they were carried along [borne along, led along] by the Holy Spirit" (2 Peter 1:20,21).

The Spirit also is the One through whom we have sanctification or consecration to God (1 Peter 1:2). He enables us to cooperate with this work by purifying our souls in obedience to the truth unto a sincere brotherly love (1 Peter 1:22).

This may involve partaking of Christ's sufferings. But if it brings reproach for His name's sake, we are happy, for the Spirit of glory and of God rests on us (1 Peter 4:14). In the natural, self-preservation is the first law of human nature. The world emphasizes self-interest, taking care of "number one." Competition leads to a desire to dominate others and play the tyrant. But Jesus was among us as the Servant of all. The greatest among us is to be the slave of all (Matthew 20:25–28; 23:11; Luke 22:27). It is only possible for us to overcome our natural drives through the power of the Spirit as Christ lives in us and His nature is being formed in us.[34] Then, the supply of God's grace will make it possible even to die for our Lord. What a contrast there is between the death of Stephen and the death of Herod Agrippa. Stephen, full of the Holy Spirit, looked into heaven, saw the glory of God, and was able to forgive his murderers (Acts 7:55–60). Herod in self-exaltation took glory to himself that belonged to God and died in agony under God's judgment (12:21–23).

Like Paul, Peter also emphasized that Jesus was "made alive [resurrected] by the Spirit" (1 Peter 3:18). By the same Spirit also, He went and "preached to the spirits in prison" (1 Peter 3:19). This has been taken by some to mean that by the Holy Spirit Christ preached through Noah to warn those who are now spirits in prison. Others take it that by the Spirit He went after His death (or resurrection) to announce or proclaim His triumph to angels now held in prison. We can be sure, however, that this passage is not teaching a second chance for salvation.

The Spirit Acting through Christ's Authority

The Book of Revelation is above all a new revelation of Jesus Christ (1:1). In the Book, the Holy Spirit reveals Christ, speaks for Christ, and acts on His behalf, all through His authority. What Jesus said to the seven churches of Asia individually, becomes His message to all the churches by the Spirit (2:7,11,17,29; 3:1,6,13,22; 14:13). This shows that the risen and glorified Christ who is now at the right hand of the Father speaks to us in the Church Age through the Spirit.[35] What John sees also, he sees as he is in the Spirit (1:10; 4:2; 17:3; 21:10).

The relation between the Holy Spirit and Christ is further clarified by comparing the visions of the seven spirits of God before the throne (1:4; 4:5) and the seven spirits in chapter 5. In chapter 4, they are seven lamps of fire indicating light, life, and wisdom. In chapter 5, they become seven horns (indicating authority and power) and seven eyes (indicating wisdom and knowledge) in the Lamb. But they are sent forth into all the world (5:6). The seven horns and seven eyes do not mean fourteen spirits. Rather, the seven spirits may refer to the sevenfold Spirit of God revealed in Isaiah 11:2. Or, the number seven may simply be the number of fullness and perfection. Thus, Christ works in the fullness of the Spirit to bring His power and His wisdom into the world. The Spirit therefore acts in this age through the authority of the Lamb who still bears the marks of having been slain. The effects of Calvary are fully ministered to us by the Spirit.

Finally, the Spirit joins with the Bride (the Church) and says, "Come!" (22:17). This invitation is to be passed on to others by all who hear. For everyone who thirsts, for everyone who wills, there is an abundant supply of the water of life. All may come and take freely and in unlimited measure. Surely this includes the outpourings of the Spirit as rivers of living water, as Jesus himself indicated when He said, "If anyone is thirsty, let him come to me, and drink" (John 7:37–39). Thus, the last book in the Bible does not end without renewing the invitation to all to enjoy not only salvation through Christ, but continuing Pentecostal outpourings.

The Spirit in Supernatural Demonstrations

The ministry of the Holy Spirit in the Early Church took place in an atmosphere of confident expectation. Not only did they expect the daily blessing and the manifestation of the gifts of the Spirit; they did not forget that Pentecost was a feast where first-fruits were offered. Pentecost was part of the final harvest. Thus, they looked ahead to Christ's return. Out of their own vital Pentecostal experience came the watchword, *Maranatha,* "Our Lord, Come!" Nor did the passage of time dim their hope. Paul, toward the end of his life came to realize he would not live to see that glorious day when the dead in Christ shall rise. But he was no less sure that Jesus would come (2 Timothy 1:12; 2:10,13; 4:7,8).

This hope of seeing Jesus again made the early Christians more conscious than ever of the necessity of carrying on His work in the power of the Spirit. In this age the Holy Spirit is the only One who can minister the life, power, and person of Jesus to us. Whether He is called the Spirit of God or of Christ, the Spirit of peace, truth, power, grace, or glory, He is always the same Holy Spirit who makes Jesus real and continues His work.

Yet He is distinguished from Jesus as *another* Counselor or Helper, and as One who bears witness to Christ by His teaching (John 14:16; 16:13,14) and by His mighty acts (Acts 2:43; Romans 15:18,19). He is distinguished also from the Father and is sent by both Father and Son (Galatians 4:6; John 14:26; 15:26; 16:7). He himself is shown to be divine by all that He does, especially by the fact that He knows the deep things of

God (1 Corinthians 2:10,11), and prays for us according to the will of God (Romans 8:27).

He also helps fulfill those prayers by directing both individuals and the Church in the will of God. Because He directed Philip to an Ethiopian eunuch (Acts 8:26–39) and Peter to the house of Cornelius (10:9–48), then gave the church at Antioch directions to send out Paul and Barnabas (13:1–3), the Church became missionary. Every Gentile Christian owes everything to the Holy Spirit who broke down the barriers and helped at least some to overcome their ingrained prejudices and move out into all the world.

A Life Wholly Dedicated to God

This dedication to God's service really grew out of a dedication to God himself. In every aspect of the life of the Christian, the Spirit points us to Jesus and pours out the love of God into our hearts.[1] We are to live in the Spirit and by the Spirit if we are truly in Christ. Thus, no aspect of our lives needs to lack His touch. What He did for the first century believers as they lived, worked, worshipped, hoped, and suffered for Christ, He wants to do for us. Who knows but what there are some work aprons and sweat cloths He can use to minister healing today! But even more important, He wants to make us one in the Spirit and one in Christ as we join together in fellowship with Him.

Actually, He is present to guide us whether we receive special manifestations of His gifts and revelations or not. Some folk have the idea they are not in the Spirit unless they receive a new revelation or new special guidance every day. But when Paul was forbidden by the Spirit to preach in Asia, that is, in Ephesus, he received no further guidance at the time. His faithfulness to his task made him go on for many days through Mysia to the borders of Bithynia. Not until then did he receive further guidance from the Spirit (Acts 16:6,7).

Much of the life of the early Christians was a matter of faithfully carrying out the work of the Lord and the business of life without spectacular interventions. Yet this was no drab existence. The gifts of the Spirit and the presence of Christ were daily their portion in both work and worship. It was a life of growth in grace and in the fruit of the Spirit as well.

Growth in grace and the development of the fruit of the Spirit was and is made possible through Christ who made us holy through His blood (Hebrews 13:12). This was made personal by the Holy Spirit who sanctified us by separating us from evil and dedicating us to God when He gave us new life and placed us into the body of Christ (1 Corinthians 6:11). But that is only one aspect of our sanctification. Paul prayed that God would sanctify us "through and through" [completely] (1 Thessalonians 5:23). There is also a continuing aspect of sanctification in which we must cooperate. We must present ourselves to God (Romans 12:1,2), and by the Spirit pursue that holiness (dedication, consecration in right relationships to God and man), for without holiness no one will see the Lord (Hebrews 12:14). This is a holiness like His, which the Holy Spirit helps us to achieve (1 Peter 1:15,16).

This means recognizing and putting into practice our identification with Christ in His death and resurrection. Daily we must count ourselves to be "dead to sin but alive to God in Christ Jesus" (Romans 6:11). Daily we must by faith yield every faculty of our being to God as "instruments of righteousness" (v. 13; 1 Peter 1:5). By the Spirit we thus keep putting to death the impulses of the old life and keep winning victories as we live for Jesus (Romans 8:1,2,14; Galatians 2:20; Philippians 2:12,13).

On one hand, we are changed from one degree of glory to another as we behold and serve Jesus (2 Corinthians 3:18). On the other hand, the same dedication to God may cause us to suffer for Christ and the gospel. Paul not only considered himself crucified with Christ and living a new life in and by Christ (Galatians 2:20), he was also willing to "fill up [on his part] in my flesh what is still lacking in regard to Christ's afflictions, for the sake of his body, which is the church" (Colossians 1:24).

That is, Paul had not yet had to die for the sake of the Church, but until that happened, he was willing to keep on suffering to establish that Body and bring more and more believers into it.

The whole work of sanctification is the work of the Spirit which receives by far the greatest attention in the New Testament. It takes precedence over witnessing, evangelism, giving, and every other form of Christian service. God wants us to be something, not just to do something. For only as we become like Jesus can what we do be effective and bring glory to Him. Our worship also, as it is guided by the Spirit and prompted by the Spirit in every aspect, encourages us in this very thing.

The Gift of the Spirit

We must avoid the idea, however, that in our Christian life our chief object is to perfect ourselves. We actually achieve more growth while in service. The saint (dedicated, consecrated one) is not the one who spends all his time in study, prayer, and devotion, important as that is. The holy vessels in the tabernacle could not be used for ordinary purposes, but their separation from ordinary use is not what made them holy. They were not holy until they were actually used in the service of God. So the saint is the one who is not only separated from evil, but separated to God, sanctified and anointed for the Master's use. This was symbolized in the Old Testament by the fact that the blood was first applied and the oil over the blood. Cleansing was thus followed by a symbolic anointing that represented the Spirit's work in preparing for service. So we too are anointed, as were the prophets, kings, and priests of old (2 Corinthians 1:21; 1 John 2:20).[2]

The means and power for service come through the gifts of the Spirit. But the *gifts* of the Spirit need to be distinguished from the *gift* of the Spirit. The baptism in the Spirit was necessary before the first disciples were to leave Jerusalem or even begin to fulfill the Great Commission. They needed power, and the very name Holy Spirit is connected with power.[3] He came as the Gift and as the Power. He himself is the firstfruits of the final harvest (Romans 8:23), come to begin a work that will bring some from every kindred, tongue, people, and nation together around the throne (Revelation 5:9). The same baptism in the Spirit was experienced by others on at least four other occasions in Acts, as we have seen, as well as by still others later on, according to Titus 3:5.

On the Day of Pentecost the reception of the gift of the Spirit was marked by the initial physical (or outward, since it was not completely physical) evidence of speaking in other tongues (languages different from their own) as the Spirit enabled them. From the fact that tongues is the evidence given, and especially from the fact that tongues was the convincing evidence at the house of Cornelius ("For they heard them speaking in tongues," Acts 10:46), there is an excellent case for regarding tongues as the initial physical (or outward) evidence of the baptism in the Holy Spirit.[4]

As many are willing to admit, it is difficult to prove from the Book of Acts that speaking in tongues is not the initial evidence of the baptism in the Holy Spirit.[5] Most who attempt to discount tongues as the evidence turn to the Epistles, looking for theological proof of their position.[6] But the Epistles are not that much divorced from the experiences of Paul, and certainly not from the experiences of the people to whom he was writing. To consider them totally theological in contrast to the Book of Acts does not fit the facts. Even where the Epistles give propositional truth, such as justification by faith, it is related back to the experience of Abraham (Romans 4). As we have seen, much of what Paul says about the Spirit in his epistles is directly parallel to the experiences in the Book of Acts.

The argument against tongues as the evidence is most often based on the question "Do all speak in tongues?" (1 Corinthians 12:30). We have already seen what a weak argument this is, especially since the verb is in a continuous present, "Do all continue to speak in tongues?" meaning, "Do all have a ministry to the Church of speaking in tongues?"

The value of tongues as a sign, in personal edification, and in teaching us to respond to the Spirit simply and in childlike faith is important. The very fact we do not know what we are saying helps us to learn to respond to the Spirit without mixing in our own ideas and wishes, for we speak as the Spirit gives utterance. There is usually no mental impression in our minds of what we are to say. Instead, our minds are most often filled with praise to the Lord, and we simply (but actively) yield our vocal organs, mouth and tongue, to the Spirit and speak whatever He gives.[7] (Some do say the Lord gave them a few words before they spoke them. When they obeyed and spoke what came to their mind, the Holy Spirit then gave the ability and the freedom in speaking in tongues.)

In the Book of Acts also the tongues came when the gift of the Spirit was received. There may or may not be an interval of time between believing for salvation and receiving the Gift. Ideally, one should reach out in faith and receive the Gift as soon as he is a believer. But there is no interval indicated in Acts between receiving the gift of the Spirit and receiving the evidence of speaking in tongues. Donald Gee tells of his experience of receiving the baptism in the Holy Spirit "by faith" and then after two weeks of new fullness in his soul, finding himself "beginning to utter words in a new tongue."[8] Many others have testified to similar experiences. In the present author's own experience, the Holy Spirit made Jesus so wonderfully real that he was not particularly conscious of speaking in tongues. (Though others said he did.) The next night he simply told the Lord that if there was a freedom in the gift of tongues, he wanted it. Immediately, the tongues poured out in overflowing abundance. Perhaps, this also is a matter of "the wind blows wherever it pleases" (John 3:8). We have an assurance, however, that we have the Gift the Bible is talking about when we speak in tongues. Thus, the Bible is the guide, and we must judge our experience by it.

This does not mean that tongues should be sought. Our attention should be on the mighty Baptizer, the Lord Jesus himself.

Faith that believes He will fulfill His promise is the key to being baptized in the Spirit. Since the Baptism is for service, consecration and surrender to God are also always in order (Romans 6:13; 12:1). But we cannot program the way He comes. Each occasion mentioned in the Book of Acts was different. Sometimes He comes in spite of what we do, again, "the wind blows wherever it pleases." He may come in a gentle stillness, with the barest whisper. He may come with the sound of a mighty rushing wind. Let us be willing to let Him come as He wills.[9]

It should be recognized also that speaking in tongues is only the initial evidence of the baptism in the Holy Spirit. Other evidence will follow as the fullness of the Spirit overflows into every avenue of life (John 7:37–39; Acts 4:8). We can expect also a deeper reverence for God (v. 43; Hebrews 12:28); a more intense dedication and consecration to God and to His Word (Acts 2:42); and an ever-increasing and more active love for Christ, for the Bible, and for the lost (Mark 16:20).

In fact, it should always be kept in mind that the baptism in the Spirit is not a climactic experience. As Pentecost itself was only the beginning of the harvest and brought men into a fellowship of worship, teaching, and service, so the baptism in the Holy Spirit is only a door into a growing relationship with the Spirit and with other believers. It leads to a life of service where the gifts of the Spirit provide power and wisdom for the spread of the gospel and the growth of the Church. This is evidenced by the rapid spread of the gospel in many areas of the world today. New fillings, new directions of service are to be expected as new needs arise, and as God in His sovereign will carries out His plan.

Generous Gifts of the Spirit

The ministry of the Spirit and His mighty deeds were the portion of the Early Church in lavish generosity (as the Greek indicates in Galatians 3:5; Philippians 1:19).[10] The abundance of gifts and the wonderful way they fitted the needs of the Body shows that God's way is always, "Not by might, nor by power, but by my Spirit, says the LORD Almighty" (Zechariah 4:6).[11]

There is, however, no special order in which the Bible lists the gifts. Romans 12:6–8 begins with prophecy. First Corinthians 12:8–10 begins with the message of wisdom. The other three lists begin with apostles. Some attempt to classify the gifts according to their nature, such as gifts of revelation, gifts of power, and gifts of speaking. Others distinguish between traveling gifts, such as apostles, teachers, and evangelists; and local gifts such as pastors, government, and helps. Or they divide them according to function, such as proclamation, teaching, service, and administration.[12] These are all legitimate, but there is no way of avoiding the overlapping that comes in any system of classification.

Some try to distinguish between public and private gifts or between functional and official gifts. But these usually fail to recognize that every Christian has his own gift, calling, or office available to him.[13]

Others attempt to distinguish between extraordinary gifts that are charismatic, completely supernatural, and which they wrongly suppose are beyond the control of the individual (as prophecy, miracles, healings, and tongues) and those they call ordinary, noncharismatic, involving natural, human abilities (as teachers, ministry, ruling, administration, helps, giving, and showing mercy). Some carry this further and suggest that since apostles and prophets were needed in the establishing or laying the foundations of the Church (Ephesians 2:20), they are not needed today.[14] But Ephesians 4:7–11 makes it clear that apostles, prophets, evangelists, and pastor-teachers were all needed in the establishing of the Church. Paul in no way distinguished between them. It seems clear also that each of these ministries involves supernatural gifts. (Some take the prophets of Ephesians 2:20 as Old Testament prophets. However, 3:5 and 4:11 definitely indicate New Testament prophets.)

Nor does the Bible distinguish between gifts that are "more supernatural" and "less supernatural." They are all part of the work of the Spirit through the Church. The statement of Harold Horton that all the gifts are "one hundred percent miraculous" with "no element of the natural in them at all"[15] has been pushed to extremes by some. He himself said later that the expression of the gift "may vary in accordance with the office or even the personality of the one through whom it is given."[16]

A problem arises here when some say that gifts such as prophecy or a message of wisdom and a message of knowledge are totally supernatural and must be manifested in an independent, distinct way that identifies them for what they are. They do not see these gifts as having anything to do with teaching or preaching. Paul contrasted what man's wisdom teaches with what the Spirit teaches and indicated that the Spirit gives the wisdom and knowledge for the preacher or teacher to use. Donald Gee's comment is appropriate: "If our conception of what is 'supernatural' stands in the way of seeing the gifts of the Spirit in the ministries of preaching and teaching, then it is clear that our understanding of the meaning of 'supernatural' needs correcting. Perhaps with some it is a confusion of 'spectacular' with 'supernatural.'"[17] Actually, the gifts are interrelated, and each one involves a variety of manifestations or ways in which it can be expressed.

Three Groups of Gifts

For the sake of convenience, the gifts will be considered in three groups. First, gifts for the establishment of the church and for bringing it to a maturity where all the members can receive their own gifts and contribute to the upbuilding of the local body (Ephesians 4:11–16). These are the apostles, prophets, evangelists, and pastor-teachers who are chosen by the Lord, taken captive by Him, and given as gifts to the Church, not just to some particular local church. In each ministry more than an occasional manifestation of a gift of the Spirit is involved. Like the first apostles, these are mature, trained people, who were not sent out until they had gained experience under the great

Teacher (Jesus, then the Teacher Spirit, the Spirit of Truth). Their ministry was not limited to one local church. They sooner or later moved on, because they were given to the Church as a whole.

Second, gifts of the edification of the local body through individual members. These are specific manifestations of spiritual gifts given as they are needed and as the Spirit wills. They may be exercised by any member of the congregation. However, in some cases, even in local congregations a ministry may develop along the line of some gift, so that in this sense some may be called prophets, interpreters, or workers of miracles (1 Corinthians 12:29; 14:28). But this does not mean they "have" the gift in the sense of the gift being resident in them. They are still the Spirit's gifts, with each expression received directly from Him as He wills. It is important also, that all these gifts are ministered in the context of the body. There is a spontaneity about them.[18] But they are not to be exercised according to the individual's own feelings, but according to the directions of the Word (1 Corinthians 14), and according to the dictates of courtesy and love. Nor do these gifts make a person independent of the help of others. Paul's letters all show how much he depended on the help and prayers of the people in the churches.

Third, gifts for service and outreach. These include administration, ruling, ministry, giving, helps, mercy, and exhortation. Other gifts overlap into this group also. Prophecy, faith, miracles, and healings certainly contribute to outreach.

Apostles, Ambassadors for Christ

Jesus is the supreme High Priest and Apostle (Hebrews 3:1; John 5:36; 20:21). The word *apostle* was used, however, of any messenger who was appointed and commissioned for some special purpose. Epaphroditus was a messenger (apostle) appointed by and sent by the Philippian church to Paul (Philippians 2:25). The missionaries in Paul's company were the messengers (apostles) sent out by and commissioned by the churches (2 Corinthians 8:23).

The Twelve were apostles in a special sense, however. After a night of prayer, Jesus chose the Twelve out of a large group of disciples and called them apostles (Luke 6:13). The fellowship of the Last Supper was limited to them (Luke 22:14). Peter recognized the Twelve had a special ministry and overseership (Acts 1:20,25,26), probably with the promise in mind that the Twelve would in the future judge (rule) the twelve tribes of Israel (Matthew 19:28). Thus, no more apostles were chosen after Matthias to be among the Twelve. Nor were any replacements chosen when they were martyred. In the New Jerusalem there are just twelve foundations with the names of the twelve apostles in them (Revelation 21:14). The Twelve were thus a limited group and performed a special function in preaching, teaching, and establishing the Church as well as in witnessing to Christ's resurrection in power. No one else can be an apostle in the sense they were.

There were other apostles, however. Jesus sent out seventy others also. These were a different group from the Twelve altogether (Luke 10:1). But Jesus used exactly the same word in sending them as He did of the Twelve (in Luke 9:2), the Greek word *apostello*, from which apostle comes. He also gave the seventy the same commission and they returned with the same results.

Paul and Barnabas are also called apostles (Acts 14:4,14). Paul also calls Andronicus and Junius "outstanding among the apostles" who were before him (Romans 16:7). However, Paul refers to all the other apostles as apostles who were before him (Galatians 1:17). In speaking of the appearances of the risen Christ, he mentions that Christ was seen by Peter, the Twelve, then five hundred, then James the brother of Jesus, then by all the apostles, "and last of all" he was seen by Paul, "as to one abnormally born" (1 Corinthians 15:5–8). Thus, it appears that the rest of those who are named as apostles in the New Testament also belonged to a limited group of which Paul was the last.

This is confirmed by the qualifications laid down in connection with the selection of a replacement for Judas (Acts 1:21,22). An apostle had to be a firsthand witness to both the Resurrection and the teachings or sayings of Jesus. This is the reason the apostle Paul constantly found it necessary to defend his apostleship. He told the Corinthians, "Am I not free? Am I not an apostle? Have I not seen Jesus our Lord?" (1 Corinthians 9:1). Then he went on to say that they are the seal, the results, the confirmation, of his apostleship. Paul also made it very clear to the Galatians that he received the facts of the gospel, not from man, not from the other apostles, but from Jesus himself (Galatians 1:1,11,12,16,17). Thus he was a firsthand witness to both the resurrection and teachings of Jesus.

Paul also fulfilled the functions of the apostles. After Pentecost, the apostles did many signs and wonders (Acts 2:43; 5:12), and with great power bore witness to the resurrection of Jesus (4:33; 5:32). They taught the people (2:42), and felt the ministry of the Word was their chief responsibility (6:4; 8:25). Paul also kept connecting his apostleship with the proclamation of Christ's resurrection, with preaching and teaching, and with the signs of an apostle: "signs, wonders and miracles [mighty deeds]" (2 Corinthians 12:12; 1 Corinthians 15:9; 1 Timothy 1:1; 2:7; 2 Timothy 1:1,11).

Yet in spite of these limitations on the office of apostle, there is a continuation of apostolic ministry indicated through the Holy Spirit (Acts 5:32). We see also that God has set in the Church apostles, prophets, teachers, "workers of miracles, also those having gifts of healing, those able to help others, those with gifts of administration, and those speaking in different kinds of tongues" (1 Corinthians 12:28). Exactly the same expression is used of these gifts as is used of the various parts of the human body in 1 Corinthians 12:18. In other words, just as eyes, ears, hands, and feet are all necessary for the proper functioning of the body, so these ministry gifts, by the very nature of the Church, are necessary for its proper functioning.[19]

Apostolic ministry, then, is a church-building, fellowship-building work, exercised with accompanying miracles that are the work of the Spirit. The apostles left behind them established churches, organized with their own elders (also called bishops or overseers, as superintendents, administrative officers elected out of the congregations) and deacons (helpers, also elected out of the congregation). Surely, such ministry has continued throughout Church history and is still needed today. False apostles have come too (Revelation 2:2), but they need to be tested by their teaching (Galatians 1:8) and by their lives. The true apostles built the Church. None of them ever tried to build a following for themselves.

Prophets, Speakers for God

Jesus himself was the great Prophet, the One the Old Testament saw as the Coming One (Acts 3:22; Matthew 21:11; John 6:14; 7:40; Deuteronomy 18:15).

The Old Testament prophet was a Spirit-filled spokesman for God, a mouth for God, yet one taught by God what to do and say. (Compare Micah 3:8; Amos 3:8; Exodus 7:1; 4:15,16.)

The New Testament word also means a speaker for God, the proclaimer of revelation directly received from God. With the apostles they revealed truths that were mysteries in Old Testament times but are now revealed by the Spirit (Ephesians 3:5), and thus helped to lay the foundation of the Church (2:20). This implies they were used in bringing truth which was later included in the New Testament.

But, just as in the Old Testament times there were many prophets who challenged the people and led them in worship, but wrote no books, so it was the New Testament church. Many brought illumination and practical application of truths already received. A good example is that of Silas and Judas who brought the decision of the Jerusalem Council to Antioch: "Judas and Silas, who themselves were prophets, said much to encourage and strengthen the brothers" (Acts 15:32). This fits in very well with the nature of prophecy as we have seen it in 1 Corinthians 14:3.

Some prophets were used also to foretell the future, as was Agabus on two occasions recorded in the Book of Acts (11:28; 21:11). In both of these cases, Agabus left his home in Judea to give the prophecy where it would bring benefit. In the first case, an offering was taken to help the Jerusalem church during the prophesied famine, which came to pass. In the second case, the church was prepared to see God's will in the arrest and imprisonment of the apostle Paul. In neither case was there new doctrine involved. Nor was there direction given for what the church was to do. This was left to their own response to the Spirit. Never was there anything akin to fortune-telling in the ministry of these prophets, nor did they ever provide a substitute for a person seeking the will of God for himself.

Those who were used regularly by the Spirit in the exercise of the gift of prophecy in the local congregation are also called prophets (1 Corinthians 14:29,32,37). The Bible also warns against false prophets who claim to speak by the Spirit and who must be put to the test (1 John 4:1).

Evangelists, Proclaimers of Good News

An evangelist is a preacher of the gospel, a proclaimer of the good news. Jesus himself was the prophesied anointed Evangelist, anointed to preach the gospel, and known for preaching the good news to the poor (Luke 4:18; 7:22).

The word *evangelist* is used in only two other places in the New Testament. Philip became known as the evangelist (Acts 21:8). Then Paul urged Timothy to do the work of an evangelist (2 Timothy 4:5). But the corresponding verb and noun are used many times of bringing good news, declaring glad tidings (Acts 13:32), preaching the gospel of God's grace, the gospel of peace, or simply preaching Christ. The gospel is the good news about Jesus Christ. The evangelist comes, like Jesus, not "to condemn the world, but to save the world through him" (John 3:17).

Using Philip as an example, we see that the ministry of the evangelist took him to people who did not know the Lord. First, it was a city where miracles brought joy and where the people believed his preaching and were baptized (Acts 8:6–8,12). Second, he was sent to an individual, and starting where the Ethiopian eunuch was reading, Philip preached (evangelized, brought the good news about) Jesus (Acts 8:35). Thus, mass evangelism and personal evangelism are both the work of the evangelist.

Here is a distinction between the evangelist and the prophet that is not often noticed. The evangelist did not go to churches. He went where the sinners were. Prophets went to the churches. As in the case of Judas and Silas, their work was to stir up, cheer up, and strengthen the believers. In a sense, then, the prophets were revival men. There may be combinations of these ministries, of course. Very often evangelism is much easier when the local church is stirred up, revived, and strengthened. But Paul indicates that some men are especially gifted as prophets, others as evangelists.

The Bible also puts us on the alert with regard to evangelists. There are those who preach another gospel and who are to be considered as accursed, for they will come under the judgment of God (Galatians 1:8,9).

Good Food from Pastor-Teachers

Though some take pastors and teachers as separate ministries in Ephesians 4:11, they seem to be united. The repetition of the word "some" indicates only four ministries are being considered and that the pastors are also teachers.

"Pastor" is not used in the modern sense of the word. (Our pastors come closer to the New Testament elder-presbyter-bishop, the administrative officer of the local church, who was also to be "able to teach"; 1 Timothy 3:2.)

"Pastor" is, in fact, translated "shepherd" everywhere else in the New Testament. The same Greek word is used of Jesus as the great Shepherd of the sheep (Hebrews 13:20), our Good Shepherd (John 10:2,11,14,16; 1 Peter 2:25). The eastern shepherd led his flock to find food and water (Psalm 23:2). The word *shepherd* in Hebrew means a feeder. The primary concern of the pastor, as the term is used here, is thus not to direct the affairs of the church, but to teach them. The good food, of course, is the Word of God. And the pastor-teacher's task is to explain it and make it easier for the people to understand, assimilate, and apply it. We live in a changing world where new problems, new questions, new circumstances surely need the help of a teacher to point out the principles of the Word and show how they relate to our daily living. This is still the work of the teacher who is gifted by the Spirit and dedicated to Christ.[20]

Jesus is also the Great Teacher. (*Master* used in the King James Version is the British word for teacher, the same word that is translated "teacher" in Ephesians 4:11.) The Holy Spirit is just as prominently the Teacher-Spirit as He is the Spirit of Power and the Spirit of Prophecy, if not more so (John 14:17,26). It is true that the Holy Spirit teaches us all directly (2 Corinthians 3:3; John 6:45; 1 John 2:20,27; Jeremiah 31:34). We do not need human authority to obtain assurance of our salvation, nor do we need some person to teach us to know the Lord in a better, more personal way. The Spirit and the Word are enough for that.[21] But teachers gifted by the Spirit and given by Christ to the Church can bring out neglected truth, and help train and inspire others to become teachers. God wants all to become teachers in the sense of being able to explain the Word to others. But teachers who can feed us with the milk and meat of the Word are needed before this can be a reality (Hebrews 5:12–14).

Apollos may be an example of a teacher who "watered" what Paul had planted in Corinth, and who helped the people to grow spiritually by his refreshing teaching (1 Corinthians 3:6; Acts 18:27). Truly, his teaching must have come with the rivers of living water, the mighty overflowing of the Holy Spirit (John 7:38).[22] Remember, too, that Apollos had a teachable spirit (Acts 18:26).

Unfortunately, there are those who are "always learning but never able to acknowledge the truth" (2 Timothy 3:7), blind leaders of the blind (Matthew 15:14), false teachers who deny the Lord who bought them (2 Peter 2:1). These people God will not spare. Christians who love and honor Jesus can enjoy a unity of the Spirit and of the faith, even if they do disagree on some points or even in some of their methods of interpreting the Bible. We do have a love for sinners, even for those who deny the Lord, as we desire to draw them back to Him. But that is different from the fellowship in the Spirit we enjoy with believers, a fellowship that grows best as we maintain a teachable spirit.

Gifts for Building Up the Local Church

As has been indicated, the gifts listed in 1 Corinthians 12:8–10 seem to be classes of gifts that are to be exercised one at a time on various occasions by various individuals as the Spirit wills. It should be further noted that each of these gifts is directed toward the needs of the Body, rather than toward the needs of the one who is used by the Spirit to minister the gift.

The Message of Wisdom

This is a proclamation or a declaration of wisdom given to meet the need of some particular occasion or problem. It is not dependent on human ability or natural wisdom but is a revelation of divine counsel.[23] Through this gift supernatural insight into both the need and into God's Word bring the practical application of that Word to the need or problem at hand.

Because it is a "message" of wisdom, it is clear that only enough is given for the need. This gift does not raise us to a new level of wisdom, nor does it make it impossible for us to make mistakes. It just lets us draw on God's unlimited storehouse (Romans 11:33). Sometimes it may bring a message of wisdom to guide the Church, as in Acts 6:2–4; 15:13–21. It is possible also that it fulfills the promises given by Jesus for "words and wisdom that none of your adversaries will be able to resist or contradict" (Luke 21:15). That Jesus was speaking of a supernatural gift of a message of wisdom is shown by His command not to meditate (prepare) beforehand what they were going to say in the synagogues or before the courts (Luke 21:13,14). This was certainly fulfilled in the case of the apostles and of Stephen (Acts 4:8–14,19–21; 6:9,10).

The Message of Knowledge

Wisdom seems to have to do with the right application of knowledge. Thus the gift of a message (proclamation, declaration) of knowledge is closely related to the gift of a message of wisdom. By searching the Scriptures one finds that much is said about "the light [enlightening] of the knowledge of the glory of God in the face of Christ" (2 Corinthians 4:6), and the heavenly fragrance of the knowledge God gives us of Christ (2:14).

Paul's prayer for the Ephesians was: "I keep asking that the God of our Lord Jesus Christ, the glorious Father, may give you the Spirit of wisdom and revelation, so that you may know him better" (Ephesians 1:17). For the Colossians he prayed also that God would "fill you with the knowledge of his will through all spiritual wisdom and understanding," so that they "may live a life worthy of the Lord and may please him in every way: bearing fruit in every good work, growing in the knowledge of God" (Colossians 1:9,10). James calls for showing knowledge by good works from a good (noble, praiseworthy) life (James 3:13).

There is great emphasis on the knowledge of the truth, that is, the truth revealed in the gospel (1 Timothy 2:4; Hebrews 10:26). Knowledge also includes the gospel requirements and their application (1 Peter 3:7; 2 Peter 1:5,8). Paul says the Jews had a zeal for God, but not according to knowledge (Romans 10:2). Those who have the knowledge of God's requirements won't stumble because of the scruples of those who are weak in faith, nor do they cause others to stumble (1 Corinthians 8:1,8,10; compare Romans 14:1–18).

Knowledge clearly has to do with the knowledge of God, Christ, the gospel, and the applications of the gospel to Christian living. Paul further said, "We have not received the spirit of the world but the Spirit who is from God, that we may understand what God has freely given us. This is what we speak, not in words taught us by human wisdom but in words taught by the Spirit" (1 Corinthians 2:12,13).

All this fits in exactly with Christ's promise that the Spirit of Truth would testify of Him, teach you all things, and guide you into all truth (John 15:26; 14:26; 16:13). There can be only one conclusion. A message of knowledge comes as a declaration of gospel truth or the application of it. It is a gift bringing supernatural illumination of the gospel, especially in the ministry of teaching and preaching.[24] God did give knowledge of facts through visions and in various other ways, but there is absolutely no indication in the Bible that the gift of the message of knowledge is meant to bring revelation of where to find lost articles or of what disease or sin a person may be suffering from. Rather, it gives deeper insight into the Scripture.

One example may be seen at the house of Cornelius. The disciples who were with Peter there were astonished when they heard Gentiles speak in tongues as the Spirit gave utterance. But Peter saw it as God's seal of approval on the faith of the Gentiles and gave a message of knowledge both then and at the Jerusalem Council (Acts 10:47,48; 15:7–11).

Faith

Faith as a gift is obviously something different from saving faith and from the faith or faithfulness which is the fruit of the Spirit. Some take it to be the faith that moves mountains or the kind of faith exhibited by the heroes of Hebrews 11.[25] But just as a message of wisdom is given to the Body to meet the need for a specific bit of wisdom, so the gift of faith may be the impartation of faith to the Body. The Holy Spirit may use a song, prayer, testimony, or preaching as a channel to communicate faith or raise the level of faith in the Body. This communication of faith made Paul an able minister of the new testament (new covenant) (2 Corinthians 3:4–6). It enabled him to help others receive the Spirit through the hearing of faith (Galatians 3:2,5). Surely, also, it was manifest in the united prayer that brought a new outpouring of the Spirit in Jerusalem (Acts 4:31). Possibly it has been expressed in power to carry out other types of ministry as well.

Gifts of Healings

Both the words "gifts" and "healing" (1 Corinthians 12:9) are in the plural in the Greek. Some take this to mean that there are a variety of forms of this gift.[26] Some of these take it that certain individuals are gifted to heal one sort of disease or sickness, some another sort. Philip, for example was used especially in the healing of the paralyzed and the lame (Acts 8:7). Others take it that God gives one a gift of a supply of healings at a particular time, and another supply is given at another time, perhaps to someone else, most probably in the ministry of the evangelist.[27] The healing of the lame man at the Gate Beautiful is taken as an example (3:6,7).

Still others take it that every healing is a special gift[28]—that is, the gift is for the sick person who has the need. Thus, in this view, the Spirit does not make men healers. Instead, He provides a new ministry of healing for each need as it arises in the Church. For example, the power that flowed into the body of the woman with the issue of blood brought her a gracious gift of healing (Luke 8:43–48). Acts 3:6 literally states, "What I have, this thing I give to you." "This thing" is singular and indicates a specific gift given to Peter to give to the lame man. It does not seem to mean he had a reservoir of healing gifts in himself, but he had to look to the Lord and receive from the Spirit a new gift for each sick person to whom he ministered.

There is no evidence that the apostles were able to heal whenever they felt like it by some resident power of healing. Nor did they consider healing their chief ministry. We read of "extraordinary miracles through Paul" at Ephesus (Acts 19:11). This implies that in connection with the establishing of the seven churches in Asia through Paul's ministry at Ephesus, unusual miracles were done that did not take place everywhere. Thus, Paul did not have any automatic gift in himself that made him a healer. Actually, in Ephesus God used handkerchiefs (sweat cloths) and work aprons taken from Paul while he was working at his tentmaking. Miracles were done as these things became a means of helping sick people express their faith. It is not easy for a person who is sick to express faith, and Jesus often did or had them do various things to encourage active expression of faith. At one time even Peter's shadow became such a means (5:15,16). But the means used were always varied and never allowed to become form or ceremony. Their faith was to be in the Lord, not in the means used to help them.

These things have nothing directly to do with the gifts of healings, however. The emphasis in 1 Corinthians 12:9 is on the expression of this gift through the various individual members of the Body. We do not need to find an evangelist. (His work is primarily for sinners.) It may not always be possible to call the elders of the church (James 5:14,15). But gifts of healings are available to every member of the Body to minister to the sick.

Miraculous Powers

Both words are in the plural, and again the suggestion is that many varieties of miracles or deeds of power are available. The word translated "miraculous powers" in 1 Corinthians 12:10 is the plural of the word "power" in Acts 1:8, but in the plural it means deeds of mighty, supernatural power that go beyond anything man can do. They are direct divine interventions in the world of man and nature which are distinguished from healings.

Palma points out that the word translated "miraculous powers" ("working of miracles," KJV) is used almost exclusively of the activity of God (Matthew 14:2; Mark 6:14; Galatians 3:5; Philippians 3:21) or of Satan (2 Thessalonians 2:7,9; Ephesians 2:2). He suggests, therefore, that this gift is especially operative in connection with the conflict between God and Satan. These acts of power bringing defeat to Satan might include the judgment of blindness on Elymas (Acts 13:9–11) and the casting out of demons.[29]

Some take this gift as one for raising the dead or nature miracles, such as stilling the storm and walking on the water.[30] But Donald Gee cautions that there is an absence in both Acts and the Epistles of nature miracles. Paul suffered four shipwrecks that we know of. The description of the one at Malta shows that God's providence enabled them to escape to land, but by swimming, not by a miracle (2 Corinthians 11:25–27; Acts 27:43 to 28:5). Only two occasions of raising the dead are recorded (9:40; 20:10). For the rest, they were referred to the comfort of the blessed hope of the resurrection and our Lord's return (1 Thessalonians 4:13–18).[31]

Both the gifts of healing and miraculous powers demonstrate to us and to the world around that Jesus is indeed Victor. At the Cross, the full price was paid and Satan's doom was sealed. But the full outworking of this will not be seen until we are changed and given bodies that are immortal and incorruptible and until Satan is finally cast into the lake of fire and the last enemy, death, is destroyed (1 Corinthians 15:51–54; 15:26; Revelation 20:10–14). In the meantime, there are gracious spiritual gifts that are available to give us a foretaste of this in healings and miracles, not as we make demands, but as the Spirit wills (1 Corinthians 12:11).

Prophecy

The nature of this gift has been discussed in connection with 1 Corinthians 14 and in connection with the prophet. All that needs to be emphasized here is that the gift was available to any member of the congregation, not just to those who had a regular ministry as prophets. In fact, because of the edification to the Church through this gift, all are encouraged to seek it. Prophecy is related also to the illumination of the mysteries of the gospel. Again, there may be variety in the expression of the gift.[32] But in most cases it seems to be directed to the body of believers who are gathered together. Peter's sermon, as has been indicated, was a fulfillment of Joel's promise concerning prophesying. But Peter took the tongues as part of that fulfillment as well, and as 1 Corinthians 14 indicates, the tongues do need interpretation to edify. However, in view of the nature of Peter's sermon, it is possible that during the course of preaching on other occasions in Acts the gift of prophecy might be in operation. A preacher does need to prepare, but there may still be times when the Spirit will give him something beyond what he has in his notes. If the experience of the Old Testament prophets is any guide, we see that God often dealt with them while they were alone with Him, and then sent them forth to prophesy, to speak for Him. Through prophecy also, the Spirit touches the sensitive spots, reveals what was secret, and brings conviction and worship, as well as encouragement and stimulation to action.[33]

Distinguishing between Spirits

Again, the plurals indicate a variety of ways in which this gift may be manifest. It involves a "distinguishing between spirits." Since it is mentioned directly after the gift of prophecy, it has been suggested that it is involved in the judging of prophecy mentioned in 1 Corinthians 14:29.[34] In fact, the word translated "distinguishing" involves forming a judgment and is related to the Greek word used of judging prophecy. It involves a supernaturally given perception, differentiating between spirits, good and evil, true or false, in order to make a decision.

John says we are not to believe every spirit, but must put them to the test (1 John 4:1). Sometimes, a gift of the Spirit is needed to do this. Actually, the Bible speaks of three kinds of spirits, the Spirit of God, the spirit of a person, and the spirit of the devil (plus the evil spirits or demons associated with him). In the operation of this gift in the local assembly or gathering of believers, it would seem that the spirit of a person might be the chief offender. Even with the best of intentions, it is possible that some people will mistake their own deep feelings for the voice of the Spirit. Or because of excessive zeal or spiritual ignorance in not knowing how to yield to the Holy Spirit, one's own spirit may intrude.[35]

Like the other gifts, this one does not raise an individual to a new level of ability. Nor does it give anyone the power to go around looking at people and telling what spirit motivates them. It is a specific gift for a specific occasion. Some examples may possibly be found in Acts 5:3; 8:20–23; 13:10; 16:16–18.

Tongues, Kinds or Families of Languages

The nature of this gift has also been described in connection with 1 Corinthians 14. It is part of the wealth of gifts operating through the multitude of believers through the one Spirit. The New Testament indicates it was common and considered desirable.[36]

The parallels between Acts and 1 Corinthians 14 indicate that the gift is the same in form as the evidence in Acts; however, the purpose of tongues in 1 Corinthians 12 is as a gift used in the church and needing interpretation to bring edification.

It is often called "ecstatic gibberish" by people who do not have the experience, but this is not Paul's view of the gift. By it we speak to God. It involves communication. By it we speak mysteries, which to Paul always meant spiritual truth (1 Corinthians 14:2). The Greek word clearly means languages, not mere nonsense syllables.[37]

If speaking in tongues seems like nonsense syllables, so did the language of the Assyrians to the Hebrews (Isaiah 28:11,13). To those who do not know Hebrew, it would sound like nonsense syllables. "Our Father" in Hebrew is pronounced *"ah-vee-noo."* "I will fear no evil" is *"lo ee-rah ra."* Since tongues is often a matter of worship and praise, spontaneous utterance and repetition should be expected, as in many psalms. Psalm 150:2, "Praise him for his acts of power," is pronounced, *"hah-le-loo-hoo bih-g'voo-roh-taw."* Then *"ha-le-loo-hoo"* is repeated again and again in the next few verses.

No matter how speaking in tongues sounds, and whether it is the languages of men or of angels, tongues means languages both in Acts and in Corinthians. When we pray in tongues our spirit prays, since our spirit is the medium through which the gift operates, and thus involves yielding our spirits and our wills to God as well as our tongues and vocal organs for the operation of the gift (1 Corinthians 14:14).[38] The result is language, as the Spirit gives utterance.

Interpretation of Tongues

Interpretation of tongues is usually taken as giving the meaning or essential content of speaking in tongues.[39] The basic meaning of the word is translation. The corresponding verb is used of translation in John 1:42; 9:7; and Hebrews 7:2. But it may mean either translation or interpretation.[40] Even when it means translation, this does not necessarily mean word for word. The job of the translator is to put the words into good sense and good grammar. Thus Psalm 23:1 is only four words in Hebrew, but needs eleven words to translate it into English in the New International Version.

The gift, of course, does not imply any knowledge of the language on the part of the interpreter. It is received directly from the Holy Spirit, and comes as one gives attention to the Lord, rather than to the tongues that are being given. Again, the gift may come in a variety of ways, "either by vision, by burden, or by suggestion, just as the Lord may choose."[41] A step of faith may be required also in that the Spirit very often gives only a few words of the interpretation at first. Then, when these are given in faith, the rest comes as the Spirit gives the interpretation.[42]

Administration (Governments)

The plural seems to indicate a variety of expressions of this gift to meet the needs of a position of leadership or administration (1 Corinthians 12:28). Other uses outside the New Testament imply giving wise counsel. A closely related noun means a steersman or pilot of a ship (Acts 27:11). It would seem to imply managing the business affairs of a congregation as well as giving spiritual leadership.

Probably, this was the Spirit's gift especially for the chief administrator, called the elder or presbyter (by comparison with the rulers of the synagogues), and called the bishop or overseer (superintendent) in Greek. This was an elected official. But the person was to be chosen, not through politics or power plays, but through the Spirit's wisdom given to the body. Then that person would be equipped with and depend on the Spirit's gifts, not just his or her own leadership ability.

The plural may also indicate that the gift was available to other positions involving leadership or administration as well.

Helps, Helpful Deeds

The plural again indicates a variety of helpful deeds that may be inspired by this gift. The corresponding verb means to take someone's part, or come to the aid of someone. It is used of helping the weak (Acts 20:35) and of devoting ourselves to kindness (1 Timothy 6:2).

The word was sometimes used in ancient times as a technical banking term for a chief accountant, however.[43] This would fit in with the work for which the seven were chosen in Acts 6:2,3. There, the word "tables" means money tables, and refers to a cash fund, a fund which Paul brought offerings to replenish at least twice. Paul was always very much concerned that finances be handled carefully and according to the instructions of the churches. There is nothing "unspiritual" about money matters in the work of the church. This would indicate also that deacons who were "full of the Spirit and wisdom" (v. 3) continued to carry this responsibility, and the Spirit continued to supply them with the gifts they needed in their work. The deacons also ministered the church's help to the poor, the weak, and the sick. Thus, the ordinary meaning of helpful deeds also fits their office as we see it in the Early Church.

Ministry, Service, Deaconship

Romans 12:7 uses the word "serving" or *ministry,* probably for the ministry of a deacon. The same Greek word is used of both the ministry of the Word and the ministry of the seven in Acts 6:2,4. It was often used for the preparation of a meal, and also of various types of spiritual service, such as the ministry of reconciliation (2 Corinthians 5:18). Another common use was of aid or distribution of help to the poor. This too fits the work of the deacon. Thus the meaning here of the gift of ministry is most probably that gift of the Spirit which enables the deacon to fulfill the office with power and wisdom. Of course, it is not limited to deacons.

Encouragement (Exhortation)

Though 1 Corinthians 14:3 includes this gift with prophecy, Romans 12:8 lists it as a distinct gift. It includes the ideas of urging, challenging, or making an appeal. It is possible also that the verb has the idea of conciliating, encouraging friendship, bringing about the unity of the Spirit.

Specific encouragement to endure to the end and to keep the hope of Christ's coming before us is another important aspect of this gift. Our hope is a vital element in our Christian life, and though the study of the Scripture is important in maintaining it (Romans 15:4), this gift of the Spirit can urge us on in the light of this hope and can make it live.

Giving, Sharing

This implies giving a part of what you have, sharing with others, especially of giving to the needy (Ephesians 4:28, Romans 12:8). As Ephesians indicates, this is not primarily a gift of the Spirit to help the wealthy share their wealth. The poor are urged to work with their hands in order to be able to share with the needy. It was the gift or ministry of the Spirit in which all participated immediately after Pentecost (Acts 2:44,45; 4:34,37). It was to be done with simplicity, sincerity, and generosity. Barnabas is one of the best examples, while Ananias and Sapphira show how it was not to be done.

Ruling, Directing, Caring, Giving Aid

Though ruling is used of having oversight of something, it is also used of showing concern, caring for people, and giving aid. Once again, leadership is not a matter of dominating others or playing the tyrant, but of service.[44] There is no thought here of ruling in the sense of directing the work of the Spirit or destroying spontaneity of worship. This is rather the gift that helps our leaders care for our souls and makes the whole church concerned about helping one another under the leadership God has given us.

Showing Mercy

This final gift in Paul's list in Romans 12 (v. 8) has to do with a ministry of doing acts of mercy, of helping others graciously and with compassion. It involves the personal care of the needy, the sick, the hungry, the naked (those with insufficient clothes), and the prisoners. It is one of the most important of gifts, as Jesus himself indicated (Matthew 25:31–46).

It may include such ministry as was done by Dorcas (Acts 9:36–39). But as we look through the Scriptures we see the blind man calling on Jesus for an act of mercy that he might see (Mark 10:47,51). The rich man in Hades asked that Lazarus be sent for an act of mercy to take a drop of water and cool his tongue (Luke 16:24). The Samaritan showed acts of mercy to the man who fell among thieves (10:37). But the same word is often used of God's mercy in giving salvation, blessing, and ministry (Romans 11:30; 1 Peter 2:10; 2 Corinthians 4:1), for God is rich in mercy (Ephesians 2:4). Thus, this gift may minister God's mercy and help to those in need, whether their need is physical, financial, mental, or spiritual.

This gift is to be ministered with cheerfulness, gladness, and graciousness. Doing these deeds of mercy out of a sense of duty or in the hope of reward or as an expression of human kindness can never be enough. In fact, the effectiveness of an act of mercy is often more dependent on the way it is done than on what is done or how much. It takes the gift of the Spirit to have a ministry along these lines. Yet it, along with the gift of giving, is open to all of us and, in fact, very necessary for all of us. Perhaps it would be well if every Christian would read Matthew 25:31–46.

No matter how the passage is interpreted, the principles are there. Though our salvation does not depend on works, if it is real it will go to work. The Spirit who loves to glorify Jesus will help us do all these things as unto Jesus.

All the Gifts Are Needed

Over most of the history of the Church there has been too much dependence on human resources. As long as the funds, equipment, people, materials, and technical skill are available, projects are pushed with every expectation of success. Yet many times they fail in spite of everything. On the other hand, some have started with almost nothing but with a tremendous confidence in God and a dependence on His gifts and help of the Holy Spirit, and the impossible has been done.

It is a great thing to learn to use the human resources available, while depending on the Spirit. The gifts of the Spirit are still God's primary means of building the Church both spiritually and numerically. Nothing else can do it.

Imagine a Rolls Royce, Cadillac, or some other fine car with all the best options: leather upholstery, heated seats, CD/DVD, On-Star, satellite radio. But then suppose that instead of a motor it had a set of pedals for the driver to push it along by his or her own power. Ridiculous? But in God's eyes, so is a church that has tremendous human drive, wonderful buildings and equipment, beautiful organization and planning, but lacks the gifts of the Spirit!

Just as the gift of the Spirit—the baptism in the Spirit—is for us, so all the gifts are for us. Why not claim them, exercise them, depend on them? They are the means God has provided so that we can advance on the foundation that is laid in Christ Jesus our Lord. The Holy Spirit who loves to honor and reveal Jesus will minister His power to and through us. He will not disappoint us. For all the gifts will glorify Jesus and prepare us for His return. Then they will be no longer needed. But until then, they are.

Appendix:
Is Mark 16:9–20 Inspired?

Pentecostals have long proclaimed that "these signs shall follow them that believe" (Mark 16:17, KJV). Recently, some opponents have tried to use critical theories to undermine confidence in this by casting doubt on the last twelve verses of Mark. Some versions in modern English have drawn attention to this.

The Phillips translation refers to this passage as "an ancient appendix." *The New English Bible,* according to R. V. G. Tasker, professor emeritus of the University of London, sets forth the two later endings of Mark's Gospel "in a way in which they can be seen by the reader to be not casual variants, but deliberate attempts to bring the Gospel to what was considered a more satisfactory conclusion."[1] This is an example of the increasing boldness of those who hold that Mark 16:9–20 is a product of human ingenuity, not of divine inspiration.

It is difficult, however, for Bible-believing Christians to accept the conclusions of these critics. Samuel Zwemer, former professor at Princeton and a great missionary, pointed out that they "leave the Gospel to end abruptly and rob us of the Great Commission there recorded."[2]

For more than one hundred years an impressive array of scholars and critics have rejected these verses. My grandfather's Greek Testament (Scholz text, 1875) indicates by a marginal note in Latin that they should probably be omitted. The modern Nestlé text puts them in brackets. On the other hand, the Marcan authorship of these verses has been defended by many fine scholars including Belser, Bengel, Bleek, Broadus, A. C. Clark, Canon Cook, De Wette, Ebrard, Eichhorn, G. Hartmann, Lange, E. Miller, Olshausen, and in great detail, Dean J. W. Burgon of Oriel College, Oxford.[3] A fine summary of Dean Burgon's book is given by Zwemer.[4]

The problem comes from the fact that ancient copies of the Gospel of Mark have been found ending in four different ways.[5]

1. A few ancient manuscripts and versions end at Mark 16:8. These include two very important manuscripts, the Sinaitic manuscript (Aleph), and the Vatican manuscript (B), both copied in the fourth century AD Westcott and Hort (followed by Nestlé) chose these two as the best ancient manuscripts available and made them the chief basis for their Greek text. The Vatican manuscript (B), however, does have a blank space long enough for these verses, indicating that the ancient scribe knew of these verses but may have been copying from a manuscript which ended at 16:8.[6] Eusebius, the fourth-century church historian, stated further (Quest. ad. Marium 1) that in his day almost all Greek manuscripts ended with 16:8. Jerome

referred to this also (Ep. 120.3) but included verses 9–20 in the Vulgate because they were found in the Old Latin manuscripts.

2. The vast majority of ancient manuscripts and versions in existence today include verses 9–20 without a break. Justin Martyr, about AD 150, knew it, and his disciple, Tatian, included it in his *diatessaron* (a sort of harmony of the four Gospels). Irenaeus, who also lived in the second century, quoted it.[7]

3. A very few manuscripts, mostly late, have a shorter ending after 16:8. It may be translated: "But they reported all these things briefly to Peter and those with him. And afterward Jesus Himself sent out by them from east to west the sacred and imperishable message (*kerygma*) of eternal salvation." In most of these manuscripts this is followed by 16:9–20.[8]

4. One fifth-century manuscript (W) has 16:9–20 with an added expansion within it, part of which is referred to by Jerome.[9]

The shorter ending and the longer expansion give evidence of being later additions and are rejected by practically all scholars. This leaves us with two questions. First, why do some early manuscripts end at 16:8? Second, what is the origin of 16:9–20?

In answer to the first question, a growing number of liberal scholars say Mark intended his Gospel to end with 16:8. Some have gone to great lengths to find instances in ancient Greek literature where a sentence ends with the preposition *gar* ("for") as it does in this verse.[10] One suggestion is that Mark simply meant that for the time the women were hushed into silence, not by terror, but by awe, at the wonder of the Resurrection message they were carrying. These critics thus consider Mark 16:8 an appropriate conclusion to the Book.[11]

Another suggestion is that the promise of an appearance in Galilee in verse 7 is eschatological, referring to the Second Coming, thus supposing that Mark ended by looking ahead to the future and had no intention of telling of the other Resurrection appearances of Jesus. The Greek, however, indicates that Jesus was going before His disciples to Galilee, which may be taken in the sense of leading the way. This fits the expectation of an appearance in Galilee in the near future, not at the *parousia*.[12]

Actually, it seems unlikely that Mark's Gospel could have ended abruptly at 16:8 in its original form. Archaeologists and other scholars have found thousands of ancient Greek writings, both secular and religious. In all of these it is extremely rare to find a Greek sentence ending with *gar*, and no one has yet found an example of *gar* at the end of a book.[13] Many find it impossible to believe that any account of the gospel or good news could end on a note of fear. Nor is it likely that the word "afraid" in 16:8 means awe or wonder. In four places in this Gospel, Mark uses the same verb (*ephobounto*) to mean "they were afraid of." This would suggest that the original manuscript of Mark's Gospel was somehow broken off or torn off in the middle of a sentence here.[14]

A few modern writers suggest that someone deliberately cut off the end of Mark's Gospel because they did not like what it said. But this is not likely, and would hardly be done by those who first circulated the Book.

Others suggest that death prevented Mark from finishing the Book. But the majority of both Protestant and Catholic scholars today believe the original ending was accidentally torn off soon after it was written and was lost. All the evidence points to the conclusion that Mark was circulated at an early period without an ending.[15]

We must therefore face our second question: What is the origin of Mark 16:9-20? As we have seen, it can be traced back to the early part of the second century within a generation or two of those who were alive when Mark wrote the Gospel. Many scholars, both Catholic and Protestant, consider it a dependable part of the Bible whether Mark himself wrote it or not.[16] Yet, even those who say this often have doubts about Mark's authorship, and some who are otherwise generally conservative seem to want to get rid of it.

Those who reject Mark's authorship do so on two grounds, one stylistic, the other thaumaturgic (due to the miracles mentioned at the end). They also lay great emphasis on the fact that the verses are missing from the great manuscripts Aleph and B. Hort has been the most influential here.[17] Yet all scholars, even today, are not as sure as Westcott and Hort were that where Aleph and B agree we must accept them. Nor do they exactly agree here, for the Vatican manuscript (B) at least left room for these verses. We know also that these verses were known and quoted as Scripture long before these two manuscripts were copied. We know too that both Aleph and B contain other omissions as well as interpolations.[18] It is not absolutely necessary to accept their verdict as final when many ancient manuscripts do have the ending.

The argument from style is based on seventeen words in 16:9-20 which the critics say are not found in the rest of Mark or at least are not used in the same sense as they were used earlier in the Book. These include "the first day of the week" (which Mark may not have had occasion to use before), "afterward" (v. 12), and "creature" (v. 15). They point out also that it seems strange that Mary Magdalene is mentioned as the woman "out of whom he had cast seven devils" (v. 9), as if the writer did not know she had been mentioned in 16:1.[19]

Arguments of this sort from style are always weak. A change in subject matter, situation, or circumstances can account easily for new words or words used in a different manner. Broadus examined the preceding twelve verses (Mark 15:44 to 16:8) and found seventeen words there not found elsewhere in Mark.[20] It is not unusual for any author to use new words or to use them in a new sense. Nor is the mention of seven devils merely a matter of introducing Mary Magdalene. Rather, it is a preparation for us to understand why the disciples did not believe her when they first heard (v. 11). They apparently thought one of the demons had returned or that she was now possessed with an eighth.

We suspect, however, that the real reason so many wish to reject 16:9–20 as coming from Mark may be found in verses 17 and 18: "And these signs shall follow them that believe; In my name shall they cast out devils; they shall speak with new tongues; they shall take up serpents; and if they drink any deadly thing, it shall not hurt them; they shall lay hands on the sick, and they shall recover."

Some who are otherwise conservative do admit that these verses might fit in with the heavy emphasis on the miraculous and on the deeds of Jesus we find in Mark's Gospel, but they would rather classify verses 17 and 18 with the magic-type miracles, the show-off miracles found in the apocryphal Gospels.[21]

The Book of Acts and the Epistles show us, however, that these things were part of the experience and teaching of the Early Church. Zwemer, who was a Presbyterian, put it well when he wrote: "And as for 'the signs' that shall follow those who believe, all of which the critics reject as thaumaturgic and fantastic (v. 17), we are content with the miracles of missions, since the day when Paul shook off the viper at Melita to the experiences of David Livingstone in Africa, the exorcising of demons in China, and the providential deliverances among the headhunters of Borneo in our own day. The Lord is still working with His apostles and 'confirming the word with signs following. Amen.'"[22]

Before leaving the subject, we should mention that many have seen another possibility for the authorship of this passage. In November 1891, F. C. Conybeare found in the Armenian manuscript (dated AD 986) a marginal note or heading printed in red which said simply "of the Presbyter Ariston." Many jumped at this and concluded it was a reference to Aristion, mentioned by Papias early in the second century with the presbyter or apostle John as a disciple of John or perhaps of the Lord. Some suggest that this explains "the Johannine style"[23] (though others make this passage strongly dependent on Luke).[24] The discovery of this Ariston or possibly Aristion so pleased Gregory that he declared 16:9–20 "is neither part nor parcel of Mark's Gospel," yet they can be accepted as truth for the words of Aristion as "a disciple of the Lord's" are "every whit as good as Mark's words."[25] There seems to be some evidence, however, that the note or rubric attributing these verses to the Presbyter Ariston was not added to the Armenian manuscript until the thirteenth or fourteenth century AD. So it is unlikely the note is of genuine value.[26]

A few writers today follow Zwemer and Dean Burgon in insisting that there should be "no break and no mutilation of the Mark text."[27] Merrill Tenney of Wheaton College suggests more cautiously that "if" Mark wrote verses 9–20, "he probably added it as an epilogue."[28] This still does not explain the apparent breaking off at the end of verse 8 and the seeming lack of transition to verse 9.

One thing the critics seem to have overlooked. Verses 9–20 are missing primarily from the Greek manuscripts from the east. The so-called Western Text (as D) and the Old Latin manuscripts all have it. It is generally held that Mark wrote his Gospel with the Romans in mind. Many details in the Gospel substantiate this. It may be that Mark's original writing was broken off at verse 8 and was then copied and distributed in the east without any ending. Then, it may be that someone at Rome who knew Mark wrote asking how he intended his Gospel to end. Mark, not knowing just where it was broken off, would then have written verses 9–20 as a summary of the Resurrection account.

In any case, what we find in these verses is in line with the accounts given us in the other Gospels. Like them, it shows the initial unbelief of the disciples and the exhortations of Jesus to faith and to be witnesses.[29] Certainly, the ending was known when there were people still alive who could verify what the apostles said. We have every reason to believe that these verses are genuinely inspired of the Spirit and meant for our edification and obedience. No one would have dared add them to the Gospel of Mark as early as we have witnesses that they were there. That is, no one but Mark himself.

This article first appeared in *Paraclete*, Volume 4, Number 1, Winter 1970.

Appendix Notes

1. *The Greek New Testament*, ed. R. V. G. Tasker (London: Oxford University Press; Cambridge: Cambridge University Press, 1964), 417.

2. Samuel M. Zwemer, *Into All the World* (Grand Rapids: Zondervan Publishing House, 1943), 69.

3. A. T. Robertson, *Studies in Mark's Gospel* (Nashville, Tenn.: Broadman Press, 1958), 127.

4. Zwemer, *Into All the World*, 69–86.

5. Bruce M. Metzger, The Text of the New Testament (London: Oxford University Press, 1964), 226.

6. Everett F. Harrison, *Introduction to the New Testament* (Grand Rapids: Wm. B. Eerdmans Publishing Co., 1964), 87; Metzger, *Text of the New Testament*, 228.

7. Metzger, *Text of the New Testament*, 227; Alfred Wikenhauser, *New Testament Introduction*, trans. Joseph Cunningham (New York: Herder and Herder, 1960), 171.

8. Harrison, *Introduction to the New Testament*; Metzger, *Text of the New Testament*, 226.

9. Metzger, *Text of the New Testament*, 227.

10. Paul Feine, Johannes Behm, Werner George Kummel, *Introduction to the New Testament*, trans. A. J. Mattill, Jr. (Nashville, Tenn.: Abingdon Press, 1966), 72; Harold A. Guy, *Origin of the Gospel of Mark* (New York: Harper & Brothers, Publishers, 1955), 159–60.

11. Feine, *Introduction to the New Testament*, 72; Guy, *Origin of the Gospel of Mark*, 159–60.

12. Harrison, *Introduction to the New Testament*, 179.

13. Metzger, *Text of the New Testament*, 228.

14. Ibid.

15. Wikenhauser, *New Testament Introduction*, 172; Caspar Rene Gregory, *Canon and Text of the New Testament* (New York: Charles Scribner's Sons, 1907), 311.

16. Wikenhauser, *New Testament Introduction*, 172.

17. F. J. A. Hort, *Introduction and Appendix to the New Testament in the Original Greek* (New York: Macmillan, 1881), 28–51; cited in Robertson, *Studies in Mark's Gospel*, 127.

18. Zwemer, *Into All the World*, 76.

19. Metzger, *Text of the New Testament*, 227; Wikenhauser, *New Testament Introduction*, 172.

20. Cited from the *Baptist Quarterly*, July 1869, in Zwemer, *Into All the World*, 79.

21. Harrison, *Introduction to the New Testament*, 88.

22. Zwemer, *Into All the World*, 85–86.

23. Robertson, *Studies in Mark's Gospel*, 132.

24. Feine, *Introduction to the New Testament*, 71.

25. Gregory, *Canon and Text*, 511.

26. Metzger, *Text of the New Testament*, 227.

27. Zwemer, *Into All the World*, 85; George A. Hadjiantoniou, *New Testament Introduction* (Chicago: Moody Press, 1957), 120.

28. Merrill C. Tenney, *New Testament Survey* rev. ed. (Grand Rapids: Wm. B. Eerdmans Publishing Co., 1961), 163.

29. Ibid. The class notes of this writer, sitting under Tenney at Gordon Divinity School, indicate that Tenney then suggested that both the long and the shorter endings were written by Mark when first one and then others wrote asking how the Book ended.

Notes

Chapter 1

1. Floyd V. Filson, *The New Testament Against Its Environment* (London: SCM Press, 1950), 79.

2. John V. Taylor, *Go-Between God* (Philadelphia: Fortress Press, 1972), 64.

3. Amos D. Millard, "The Holy Spirit and Us," *Paraclete*, 2, no. 2 (1968): 20.

Chapter 2

1. J. Ritchie Smith, *The Holy Spirit in the Gospels* (New York: The Macmillan Company, 1926), 27.

2. George Johnston, *The Spirit-Paraclete in the Gospel of John* (Cambridge: University Press, 1970), 3.

3. Walter Eichrodt, *Theology of the Old Testament,* trans. J. A. Baker (London: SCM Press, 1961), 2:46.

4. Th. C. Vriezen, *An Outline of Old Testament Theology,* 2nd ed., rev. (Newton, Mass.: Charles C. Branfor, 1970), 215.

5. George Eldon Ladd, *A Theology of the New Testament* (Grand Rapids: William B. Eerdmans Publishing Co., 1974), 287.

6. E. A. Speiser, *Genesis* (Anchor Bible; Garden City, N. Y.: Doubleday and Co., 1964), comment on Genesis 1:2.

7. Vriezen, *Outline of Old Testament Theology,* 214. See also C. F. Keil, *Bible Commentary on The Old Testament* (Grand Rapids: Wm. B. Eerdmans Publishing Co., reprint), 1:48.

8. H. C. Leupold, *Exposition of Genesis* (Grand Rapids: Baker Book House, 1950), 1:49.

9. Gustave Friedrich Oehler, *Theology of the Old Testament* (Grand Rapids: Zondervan Publishing House, reprint from 1883), 118.

10. Adam Clarke, *The Holy Bible With a Commentary* (New York: Abingdon Cokesbury Press, n.d. ca. 1830), 1:42.

11. A. B. Davidson, *The Theology of the Old Testament* (Ebinburgh: T. & T. Clark, 1955 reprint from 1904), 121–22.

12. Keil, *Bible Commentary,* 1:78; Samuel R. Driver, *The Book of Genesis* 3rd ed. (New York: E. S. Gorham, 1905), 38.

13. Driver, *Book of Genesis,* 83–84; Alan Richardson, *Genesis I–XI* (Torch Bible Commentary; London: SCM Press, 1953), 95.

14. Speiser, *Genesis,* 44.

15. Smith, *Holy Spirit in the Gospels,* 26.

16. Leupold, *Exposition of Genesis,* 1:255–56.

17. William Barclay, *The Promise of the Spirit* (Philadelphia: The Westminster Press, 1960), 11.

18. A. H. McNeile, *The Book of Numbers* (Cambridge Bible; Cambridge: University Press, 1931), 63; L. E. Binns, *The Book of Numbers* (Westminster Commentary; London: Methuen & Co., 1927), 71.

19. J. A. Thompson, "Numbers," *The New Bible Commentary* rev. ed. (Grand Rapids: Wm. B. Eerdmans Publishing Co., 1970), 192.

20. Binns, *The Book of Numbers*, 191.

Chapter 3

1. A. B. Davidson, *Theology of the Old Testament*, 125.

2. Oehler, *Theology of the Old Testament*, 354; Eichrodt, *Theology of the Old Testament*, 1:308; 2:51.

3. Keil, *Bible Commentary*, 239.

4. G. A. Cooke, *The Book of Judges* (Cambridge Bible; Cambridge: University Press, 1918), 37; Paulus Cassel, *Judges and Ruth* (Lange's Commentary; Grand Rapids: Zondervan Publishing Co., reprint from 1865), 70.

5. Samuel J. Shultz, *The Old Testament Speaks* (New York: Harper & Brothers, 1960), 107.

6. A. B. Simpson, *The Holy Spirit* (New York: The Christian Alliance Publishing Co., 1895), 1:146.

7. Keil, *Bible Commentary*, 338.

8. Davidson, *Theology of the Old Testament*, 127.

9. George A. F. Knight, *A Christian Theology of the Old Testament* (London: SCM Press, 1959), 37.

10. George Foote Moore, *A Critical and Exegetical Commentary on Judges* ICC (Edinburgh: T. & T. Clark, 1895), 87.

11. Cassel, *Judges and Ruth*, 119; Cooke, *Book of Judges*, 80.

12. Oehler, *Theology of the Old Testament*, 142.

13. Keil, *Bible Commentary*, 399.

14. Moore, *Critical and Exegetical Commentary*, 325, 338. See Barclay, *Promise of the Spirit*, 17.

15. Keil, *Bible Commentary*, 400.

16. Eichrodt, *Theology of the Old Testament*, 2:52.

17. See F. E. Marsh, *Emblems of the Holy Spirit* (Grand Rapids: Kregel Publications, reprinted 1971), 38–112.

18. A. F. Kirkpatrick, *The First Book of Samuel* (Cambridge Bible; Cambridge: University Press, 1888), 150.

19. Smith, *Holy Spirit in the Gospels*, 25.

20. Mitchell Dahood, *Psalms II* (Anchor Bible; Garden City, N. Y.: Doubleday & Co., n.d.), 71.

21. *Lange's Commentary* and Smith as well as the RSV take "spirit" to mean the human mind or spirit. But this is contrary to the chronicler's usage, as *Barnes' Notes* and the Anchor Bible point out. See J. M. Myers, *I Chronicles* (Anchor Bible; Garden City, N.Y.: Doubleday & Co., 1965), 190.

22. M. H. Pope, *Job* (Anchor Bible; Garden City, N. Y.: Doubleday & Co., 1965), 216.

Chapter 4

1. George Eldon Ladd, *The Pattern of New Testament Truth* (Grand Rapids: Wm. B. Eerdmans Publishing Co., 1968), 100–01.

2. Ladd, *Pattern of New Testament Truth*, 101; Smith, *Holy Spirit in the Gospels*, 35. See also Charles Caldwell Ryrie, *Biblical Theology of the New Testament* (Chicago: Moody Press, 1959), 112, 121 and Arno Clemens Gabelein, *The Holy Spirit in the New Testament* (New York: Our Hope, n.d.), 8, 34–35.

3. This is also the conclusion of the classic work by E. B. Pusey, *The Minor Prophets* (New York: Funk & Wagnalls, 1885), 1:193; as well as Theo. Laetsch, *The Minor Prophets* (St. Louis: Concordia Publishing House, 1965), 128.

4. C. F. Keil, *The Minor Prophets* (Grand Rapids: Wm. B. Eerdmans Publishing Co., 1954 reprint), 1:211.

5. Pusey, *Minor Prophets*, 1:196.

6. Laetsch, *Minor Prophets*, 128.

7. Keil, *Minor Prophets*, 1:204.

8. Ibid. See also Pusey, *Minor Prophets*, 1:193.

9. C. Von Orelli, *The Prophecies of Isaiah* (Edinburgh: T. & T. Clark, 1895), 32.

10. Franz Delitzsch, *Bible Commentary on the Prophecy of Isaiah* (Grand Rapids: Wm. B. Eerdmans, 1949 reprint), 1:282–83.

11. Ibid.

12. Vriezen, *Outline of Old Testament Theology*, 216; Orelli, *The Prophecies of Isaiah*, 325.

13. C. F. Keil, *Biblical Commentary on the Prophecies of Ezekiel* (Grand Rapids: Wm. B. Eerdmans Publishing Co., 1950 reprint), 1:56, 62, 112, 142.

14. A. B. Davidson, *Ezekiel* (Cambridge: University Press, 1884), 15.

15. Ibid., 75.

16. Ibid., 350.

17. Laetsch, *Minor Prophets*, 393.

18. Merrill F. Unger, *Zechariah* (Grand Rapids: Baker Book House, 1965), 37.

19. Thomas V. Moore, *A Commentary of Zechariah* (London: Banner of Truth Trust, 1961 reprint from 1856), 72; Unger, *Zechariah*, 70.

20. H. C. Leupold, *Exposition of Zechariah* (Grand Rapids: Baker Book House, 1965), 81.

21. Hinckley G. Mitchell, *A Critical and Exegetical Commentary on Haggai and Zechariah* (Edinburgh: T. & T. Clark, 1912), 162.

22. Pusey, *Minor Prophets*, 101.

23. Mitchell, *Critical and Exegetical Commentary on Haggai and Zechariah*, 163; H. L. Ellison, *Men Spake From God*, 2nd ed. (Grand Rapids: Wm. B. Eerdmans Publishing Co., 1958), 129.

24. John Calvin, *Commentaries on the Twelve Minor Prophets*, trans. John Owen (Grand Rapids: Wm. B. Eerdmans Publishing Co., 1950 reprint), 108.

25. Unger, *Zechariah*, 73, 80.

26. C. F. Keil, *The Twelve Minor Prophets*, trans. James Martin (Grand Rapids: Wm. B. Eerdmans Publishing Co., 1954 reprint), 266, 275.

27. Ibid., 277.

28. Ladd, *Theology of the New Testament*, 37.

Chapter 5

1. Henry Alford, *The Greek New Testament* (London: Rivingtons, 1883), 1:447–48.

2. Ladd, *Theology of the New Testament*, 160–61.

3. Barclay, *Promise of the Spirit*, 24–25.

4. Ladd, *Theology of the New Testament*, 36.

5. James D. G. Dunn, *Baptism in the Holy Spirit* (London: SCM Press, 1970), 9–11.

6. Smith, *Holy Spirit in the Gospels*, 141.

7. Arndt and Gingrich, *A Greek-English Lexicon of the New Testament* (Chicago: The University of Chicago Press, 1957), 737.

8. A. Carr, *St. Matthew* (Cambridge: University Press, 1886), 100.

9. C. G. Montefiore, *The Synoptic Gospels* (New York: KTAV Publishing House, 1968), 2:338.

10. Smith, *Holy Spirit in the Gospels*, 142.

11. *Basil the Great on the Holy Spirit*, trans. George Lewis (London: Religious Tract Society, n.d.), 74. (Basil, born AD 329, was bishop of Caesarea in Cappadocia.) Also Origen and others; see Alford, *Greek New Testament*, 1:23 (though Alford disagrees).

12. Dunn, *Baptism in the Holy Spirit*, 33, 36.

13. Ibid.

14. Barclay, *Promise of the Spirit*, 28–29.

15. Gerhard Kittel, *Bible Key Words* (New York: Harper and Row, 1960), 3:26.

16. Alan Richardson, *An Introduction to the Theology of the New Testament* (New York: Harper & Brothers, Publishers, 1958), 108.

17. Filson, *New Testament Against Its Environment*, 81.

Chapter 6

1. Rene Pache, *The Person and Work of the Holy Spirit* rev. ed., (Chicago: Moody Bible Institute, 1966), 22.

2. Alford, *Greek New Testament*, 1:551.

3. J. J. Van Oosterzee, *The Theology of the New Testament*, trans. J. J. Evans (New York: Dodd, Mead and Co., 1871), 84.

4. Gabelein, *Holy Spirit in the New Testament*, 18.

5. Pache, *Person and Work of the Holy Spirit*, 83.

6. Smith, *Holy Spirit in the Gospels*, 214.

7. Montefiore, *Synoptic Gospels*, 2:473.

8. Smith, *Holy Spirit in the Gospels*, 138, 252.

9. Irving F. Wood, *The Spirit of God in Biblical Literature* (New York: A. C. Armstrong and Son, 1904), 130–31.

10. Basil the Great, *Basil the Great on the Holy Spirit*, 72–73. Basil also preached a threefold immersion, as was common in the East.

11. Archibald M. Hunter, *Introducing New Testament Theology* (Philadelphia: The Westminster Press, 1957), 134.

12. Herman Barclay Swete, *The Holy Spirit in the New Testament* (London: Macmillan and Co., Ltd., 1910), 147; Alford, *Greek New Testament*, 1:714.

13. Hunter, *Introducing New Testament Theology*, 139.

14. Gabelein, *Holy Spirit in the New Testament*, 21.

15. Johnston, *Spirit-Paraclete in the Gospel of John*, 42.

16. Smith, *Holy Spirit in the Gospels*, 149; T. J. Wheldon, *The Holy Spirit* (Carnarvon: The Calvinistic Methodist Book Agency, 1899), 109.

17. Ladd, *Theology of the New Testament*, 284–85.

18. Ibid., 285.

19. Simpson, *Holy Spirit*, 2:50.

20. Donald Guthrie, "John," *The New Bible Commentary*, 3rd ed. (Grand Rapids: Wm. B. Eerdmans Publishing Co., 1970).

21. Ladd, *Theology of the New Testament*, 292.

22. Ibid., 291.

23. Filson, *New Testament Against Its Environment*, 94.

24. Barclay, *Promise of the Spirit*, 38, 40.

25. Ryrie, *Biblical Theology of the New Testament*, 331–32.

26. William C. Scofield, *The Holy Spirit in the New Testament Scriptures* (New York: Fleming H. Revell Co., c. 1896), 81; George B. Stevens, *The Theology of the New Testament* (New York: Charles Scribner's Sons, 1917), 214.

27. George R. Brunk II, ed. *Encounter with the Holy Spirit* (Scottdale, Pa.: Herald Press, 1972), 10; Johnston, *Spirit-Paraclete in the Gospel of John*, 91.

28. Ladd, *Theology of the New Testament*, 293.

29. Marcus Dods, "The Gospel of St. John," *Expositor's Greek Testament*, ed. W. R. Nicoll (Grand Rapids: Wm. B. Eerdmans Publishing Co., n.d.), 824.

30. Marvin R. Vincent, *Word Studies in the New Testament* (Grand Rapids: Wm. B. Eerdmans Publishing Co., 1946 reprint of 1889), 243–44.

31. R. Richardson, *Scriptural View of the Office of the Holy Spirit* (St. Louis: Christian Publishing Co., 1872), 27.

32. J. H. Bernard, *A Critical and Exegetical Commentary on the Gospel According to St. John*, ed. A. H. McNeile (Edinburgh, T. & T. Clark, 1928), 2:496; Stevens, *Theology of the New Testament*, 213.

33. Johnston, *Spirit-Paraclete in the Gospel of John*, 81.

34. Ibid., 96, 99–101; Lindsay Dewar, *The Holy Spirit and Modern Thought* (New York: Harper & Bros., 1959), 37.

35. Smith, *Holy Spirit in the Gospels*, 322; J. Worthington-Atkin, *The Paraklete* (London: Marshall Brothers, 1906), 1–2.

36. Hunter, *Introducing New Testament Theology*, 137.

37. Ryrie, *Biblical Theology of the New Testament*, 331.

38. Edward H. Bickersteth, *The Holy Spirit* (Grand Rapids: Kregel Publications, 1959 reprint), 129–31.

39. Ibid., 131.

40. Johnston, *Spirit-Paraclete in the Gospel of John*, 11.

41. Simpson, *Holy Spirit*, 2:22; R. Richardson, *Scriptural View of the Office*, 90–93; Ladd, *Theology of the New Testament*, 288–89; James E. Cumming, *Through the Eternal Spirit* (Minneapolis: Bethany Fellowship, 1965), 90.

42. Pache, *Person and Work of the Holy Spirit*, 39.

43. R. Richardson, *Scriptural View of the Office*, 90–91.

44. William E. Biederwolf, *A Help to the Study of the Holy Spirit* (Grand Rapids: Baker Book House, 1974 reprint from 1903), 56; Dunn, *Baptism in the Holy Spirit*, 178; Smith, *Holy Spirit in the Gospels*, 371–73.

45. A. Richardson, *Introduction to the Theology of the New Testament*, 116.

46. Pache, *Person and Work of the Holy Spirit*, 38–39.

47. Scofield, *Holy Spirit in the New Testament Scriptures*.

48. Biederwolf, *Help to the Study of the Holy Spirit*, 55–57

Chapter 7

1. J. H. E. Hull, *The Holy Spirit in the Acts of the Apostles* (London: Lutterworth Press, 1967), 27.

2. W. T. Conner, *The Faith of the New Testament* (Nashville: Broadman Press, 1940), 198.

3. R. Richardson, *Scriptural View of the Office*, 228.

4. Ladd, *Theology of the New Testament*, 346.

5. Scofield, *Holy Spirit in the New Testament Scriptures*, 120.

6. Biederwolf, *Help to the Study of the Holy Spirit*, 82.

7. R. Richardson, *Scriptural View of the Office*, 110.

8. Taylor, *Go-between God*, 6.

9. Pache, *Person and Work of the Holy Spirit*, 23.

10. Dunn, *Baptism in the Holy Spirit*, 40.

11. Adolf Schlatter, *The Church in the New Testament Period*, trans. Levertooff (London: S.P.C.K., 1961), 17.

12. Thomas D. Bernard, *The Progress of Doctrine in the New Testament* (Grand Rapids: Zondervan Publishing House, 1939 reprint from 1864), 108.

13. Arthur W. Pink, *The Holy Spirit* (Grand Rapids: Baker Book House, 1970), 41.

14. Hans Conzelmann, *An Outline of the Theology of the New Testament*, trans. John Bowden (New York: Harper & Row, 1969), 37.

15. Gaebelein, *The Holy Spirit in the New Testament*, 34.

16. R. Richardson, *Scriptural View of the Office*, 110.

17. Schlatter, *Church in the New Testament Period*, 18–19; Arthur T. Pierson. *The Acts of the Holy Spirit* (New York: Fleming H. Revell Co., 1895), 44.

18. Howard M. Ervin, *These Are Not Drunken As Ye Suppose* (Plainfield, N.J.: Logos, 1968), 62–63. See a good answer to this and other arguments of Ervin against refillings by Larry W. Hurtado. "On Being Filled With the Spirit," *Paraclete*, 4, no. 1 (1970): 29–32. See also Wheldon, *Holy Spirit*, 257.

19. Joseph A. Alexander, *Commentary on the Acts of the Apostles* (Grand Rapids: Zondervan Publishing House, 1956 from 1875 3rd ed.), 307.

20. Hull, *Holy Spirit in the Acts of the Apostles*, 48.

21. Rudolf Bultmann, *Theology of the New Testament* (New York: Charles Scribner's Sons, 1951), 1:159.

22. Kittel, *Bible Key Words*, 52–53. But see Bruce on this passage.

23. Alexander, *Commentary on the Acts of the Apostles*, 426.

24. Kittel, *Bible Key Words*, 52.

25. Wheldon, *Holy Spirit*, 111.

26. A. Richardson, *Introduction to the Theology of the New Testament*, 120.

27. F. F. Bruce, *The Acts of the Apostles* (Grand Rapids: Wm. B. Eerdmans Publishing Co., 1960), 303.

28. Dunn, *Baptism in the Holy Spirit*, 86.

29. Hull, *Holy Spirit in the Acts of the Apostles*, 110.

30. Ernst Kasemann, *New Testament Questions of Today*, trans. W. J. Montague (Philadelphia: Fortress Press, 1969), 74.

31. Bruce, *Acts of the Apostles*, 385; Alexander, *Commentary on the Acts of the Apostles*, 222.

Chapter 8

1. Barclay, *Promise of the Spirit*, 80.

2. Ladd, *Theology of the New Testament*, 520.

3. R. A. Torrey, *The Person and Work of the Holy Spirit* rev. ed. (Grand Rapids: Zondervan Publishing House, 1974), 148.

4. Dunn, *Baptism in the Holy Spirit*, 107.

5. Frederic Rendall, "The Epistle to the Galatians," *The Expositor's Greek Testament* (Grand Rapids: Wm. B. Eerdmans Publishing Co., reprinted 1970), 3:170.

6. Herman N. Ridderbos, *The Epistle of Paul to the Church of Galatia* (Grand Rapids: Wm. B. Eerdmans Publishing Co., 1953), 128; Ernest D. Burton, *A Critical and Exegetical Commentary on the Epistle to the Galatians*, ICC (Edinburgh: T. & T. Clark, 1921), 175.

7. Burton, *Critical and Exegetical Commentary on the Epistle to the Galatians*, 176–77; John Eadie, *Commentary on the Epistle of Paul to the Galatians* (Grand Rapids: Zondervan Publishing House, reprint from 1894), 252–53.

8. Burton, *Critical and Exegetical Commentary on the Epistle to the Galatians*, 221.

9. Ibid., 224

10. Ibid., 278.

11. Donald Gee, *A New Discovery* (Springfield, Mo.: Gospel Publishing House, 1932), 42.

12. Burton, *Critical and Exegetical Commentary on the Epistle to the Galatians*, 315

13. Willibald Beyschlag, *New Testament Theology*, trans. Neil Buchanan (Edinburgh: T. & T. Clark, 1895), 2:213.

14. J. S. Murray, "What We Can Learn From the Pentecostal Churches," *Christianity Today*, June 9, 1967, 11 (899).

15. W. Sanday and Arthur Headlam, *A Critical and Exegetical Commentary on the Epistle to the Romans* (Edinburgh: T. & T. Clark, 1968 reprint from 1902), 9.

16. M. R. Vincent, *Word Studies in the New Testament* (Wilmington: Associated Publishers and Authors, 1972 reprint), 664.

17. Taylor, *Go-between God,* 102.

18. John Murray, *The Epistle to the Romans* (Grand Rapids: Wm. B. Eerdmans Publishing Co., 1968), 1:10–11.

19. F. F. Bruce, *Epistle of Paul to the Romans* (Grand Rapids: Wm. B. Eerdmans Publishing Co., 1963), 73.

20. Barclay, *Promise of the Spirit,* 100–01.

21. Kittel, *Bible Key Words,* 3:56.

22. Ladd, *Theology of the New Testament,* 418, 489.

23. Beyschlag, *New Testament Theology,* 2:210; Stevens, *Theology of the New Testament,* 437.

24. Beyschlag, *New Testament Theology,* 2:209.

25. Bruce, *Epistle of Paul to the Romans,* 160.

26. Murray, *Epistle to the Romans,* 285.

27. Ladd, *Theology of the New Testament,* 471.

28. Ladd, *Pattern of New Testament Truth,* 100.

29. Bruce, *Epistle of Paul to the Romans,* 91.

30. Ernst Kasemann, *New Testament Questions of Today,* trans. W. J. Montague (Philadelphia: Fortress Press, 1969), 190.

31. Donald Gee, *Concerning Spiritual Gifts* (Springfield, Mo.: Gospel Publishing House), 78.

32. Murray, *Epistle to the Romans,* 122; W. M. Greathouse, "Romans," *Beacon Bible Commentary* (Kansas City: Beacon Hill Press, 1968), 242.

33. Donald Gee, *The Ministry Gifts of Christ* (London: Assemblies of God Publishing House), 41. (Incorporated as Part II, in Donald Gee, *Now That You've Been Baptized in the Spirit* (Springfield, Mo.: Gospel Publishing House, 1972.)

34. Bruce, *Epistle of Paul to the Romans,* 229.

35. Ladd, *Theology of the New Testament,* 411, 630.

36. Barclay, *Promise of the Spirit,* 70–75.

Chapter 9

1. Gee, *Now That You've Been Baptized in the Spirit,* 141.

2. Donald Gee, *Spiritual Gifts in the Work of the Ministry Today* (Springfield, Mo.: Gospel Publishing House, 1963), 8.

3. Conner, *Faith of the New Testament,* 363.

4. R. Birch Hoyle, *The Holy Spirit in St. Paul* (Garden City, N. Y.: Doubleday, Doran & Co., 1929), 47. (A book with many good points.)

5. Ladd, *Theology of the New Testament,* 518.

6. A. H. Leitch, "The Holy Spirit and These Days," *Christianity Today,* May 21, 1971, 15; Taylor, *Go-between God,* 108.

7. Norman Hillyer, "1 & 2 Corinthians," *The New Bible Commentary* 3rd ed. (Grand Rapids: Wm. B. Eerdmans Publishing Co., 1970), 1059.

8. Some take "harlot" here to mean a temple prostitute in the heathen worship. But it is hardly likely that even the Corinthian believers, babes in Christ though they were, would go that far. Paul's usage of the word seems to be more general here.

9. Ladd, *Theology of the New Testament*, 466, 469.

10. Hillyer, "1 & 2 Corinthians," 1062.

11. See Hillyer, "1 & 2 Corinthians," 1065–66, for a clear discussion of the customs dealt with in this passage.

12. Gee, *Concerning Spiritual Gifts*, 86.

13. Ibid., 17.

14. R. B. Chapman, "The Purpose and Value of Spiritual Gifts," *Paraclete*, 2, no. 4 (1968): 25.

15. John Owen, *The Holy Spirit* (Grand Rapids: Sovereign Grace Publishers, 1971 reprint), 16.

16. Harold Horton, *The Gifts of the Spirit* (London: Assemblies of God Publishing House, 1962 from 1934), 80. (U.S. edition published by the Gospel Publishing House, 1975.)

17. Ladd, *Theology of the New Testament*, 534–35.

18. Arnold Bittlinger, *Gifts and Graces*, trans. H. Klassen (Grand Rapids: Wm. B. Eerdmans Publishing Co., 1967), 17–18.

19. Hillyer, "1 & 2 Corinthians," 1067.

20. Simpson, *Holy Spirit*, 2:42.

21. Kasemann, *New Testament Questions of Today*, 192–93.

22. Conner, *Faith of the New Testament*, 373.

23. H. Horton, *Gifts of the Spirit*, 35–36.

24. A. Robertson and A. Plummer, *A Critical and Exegetical Commentary on the First Epistle of St. Paul to the Corinthians* ICC (Edinburgh: T. & T. Clark, 1967 reprint from 1914), 272.

25. Dunn, *Baptism in the Holy Spirit*, 128.

26. Ladd, *Theology of the New Testament*, 542; James O. Buswell, *A Systematic Theology of the Christian Religion* (Grand Rapids: Zondervan Publishing House, 1962), 2:208.

27. L. Thomas Holdcroft, "Spirit Baptism: Its Nature and Chronology," *Paraclete*, 1, no. 1 (1967): 30.

28. Bultmann, *Theology of the New Testament*, 1:159.

29. Stevens, *Theology of the New Testament*, 437.

30. Bittlinger, *Gifts and Graces*, 75.

31. Chapman, "The Purpose and Value of Spiritual Gifts," 27.

32. Conzelmann, *Outline of the Theology of the New Testament*, 260.

33. Taylor, *Go-between God*, 201.

Chapter 10

1. Gee, *Concerning Spiritual Gifts*, 65.

2. Filson, *New Testament Against Its Environment*, 79.

3. Bittlinger, *Gifts and Graces,* 50.

4. Dennis and Rita Bennett, *The Holy Spirit and You* (Plainfield, N.J.: Logos International 1971), 95; Ralph Harris, *Spoken by the Spirit* (Springfield, Mo.: Gospel Publishing House, 1973), entire book; John L. Sherrill, *They Speak With Other Tongues* (Spire Books, Westwood, N.J.: Fleming H. Revell, 1964), 45, 91–92, 96–100.

5. Bittlinger, *Gifts and Graces,* 66.

6. Beyschlag. *New Testament Theology,* 2:247.

7. H. Horton, *Gifts of the Spirit,* 172–74.

8. Gee, *Concerning Spiritual Gifts,* 88.

9. Beyschlag, *New Testament Theology,* 2:18.

10. Wood, *The Spirit of God in Biblical Literature,* 161.

11. Schlatter, *Church in the New Testament Period,* 68

12. Gee, *Concerning Spiritual Gifts,* 89.

13. Pache, *Person and Work of the Holy Spirit,* 25.

14. Ladd, *Pattern of New Testament Truth,* 101–02.

15. Barclay, *Promise of the Spirit,* 15.

16. Athanasius, *The Letters of Saint Athanasius Concerning the Holy Spirit,* trans. C. R. B. Shapland (New York: Philosophical Library, 1951), 172. (Written AD 356–361.)

17. Dunn, *Baptism in the Holy Spirit,* 158–59.

18. See Biederwolf, *Help to the Study of the Holy Spirit,* 30, for a listing of a number who take this view.

19. Ibid., 31.

20. Hunter, *Introducing New Testament Theology,* 95.

21. Cumming, *Through the Eternal Spirit,* 82.

22. Taylor, *Go-between God,* 108.

23. Conner, *Faith of the New Testament,* 364.

24. Owen, *Holy Spirit,* 770.

25. Ladd, *Theology of the New Testament,* 518.

26. Owen, *Holy Spirit,* 832.

27. A. T. Robertson, *Word Pictures in the New Testament* (Nashville: Broadman Press, 1931), 4:581.

28. Donald Guthrie, *The Pastoral Epistles* (Grand Rapids: W. B. Eerdmans Publishing Co., 1960), 134.

29. Ladd, *Theology of the New Testament,* 445.

30. Robertson, *Word Pictures in the New Testament,* 4:607; Guthrie, *Pastoral Epistles,* 206.

31. Guthrie, *The Pastoral Epistles,* 206.

32. Owen, *Holy Spirit,* 890.

33. Ryrie, *Biblical Theology of the New Testament,* 234.

34. Taylor, *Go-between God,* 109.

35. Filson, *New Testament Against Its Environment,* 75; Pache, *Person and Work of the Holy Spirit,* 170.

Chapter 11

1. Hunter, *Introducing New Testament Theology,* 97.

2. Wheldon, *Holy Spirit,* 47.

3. E. W. Bullinger, *The Giver and His Gifts* (London: The Lamp Press, 1953), 26–27.

4. D. V. Hurst, "The Evidence Points to the Evidence," *Paraclete,* 2, no. 1 (1968): 22–30.

5. Including Ryrie, *Biblical Theology of the New Testament,* 113.

6. Ibid., 114.

7. Albert Hoy, "Public and Private Use of Tongues," *Paraclete,* 2, no. 4 (1968): 11–12.

8. Gee, *A New Discovery* (Formerly *Pentecost),* 8.

9. See Addison H. Leitch, "The Holy Spirit and These Days," *Christianity Today,* May 21, 1971, 15 (791).

10. Barclay, *Promise of the Spirit,* 63, 85.

11. Scofield, *Holy Spirit in the New Testament Scriptures,* 12.

12. Brunk, *Encounter with the Holy Spirit,* 58–59.

13. Kasemann, *New Testament Questions of Today,* 194.

14. Ladd, *Theology of the New Testament,* 535–36.

15. H. Horton, *Gifts of the Spirit,* 35.

16. Ibid., 80.

17. Gee, *Spiritual Gifts in the Ministry Today,* 24.

18. Taylor, *Go-between God,* 202.

19. According to Bittlinger, *Gifts and Graces,* 68, on this basis Luther said there were apostles in all churches and Calvin said apostles would be called forth as needed.

20. Schlatter, *Church in the New Testament Period,* 24.

21. Oehler, *Theology of the Old Testament,* 508.

22. Gee, *Ministry Gifts of Christ,* 64.

23. Ralph M. Riggs, *The Spirit Himself* (Springfield, Mo.: Gospel Publishing House, 1949), 123.

24. Gee, *Spiritual Gifts in the Work of the Ministry Today,* 20–39, gives a sensible discussion of this. See also his *Concerning Spiritual Gifts,* 111–19.

25. Bittlinger, *Gifts and Graces,* 32–33.

26. Gee, *Concerning Spiritual Gifts,* 45; Howard Carter, *Spiritual Gifts and Their Operation* (Springfield, Mo.: Gospel Publishing House, 1968), 49.

27. L. Thomas Holdcroft, "The Gift of the Gifts of Healings," *Paraclete,* 2, no. 2 (1968): 10–11.

28. Bittlinger, *Gifts and Graces,* 37.

29. Anthony D. Palma, "The Working of Miracles," *Advance,* October 1974, 36.

30. Bittlinger, *Gifts and Graces,* 41; H. Horton, *Gifts of the Spirit,* 126.

31. Gee, *Spiritual Gifts in the Work of the Ministry,* 78–79.

32. E. H. Merrill, "Who Are Today's Prophets?" *Christianity Today,* March 12, 1971, 9–10 (541–42).

33. Bittlinger, *Gifts and Graces*, 106–07; Gee, *Concerning Spiritual Gifts*, 48, 51.

34. Anthony D. Palma, "Discerning of Spirits and Prophecy," *Advance*, May 1973, 16.

35. Ibid., 16; L. T. Holdcroft, "Spiritual Gifts We May Fail to Recognize," *Paraclete*, 3, no. 2 (1969): 22.

36. Wood, *The Spirit of God in Biblical Literature*, 162; Bittlinger, *Gifts and Graces*, 98.

37. Bittlinger, *Gifts and Graces*, 97–98; John Ruthven, "Is Glossolalia Languages?" *Paraclete*, 4, no. 2 (1970): 27–30.

38. Bittlinger suggests that even Jesus may have prayed in tongues, since the Greek verbs *stenazein* and *anastenazein* for sighing or groaning were used as technical terms for prayer that did not involve the mind. The terms are used of Jesus in Mark 7:34; 8:11–12; Bittlinger, *Gifts and Graces*, 49.

39. Ibid., 51; H. Horton, *Gifts of the Spirit*, 168.

40. Howard M. Ervin, "As the Spirit Gives Utterance," *Christianity Today*, April 11, 1969, 10 (626).

41. Gee, *Concerning Spiritual Gifts*, 66.

42. S. M. Horton, *Tongues and Prophecy* (Springfield, Mo.: Gospel Publishing House, 1972), 24.

43. Bittlinger *Gifts and Graces*, 70.

44. Kasemann, *New Testament Questions of Today*, 193; Conzelmann, *Outline of the Theology of the New Testament*, 260.

SUBJECT INDEX

Scripture Index

Old Testament

New Testament